The Wandering Widow

A curious woman takes on the world

Andrea Granahan

Published by Joy Woods Press, P.O. Box 25, Bodega, CA 94922

Printed on acid-free paper.

First Edition

Granahan10@gmail.com

WanderingwithAndrea.com

Dedicated to my sons David and Devin

And Mary Gaffney for her editing help,

And my travel companions

But do not hurry the voyage at all.
It is better to let it last for many years;
and to anchor at the island when you are old,
rich with all you have gained on the way

Ithaca, by Constantine Cavafy

Other books by Andrea Granahan

It's Greek to Me

The Man with the Portable Love Room and
Other Stray Thoughts

Backstories from the West Edge

Loving David

Contents

Prologue

When you find yourself completely alone after decades of sharing a life with a mate, raising children, running a business now sold, your jobs now complete, what do you do with yourself?

Even as I raised my family, I had worked as a journalist and published a newspaper. I knew how to write and I loved to travel. I was always a curious person and after my two year sojourn in rural Greece, I became even more curious. How did other cultures solve basic human problems such as earning a living, finding a mate, raising and educating children, healing the ill, caring for the helpless? What did other cultures honor on a daily basis, even hold sacred?

When I was widowed, I discovered many things about myself. After the shock and sorrow, along with bleak loneliness, there was another new sensation. It took me a while to realize what it was.

Freedom.

Married as a teenager, becoming a mother, attaining an education, owning a business, freedom from responsibility was such a novel sensation, it shocked me.

I had sold the newspaper that had claimed so many hours and years of my life. My time as a caregiver was over. My children were all independent. I had a small income from a rental. With care, I could survive as a freelance travel writer.

The emptiness which I felt at first as a widow I now saw had become a blank slate. I wanted, no, needed, to fill it and for the first time, I consciously realized it was a matter of choice.

I chose the world.

Section 1.
Africa

The lioness was four feet away from me. She stopped walking beside the electric tram and started sniffing at me. I gasped in spite of my effort to remain absolutely silent. I remembered the rules.

"Stay still. Keep the lights out of her eyes, let her explore. I can shoot her, but she can strike faster than I could shoot anyway," the guide had whispered over the microphone when we stopped. Africa is one place where one gladly heeds the rules. I was seated on the outside edge of our open, awning-covered tram. I sat perfectly still after my involuntary sharp intake of breath. I kept my hands and head inside the perimeter of the tram.

"She'll think you are part of a larger animal. But if you put out a hand or your head she will know you are prey," the guide warned.

She looked confused. I smelled edible but I was part of a huge creature. Perhaps it had eaten me? I did not look her in the eyes, I did not take her photo until she suddenly lay down on the warm pavement below me. Then I got a quick shot.

She got up and slowly strolled all around the tram puzzled. Everyone gasped as she stopped to check them out. I kept track of her by the sound of terrified breaths.

Eventually she sauntered up the road. A short way ahead we came upon five lionesses all laying on the road. We were all very still until the cats decided to walk off into the bush. I had not come to South Africa to frighten myself.

Why had I come there of all places when I was first widowed?

I was ten and in fourth grade when I heard an African explorer speak at my school. He fired my imagination as he spoke of the wonderful people and animals of that far-away continent. Africa took center place in my imagination. I read everything I could get my hands on about the then "mysterious continent". Sheena Queen of the Jungle comic books littered my room.

When my husband David was ill, we had planned a Caribbean cruise, but he died the week before we planned to leave. Two months later I saw two things in my mail: a credit card showing that travel insurance had refunded the cruise money and a mailer from a company offering a "shoestring" African safari for less than the cruise cost. Suddenly my ten-year-old self came roaring back. I picked up my phone and booked the safari.

I had felt so sedentary during the many months of caregiving, I longed to toughen up, feel strong again, get outdoors once more. I used the intervening weeks before I was to leave to work out at a gym and get myself in shape for the trip.

I finally boarded my plane to Johannesburg. It was a fourteen hour overnight flight. I realized I would be flying over the Equator for the first time. I wanted to be awake for it. Then I noticed I was near the cockpit and asked the flight attendant in those idyllic pre 9/11 days, if I could go into the cockpit when we passed over the belt of the earth. After a while the attendant fetched me.

The belly of the plane was dark since everyone was sleeping, but in the cockpit it was a beautiful dawn over the Atlantic. The pilot, co-pilot and a navigator made me welcome and the attendant brought us all some coffee. We chatted, and in a while the pilot pointed down at the sea. "We are now crossing the Equator," he said. There was a moment of silence, then he ruefully said in his South African accent, "Oh, no. They've erased the white line again!"

The flight attendant took me back to my seat still laughing, and I watched the Kalahari Desert unfold beneath us. And at last we landed. I was finally, truly in Africa

Sawubona Soweto

I had foolishly thought I could easily buy mosquito netting in Johannesburg. I asked Millie, the busy assistant at the safari lodge, about public transport downtown to a camping supply store. She looked at me aghast.

"You can't do that! You'd be toast in two minutes," she said.

"Well, I need to change money and I want to buy a mosquito net," I told her.

"There's a shopping center down the block with a bank. Just go there in the daylight."

I left and found the small enclosed mall with an armed security guard at the entrance. At the bank, another armed guard gestured me into a cubicle that had two locked doors, one to the mall and the other into the bank. While locked away a third guard inside had me hold up my passport and eventually let me in to get my rands.

As I walked back to the lodge I passed high razor wire topped walls and saw signs warning there was twenty-four hour armed response to alarms. I was afraid to open the gate to the lodge. Their resident watch dogs growled at me. I called and eventually Millie came to let me into the lovely gardens and swimming pool at the lodge. I thought I'd spend a day trapped there.

Then I saw that the lodge offered an afternoon tour of Soweto and Nigel, the owner, explained it was conducted by a young Zulu man named Juda. Juda showed up in a van and greeted me in Zulu "Sawubona", a lovely greeting which means I see you and value you. The response is Yaybo which means one returns the same feeling. We drove to a hotel to pick up another tourist, a young, dingbat woman who when asked if she was American, breezily replied, "No, I'm a Texan." Juda looked puzzled so I told him "Texas is in

3

America." Judah nodded and she looked at me with daggers in her eyes.

I was startled when Juda stopped his van and ushered us into a smaller beat up old auto and turned us over to Chris and Simba, two younger Zulu lads. I considered the situation a moment and realized Juda's new van might be at risk in a poor neighborhood, and thus the change of vehicles for something less conspicuous.

The lads were very good-natured and funny. They pointed out a large grim building "Free hotel, and they give you free food and a blanket," Chris told me. "Everything free, except the guests." It was the penitentiary.

A sudden furious downpour flooded streets that couldn't keep up with the intense rain. But the rain ended as suddenly as it had begun. I started humming Paul Simon's tune about the rains in Africa as we drove through the floods.

Most of Soweto was filled with small cinder block houses that were cubicle in shape reminding me of sugar cubes. There were shipping containers everywhere, much larger than the cube houses, outfitted as offices offering fax and copy services. People were roasting corn over small braziers and selling it on the streets. Then we went to what Chris said was now called "an informal settlement" and I got my first culture shock.

A cyclone fence surrounded it, but there were gaps cut into it everywhere, and it was flooded from the rain.

"First sweets," said Chris as he led us on some planks that had been thrown down over the temporary flood into a tiny shop where a narrow board on sawhorses made a rudimentary table that had a display of poisonous looking candies. Kids were gathering outside the shop as we selected a handful of the garish sweets and then dutifully handed them out to the kids. I had guilt pangs over creating dental problems, but the kids were very happy.

The squatters in the settlements can get on a list for permanent housing that was slowly being built, but in the meantime, everyone was squeezed into oppressively close quarters. It was hard to find a path to walk on, but Chris skillfully guided us around. He told us eleven tribes had been thrown on top of one another. Here and there the government put in a porta-potty. It was like walking through a junkyard, but somehow the people had established their tribal way of life in this awful urban setting. I had to admire them. I wondered how bad things were in their homelands that they immigrated to South Africa and these intolerable conditions.

Eleven languages were spoken, but Zulu was the lingua franca, and the Zulus, especially Chris, were the cocks of the walk. Everyone greeted him respectfully. A schoolgirl in a uniform walked by.

"Hey, how are your grades in your classes?" Chris asked her. "You doing your homework?"

She answered him in English, "I am doing good. My teacher gave good grades in English."

"Good, good. Go do your homework."

Chris told us a lot of kids in the settlement did not go to school and he constantly encouraged them to get an education and learn English. The girl was one of his successes.

It was clear that Chris was more than just a tour guide to the settlement. The Texan didn't seem to care and began demanding to meet an ishangoma, a witch doctor. He took us to a small thatched dome where we had to crawl inside. There sat an old woman in tribal garb surrounded by drums, animal skins and drying herbs. He offered to translate if the girl paid the old woman to tell her future. I opted out.

We had picked up an entourage of children. They gathered around me as I waited outside the hut. I took a notebook and asking one child's name wrote it on a piece of paper. I gave it to him. He looked as if I had handed him a valuable treasure. All the kids began begging for me to give them a piece, so I began drawing hearts because it was faster, and they gleefully grabbed their pieces of paper shouting with excitement. Finally, I tore out the last piece of paper and the kids departed to show their families their new acquisitions. Eventually Chris and the Texan came out of the hut and she looked very disturbed. I didn't ask what her future held. I gathered it wasn't pleasant.

Then Chris took us to a small house made of scrap materials. He told us it was an unofficial orphanage. A young couple was bathing a baby. There were four children quietly playing. I looked through an open door and saw there were cots and a bunkbed in the single adjoining room, and children were sleeping in them.

"There are fifteen children sharing the space. They have to take turns using the beds," Chris explained. I looked at the couple realizing they had taken on all these kids – most of them AIDS orphans. A cigar box was on a small stand by a candle under a picture of Christ to collect donations. I emptied my purse and told the Texan she should, too.

I was shaken as we left the settlement. I had never seen poverty like this before. We drove to the elite part of Soweto where Winnie Mandela lived as the white South Africans did in a walled compound. South Africans with any money have successfully built their own prisons where dogs patrol the walls, lethal electric fences surmount them and where signs promise armed response to any who dare to breach the walls.

Chris told me construction could not start until a wall was completed because insurance companies demanded the walls.

We reconnected with Juda and his van, Chris and Simba joining us. We dropped off the Texan and they took me to the lodge. There the Zulu fellows taught me their intricate handshake and bid me farewell. Thinking of the unofficial orphanage and the children sharing beds, I entered the lodge walls of my protected prison.

Peter and the Sand Elephant

I came to South Africa for solace, for the comfort animals offer. How on earth did I, so recently widowed, still deeply grieving end up next to a drunken Great White Hunter, generations out of date?

My South African chardonnay was too good to rush. I wouldn't let him drive me out of the small, stonewalled bar, rife with character, and back to my thatched room upstairs – yet.

Peter was just now back from safari. The bartender, Nigel, also the safari group owner, therefore, Peter's boss, apologized as he poured himself a drink.

"Just off safari, so he's letting off some steam," Nigel said.

That excused this loud, hulking redneck on the barstool next to me? My host hoped so. At least I was relieved Peter wouldn't be my guide. He got a week's break between safaris, I was told, and I was to leave for the bush the next day.

The barmaid, Millie, hustled to serve the noisy men quickly. Jet-lagged, I decided to try to get some sleep as soon as I finished my wine. But Peter unexpectedly redeemed himself, so I will remember him with fondness forever because he revealed himself to be a good storyteller, and he presented me with a lovely gift – a sand elephant.

"I was in Namibia," he said to me abruptly. My mind instantly turned to great red dunes of sand, massive as the mountains at home (my children had not subscribed to National Geographic for me in vain). "It was the dry season."

I know dry. My spring at home ran dry each summer for years in a prolonged drought, forcing me to abandon my beloved garden several seasons until we drilled a very deep well. I reused bath water; I even hauled in water for my bath. Raccoons invaded my house to drink our cat's water. Dry, I can understand.

"I came to an oasis."

Oh, my God, an oasis. I was reminded that there is such a place to retreat to in times of great dryness. I needed an oasis. I hoped it was Africa.

"I didn't pitch camp because I was too tired. I found a nice palm tree and unrolled my bag. Hey, another round – and don't forget the lady," Peter called.

"So, then what happened," I asked, discreetly indicating that I want to pay for my Great White Hunter's round. I may not have had much money, but the rand was so devalued I could afford it and I knew he couldn't. Everyone leaned forward to hear what Peter had to say next. Millie quietly picked up my cash.

"Well, I was sleeping under this great effing palm tree at the edge of the oasis. I woke up to this rather odd sound and turned over in my sleeping bag."

"And found a bleeding 'or'" sang out his even more drunken safari companion.

The others in the bar turned immediately upon the insensitive fellow. "Stow it!" they said and turned their gaze back to Peter. I was fixated upon him and he responded to my questioning eyes. "I opened my eyes and saw this great elephant foot not more than a hand's width from my head."

We all gasped.

"All my life I have wanted to see one of those great sand elephants of Namibia. It's so hard. You lead safari after safari, but they keep out of sight. They're elusive you know."

We were now mesmerized. He was looking at me, so I nodded although I didn't know, and I realized the others in the bar were relying on me to keep him talking. They all wanted to hear this story.

"So I was lying there, and there's this huge animal and if he wants, he can move his foot a bit and squash me out of existence."

"Were you scared?" I asked.

Peter paid no attention to my question. He was a storyteller in the midst of a tale. I no longer mattered. I relaxed and everyone else sat back. We would hear the story with or without my help.

"Well, just about then this animal who's eating the palm branches from the tree above, which was the sound that woke me, realizes I am there and lowers his trunk. It's a male; I can see his tusks. Hell, I can see his bloody balls. And he runs his trunk up and down my body – never touching me, mind. Just an inch over my skin if I'm still. You better believe I was still!"

Nigel refilled Peter's glass, as Peter looked me in the eyes. He was drunk but focused, I could see.

"Do you know what that feels like?" he demanded.

"Of course not," I responded.

Peter sat back for a moment feeling self-satisfied. We were hoping the tale isn't over. "This animal was bigger than I had seen an elephant. Mind you, I usually don't see them from the feet up."

I had yet to see an elephant outside of a zoo or circus, but I understood.

Nigel, Millie, the other safari guide, and I were all riveted on Peter. And he was in form. "It ran its trunk up and down my body again, ran the tip over my face a long while. Then it went back to stripping the palm of its fronds. Then it would run its trunk over my whole body length again. Frond, me, frond, me. I could feel his body heat, he was that close. I didn't dare move seeing his great foot next to my skull."

For a moment I could clearly see the heart-shaped rosy tip of an elephant's trunk up close, inquisitive next to my face.

"I just lay there frozen. And this great sand elephant ate the palm fronds and checked me over. Again and again."

We sat silent while Peter refreshed himself from his glass and Nigel, standing in readiness, replenished it. "It went on for over an hour at least, even allowing for my fear. The elephant ate the whole bloody palm tree then gave me one final going over out of curiosity and shambled off into the desert again."

"Did you feel lucky to have seen the sand elephant or just relieved it didn't step on you?" I asked. I really wanted to know. The other South African males and the barmaid looked at me and backed off. They weren't used to outspoken American women. He was done with his story, and I was definitely pushing it.

Peter sat back thoughtfully, sipped his drink and then looked me in the eye once more. The drunken glaze seemed to fade from his eyes as he groped for what he was trying to say. "I felt, I felt – honored," he finally said.

I smiled at him and he at me. "Thank you," I told him.

The others were dismayed for a moment that burly Peter hadn't put me in my place with a rowdy joke. The bar was silent. Then the other guide made a joke about Peter getting sexual thrills from elephants out of frustration. Raucous laughter broke out. I excused myself and later in my room, heard a giant racket in the bar that woke me from dreams of greathearted, red-dusted, giant elephants that were very gentle. The sweet smell of the thatch roof lulled me back to sleep.

In the morning I learned from Millie that the guides had gotten into a brawl and knocked over the bar counter. "We have got to get that bolted down once and for all," she said distracted as she attended to organizing our breakfast.

Nigel stopped me in the grounds while we were loading our packs into our safari vehicle as we prepared to leave. "I think I must apologize for my rude guide," he said.

I was puzzled.

"Peter was quite over the bounds last night," he explained. "He is our oldest guide and he has never before spoken of his ventures before he joined us. I'm afraid we allowed him to go too far."

I smiled, "No, Peter was fine. No apology necessary."

"Well, if you are quite sure," my worried host said. He rubbed his forehead and I realized he is suffering from a hangover.

"I am," I reassured him.

"Well, that's good then," he said and left me to finish getting ready for my adventure. I heaved up my pack into our truck and for a moment imagined the rosy, heart-shaped tip of a curious elephant's trunk. I thought of its great beating heart.

Sometimes solace comes in unexpected forms, and just maybe, armed with Peter's vision, I would find my oasis here.

South African Males

There were ten of us on the safari and we realized right away that Philip had problems. He was an English South African. Most of them seemed to have some sort of masculinity security problem. They had to constantly show they were more macho than anyone else. They totally disregarded any ideas women might have and just ordered them around.

But Philip was our guide, or so we thought, and we were all determined to enjoy our safari. We had an unspoken agreement to put up with him. Philip was in his mid-twenties, about the age of my youngest son.

There were a German couple Ziggy and his very sweet girlfriend Ushi, a single Scandinavian man, Chris, a young English woman named Rose, an older Canadian woman named Joyce who had been in Africa for over two years and was a nurse, me, the only American, and a group of four young married Dutch women, one of them Black, Gretchen, a lively and very outspoken woman. The four were all friends vacationing together. All of them had been on safaris before. They explained with six weeks of vacation a year their families vacationed for two, the husbands vacationed together for two, and the women vacationed together the last two.

There was a young Boer South African woman named Sandy whom we first thought was there to assist Philip. Only well into the trip did we learn this was actually Sandy's safari. Philip was along for the ride to pick up a vehicle he had left behind in Mozambique when he had been caught in typhoon and forced to abandon a safari, flying the clients home early. Sandy was so meek mannered she simply let Philip take over. Us women were appalled. But in South Africa it was expected behavior despite Sandy having been through the same vigorous guide training program required by the government as

Philip. Certified guides there are highly well-trained people. Sandy had earned her way.

Philip had a redeeming quality – he was a great cook, while Sandy seemed incapable of producing anything but unending macaroni and cheese. He was also a good storyteller when properly primed with alcohol supplied by the rest of us. He made a preliminary play for Rose. Apparently one perk for male guides is winning over lady safariers with their manly ways. You can blame Hemingway, Clark Gable and Ava Gardner for that one. He was promptly rejected in favor of the attentions of the Scandinavian. It made Philip extremely grouchy for two or three days.

While he was grouchy, he began shouting and swearing at us often; once for not having folded our tents properly, so they did not fit into the designated bin of the truck. He positively ranted about it. Gretchen had little patience with Philip and shouted back at him, telling him to mind his manners and watch his language. I finally demanded he show us how to properly fold them.

"You've been trained, we haven't," I scolded him. "You want it done right, then show us how to please you."

He grumbled but then demonstrated that the tents had to be folded in thirds then folded small, not simply rolled up as we had been doing. We had had no idea.

He got over his snit as we went on our first real game drive in Kreuger Park.

We saw fields of beautiful dew-covered, golden colored spider webs and were told they came from the Golden Orb spider and were the first material used for Kevlon bullet proof vests, they are so strong. Finally, scientists were able to replicate the webs in a lab and leave the poor spiders alone.

A tortoise crossed the road. Sandy cracked a joke – her one and only during the three-week trip – "We are hunting for the Small Five." as opposed to the Big Five, the most dangerous animals according to old time trophy hunters. The Big Five were lion, leopard (because it strikes faster than the human eye can follow), elephant (because they have no other predator but man and get very angry when someone kills one of their own), rhino, and Cape buffalo (because they are so bad tempered and can carry a grudge a long time).

Suddenly we happened on a herd of impala – the lovely antelope. I quickly wrote down how many male and females we saw – our first sizable game. Ziggy began laughing at me. I asked why and he just said, "You will see." He was right. Before the day was done we had seen perhaps a thousand impala. They are fast, prolific and low on the food chain.

Before long we happened on a group of giraffes feeding off the tops of the trees. I was instantly enchanted. We stopped for photos, but a vehicle coming the other way stopped and the driver told us, "Leopard, a mile down the road on the bough of a tree over the road."

Philip immediately started the safari-mobile.

"But we have giraffes!" I said. Ziggy knelt before me, holding my hands.

"Andrea, I have been on six safaris and have never seen a leopard. Please, please. I promise you many giraffes, but this is our one chance for a leopard," he pleaded. I smiled, and called out "To the leopard."

Ziggy afterwards claimed as this was my first safari, unlike the rest of my fellow travelers, I was their good-luck charm. The leopard was napping on a low bough. We were all silent. Most of us had not yet switched to the then new digital cameras and whenever an automatic film winder made a short whirring noise, the leopard would open his eyes, yawn, then go back to sleep. For a half hour we sat enthralled watching it sleep away the hot part of the day.

As we drove away to find a safe place to have lunch, Philip was quite pleased with himself. It was everyone's first leopard, and he took personal credit for having produced it for us, bragging non-stop until

Gretchen sharply told him to "stuff it.". Before the end of the day we had seen all of the Big Five, and my reputation as a good luck charm was solidified.

"Never before a leopard, and never before all five in one day. Thank you, Andrea," Ziggy exclaimed. My fellow travelers applauded me though I hadn't done a thing. I think they just wanted to puncture Philip's ego balloon.

Krueger Park was a paradise. There were enclosures I thought of as people cages where one had to be at night. There were a lot of rules, be in an enclosure before dark, stay in your vehicle when on a game drive, etc. all of which made sense and were enforced not much by the rangers, but by the animals. Guides who conducted night drives had special training and were armed. They drove open sided, quiet electric trams.

The guide handed out spotlights to us all so we could scan the landscape. If we saw eyes reflected we pushed a button that lit a signal that alerted the driver who would stop. We'd pass up the information in a whisper "twenty meters back on the right". Then we'd be very silent as the driver backed up and we all aimed our lights at the animal. The guide on our first night drive told us he had been doing the drives for eleven years and had never seen so much game. We came upon an entire pack of hyenas with their cubs licking up after a kill. We even saw the wild African cat (apparently the Eve of all our housecats) nursing a litter – a first for all, even the guide.

Everyone told the guide it was because of my luck.

We learned during the unending war in neighboring Mozambique all the lions in the South African park had become man eaters. Desperate, starving Mozambiquans had taken the chance to scale the park fence at the border and all that would be left were the remnants of their clothing that the rangers would find.

Philip fell into another foul mood as soon as we neared the border into Mozambique. He snapped at everyone, and swore as he navigated bad roads. He learned we could not get to Zimbabwe as planned because a typhoon had washed out the only road there. The storm had displaced land mines that had to be relocated by experts before road repairs could be made which would take months. The entire safari had to be rerouted and new plans made. Then our safari-mobile truck got stuck in sand and we all had to help dig it out. He swore continually until we were finally at a camp on a stunningly beautiful and empty beach and the Dutch women bought him enough beer for him to get drunk.

A conversation about birthdays and astrological signs sprang up. Gretchen, the black Dutch woman, had a birthday close to Philips.

"But you are on the cusp of Cancer, whereas I am a complete crab," he said.

"Oh, we all know that, Philip," I said, and the entire group burst into laughter. He pretended to punch me.

Then he began speaking about someday having to give up being a guide if he wanted to start a family. He would be a good father, he declared, and would regularly beat his sons. We were horrified. Gretchen challenged him about that sort of parenting and he replied his father had beat him regularly and look how splendidly he turned out. Then he also spoke of canings he received in his boarding schools.

When he went off to the campground bar the rest of us talked and agreed it was no wonder Philip had problems and we speculated if being brutalized as children had turned all white African males into such parodies of machismo. Every stroke of the cane driving out a little more joy, a little more security until a man could become hollow. Even Gretchen seemed to take pity on Philip after that.

Tales from an African Guide

We took it in turns to ply Philip with alcohol after dinner when we gathered around the fire. We did it to get stories out of him. When he wasn't having a temper tantrum or in one of his boasting moods, he was a good storyteller.

Philip and the Swede

It cost me a bottle of whiskey to get this story and it was worth it.

Philip was on a canoe safari down the Zambezi River. The safari was made up of eight men and one woman, a very tall, ("almost two meters high") blonde, beautiful Swedish woman who was traveling with her boyfriend.

There were permanent camps set up at infrequent intervals on the banks of the river, but they were far apart and in between the safari had to rough it, sleeping on the ground.

The safari was a sweaty, dirty affair. The river was too full of crocodiles, hippos, and other dangers to chance bathing in it. The water supply the safari carried was reserved strictly for drinking and preparing food. The group was grimy and uncomfortable after just a few days. They had to regularly apply bug repellent because of dangerous mosquitos, adding to the discomfort.

Finally, their canoes reached a real camp and cheers went up as they beached their crafts. Philip decided to prepare a special meal for dinner. There was a shower rigged up with a five gallon can of water on a small hill above the tents. Everyone gallantly voted to let the Swede take the first shower.

The men settled into camp chairs around a fire pit and poured out some whiskey to celebrate their hard labor on the river and having found a modicum of comfort at last.

In the shower the young lady was luxuriating in soap and water, and had lathered her hair. Her eyes were closed when she heard a loud noise and the water stopped. She wiped soap out of her eyes and looked up to see a great bull elephant drinking the last of the shower.

The terrified girl screamed and ran nude to the fire screaming in her Swedish accent, "Elephant, elephant, elephant! Help! Help!"

Philip smiled at the memory, "All of us sitting around that fire didn't move at first, just drinking in the sight. For everyone, except her boyfriend, it was the greatest moment of the safari. The sight of her was better than all the game we had seen."

Chilean Glamour Girls

African safaris are not glamorous affairs despite Hollywood's efforts to portray them as such. Unless you are on a very expensive luxury safari, you are expected to set up your own tent, pitch in with the camp cooking, and you schlep your own bags. You are limited to one soft sided bag. Philip told us a tale about an odd safari he led once.

He was startled when two young Chilean women showed up with three very large suitcases each to join his safari.

The young ladies were definitely city girls. One was a model and a beauty queen who had won a trip to Africa in a pageant. Her friend was her agent. He explained they'd have to leave their bags behind at the safari headquarters and purchase a soft bag to take on the trip.

"They had three ballgowns each and a dozen pair of high heels," said Philip. "I told them they had to pack appropriate clothing."

"But I need at least one gown in case we go out," the model protested.

"If we go out, you'll wear shorts, a tee shirt and sandals," he replied.

They weren't happy about it, but the women did as requested and set out for a taste of the wild.

They weren't on safari very long when one night as everyone was sitting around the campfire the agent heard a noise behind her. She turned and shined her flashlight in the bush and spotted a hyena.

After that the Chileans refused to sleep in the tents, and insisted on being locked into the luggage bin of the safari vehicle every night.

When they needed to use the bathroom they'd knock on the compartment door and call out, "Phee-leep" plaintively until he came and unlocked them. And each morning he'd let them out.

By the end of a couple weeks when they returned to claim their ball gowns, he didn't know who was happier the safari was over – them or him.

When Lions Moved In

"I was on safari in Namibia with a small group," Philip said. "We had been driving through desert country heading for an oasis where there were some nice trees and good camping. But we had seen some wonderful game and stopped to sightsee, so it was dark when we got there.

"We cooked dinner, and everyone pitched their tents by lantern light. I was tired and just rolled up in my sleeping bag on top of the safari-mobile (a Mercedes truck converted to a glass sided bus). In the morning I woke at dawn, stood up to stretch and then gaped in horror.

"During the night about a dozen lions had come into camp and curled up around the tents to sleep.

"I yelled to everyone not to come out of their tents. I yelled and shouted and banged the top of the bus to persuade the lions to move on, but they ignored me and went on sleeping.

"I crawled into the bus through the top opening and hauled out pot lids and banged them. The sun was up and it began to get very hot. I brought out water bottles and began pitching them to the entrance of the tents.

"I'd shout out when it was safe for someone to unzip the tent and grab their bottle or warn them when a lion looked too interested. I beeped the horn, I started the engine, but those lions just lay there.

"Some of the people were getting desperate and began using the empty water bottles for sanitary purposes.

"Finally, around noon, the lions began to rouse and stretch, and one by one they wandered off. Everyone just yanked up their tents, pitched them hurriedly into the bus and we headed off as fast as we could to find another place to make our belated breakfast."

When Rules are Broken

There was a defiant East German on one safari. After having lived so long under an authoritarian government East Germans did not like rules – any rules. I was to discover that was true of many people in previously Soviet countries. It often made them difficult neighbors. This fellow had a brand new camcorder and he wanted to use it every chance he could.

"He kept wanting to get out of the vehicle in dangerous circumstances. He challenged me again and again and almost started a fist fight once, but the other people on the safari pulled him away.

"He got it into his head that he wanted to film a Cape Buffalo. I explained how dangerous they were and that he had better film them from a distance using his zoom lens. But, of course, he had to argue with me. We reached an enclosure in Kreuger Park and settled in for the night. On the way in we spotted a herd of buffalo by the river. The enclosure didn't open its gates until five the next morning.

"We were ready to leave but we couldn't find the East German. We asked the rangers to help. They found him eventually. He had apparently scaled the fence and gone out at dawn to film the Cape Buffalo herd. He was dead of thirty-five puncture wounds. His camcorder had caught the charge. He had caught his footage but at what cost.

"I hadn't liked him, but I was horrified at his end. Awful way to go."

The Night of the Lions

During the days we were in a "safarimobile", a tall converted Mercedes truck with many windows added up high to see over the brush while we were on game drives. It was high enough it took a ladder to get on board. I climbed carefully but my safari-mates scampered up and down like the numerous monkeys we spotted. Once in a while we'd stop at a campground that offered night game drives for a small fee.

At our first camp, we were excited to learn there was going to be one leaving in a few minutes. We ran to the rendezvous spot and heard a raucous voice calling in clear English, "Go away! Go away!"

When we stopped, dismayed, a ranger began laughing and pointed to a tree, "It's the Go Away bird, a Grey Laurie."

Ten of us piled into the low-slung open vehicle with just a canvas awning. There was nothing between us and the creatures of night.

When we got back safely to camp that night we were all elated. Our guide, Sandy, had cooked our dinner in a big cast iron pot over a wood fire, knowing we'd be as hungry as lions. Someone took out a couple bottles of red wine. We sat around the fire talking rapturously about the wonderful animals. Suddenly a male lion began growling. It was very close.

The "people cage" had an impressive gate, but only a one-meter high electric fence surrounding it. It seemed any self-respecting feline, even my young cat at home, could leap it if it wanted to, much less a lion.

We all shone flashlights into the bush trying to spot it, but although it was near, we could not see it. Suddenly another lion, also male, growled back. The two seemed to be working out negotiations about whose territory ended where. I wondered uneasily if they were saying, "Okay, you take the Dutch girl, give me the American."

We stayed up a couple more hours. My tent was pitched right up against the fence. Everyone eventually was worn out and lions or not they drifted off to bed. I lay in my tent thinking I could never doze off while two lions were within just yards of my sleeping bag, but I did. The phrase "Lying down with lions" took on new dimensions for me.

A few hours later I was awakened by something making a great racket right on the other side of the fence, literally six feet from my head. I grabbed my flashlight and thought of bounding out to see what it was, then came to my senses. Lions, I told myself, lions had been right out there a short while ago, and I was prey. I didn't leave the safety of my tent, but I shone my light through the mosquito netting peering into the darkness. Believe it or not, I fell asleep again – surrounded by critters, lullabyed by lions.

Mozambique

Mozambique shares a border with South Africa. If you look at a map, it is the country that looks like an upside-down howling wolf hound on Africa's east coast. I had chosen a safari that went there for one reason – to swim in a new ocean. Mozambique has a long coastline on the Indian Ocean.

I knew the country was poor. I had done some research and was appalled to learn it had only recently come out of a thirty-year war. What started as a war for independence from the Portuguese turned into a vicious civil war funded by South Africa's Apartheid government and secretly by the US using Israel as our middleman because the newly elected Mozambique president was a Marxist.

I was to learn a lot in Mozambique, especially about landmines and poverty. Also, about simple joy. Despite being the poorest country on the planet at that time, despite the horror of landmines, at least no one was shooting at them anymore and that made almost everyone very happy.

Approaching the border which was very scary looking with two cyclone fences and razor wire filling the gap between them, watchtowers and AK 47 toting guards everywhere, Sandy and Philip warned us.

"When you go into the building to show your passports don't wear hats or sunglasses."

"Why," someone asked.

"There's a picture of their president inside and they feel hats and sunglasses are a sign of disrespect to him."

New governments of new democracies are very thin-skinned and insecure. And their border guards usually carry heavy arms.

24

Once safely away from the border we headed to Maputo, the capital, to exchange money. As we drove, I noticed something odd. There were small craters here and there, and in each there was small crop of corn growing. I learned the craters were from landmines. People knew it was safe to plant there once they had already blown up.

The war had also cost the country its wildlife. Elephants lost limbs to landmines just as people had. Hunger had driven people to hunt their animals. In South Africa when elephants crossed the borders from Mozambique, they had on average four bullet holes in them. The bush was lovely and could have supported a large game population – but not until landmines were removed.

We drove into Maputo and as we circled the central plaza where all the major government buildings were located, Philip again cautioned us not to take photos.

"I once took one of the sculpture and got arrested. My boss had to come here and pay bribes to get me out of jail and reclaim our vehicle."

I really wanted to photograph the sculpture. It was a huge monumental piece made out of welded AK 47s. The gun crossed with the short-handled mattock had become the symbol of the country and decorated its flag. The Portuguese had demanded all males over fifteen years old give six months of the year of labor working on government owned farms instead of working on their own subsistence farms for their families. For their "taxes" they got nothing. No health care, no schools. So, the war began as a right to grow food. Thus, the mattock and gun.

At the money changer's we realized that for the duration of the war Mozambique didn't have the resources to print new money. The money was filthy, battered and disintegrating. One bill fell in half as the man handed it to me. He whipped out a roll of tape and put it together again. The tape was a critical tool of his trade. At the market people maimed by landmines sold carvings. Outside a woman dying of AIDS lay on the sidewalk without even a piece of cloth under her head. People just stepped around or over her.

"Get us out of here, Philip," we all demanded.

As we drove through Maputo back to the lovely countryside, we saw bullet ridden buildings, buildings half blown up. Unlike other Mozambiquans, the people of Maputo looked shell shocked, not happy. As we passed a "market" that looked like it was a garbage dump, from inside the vehicle I raised my camera. A woman in the market saw me and raised up a coconut to throw at me. I hastily withdrew my camera.

"I've heard of camera-shy, but this is ridiculous," I told Philip who had snapped at me.

"That's because the Apartheid used to send spies disguised as tourists who took photos of people like doctors and teachers as well as government leaders and then they gave them to Renamo (a group then funded by the Apartheid to terrorize the people) to seek out and kill," Philip said and Sandy concurred.

After that I respected the justifiable paranoia.

We were headed to a place called Morangulo on the beach. We turned off the paved road that linked Mozambique to Zimbabwe on to a dirt road. It was pocked with large potholes and some of our closed lockers on the vehicle burst open breaking some bottles. We pulled up to a collection of thatched huts and were greeted by a large family. A grinning man, Sabao, welcomed us and led our guides proudly to a screened bread box atop a palm tree stump. It was full of fresh baked rolls.

"We like to support him so always stop to buy his rolls on the way to camp," Sandy said.

Sabao gave us a tour of his compound. A new son-in-law was cutting thatch for a hut for him and his bride. There were young children and a new baby that Sabao introduced us to. I had brought an old polaroid camera with me just for such occasions. I took it out and snapped a photo of Sabao and his wife holding their grandson. The family exclaimed loudly as they saw the photo take shape in front of them and were overjoyed when I gave it to them.

Sabao's oven had been fashioned out of an oil barrel and a battered sheet of metal. His ingenuity and his investment into the bread box was providing his family with a small, steady income stream. He was good baker. The rolls were crusty and delicious.

Morangulo

I was sleepless. The malaria medicine we all had been told to take was the worst possible as far as side effects went, but there was fatal form of malaria loose in Mozambique, so we endured it. We took it one day a week. It made some people become psychotic we were told, but fortunately we avoided that. It made a few feel ill the first day. For me the side effect was messed up sleep rhythms. In my entire time in Africa I never got more than four hours of sleep at a stretch. That continued for the two months afterwards at home where I had to continue taking awful meds.

But that meant I was awake for the sunrise every day in Morangulo and that made it all worthwhile.

The camp run by two men, one a Mozambique-born Portuguese and the other an English South African, was beautiful. The pristine beach protected by a barrier island was all ours. The lawns beneath the palm trees were kept cropped by men with machetes.

There was small bar with a vine covered arbor. We pitched our tents, made dinner then went off to the bar where the Dutch ladies taught us drinking games.

We settled into several days of sheer pleasure. We learned at night former army soldiers were paid to guard us. They materialized out of the bush wearing helmets and carrying the ubiquitous AK 47s. At night when we cooked our dinner in a large iron pot over the campfire we were told to help ourselves as often as we wanted but never take more that we could eat at a time so as not to waste any food. What was left in the pot was given to the guards who gratefully took it, returning the pot scrupulously scrubbed out by morning.

There was one day we were offered the chance to sign up for SCUBA diving lessons the next day. I eagerly signed on but a strong wind and current blew in during the night and the instructor called it off because he said visibility conditions would make it dangerous. To make up for it he and his partner offered to take us in their 4x4s down the beach to snorkel in a special place.

It was an extraordinary drive. We drove on the deserted beach for ten miles. Coconut groves reached for the sea. We forded two rivers. In the ten miles we saw just one family, a father, mother and two children fishing. I felt enormously privileged. These beaches were so stunning and as yet unspoiled. It was as if I found Hawaii before tourism. Mozambique has tremendous resources I am sure someone will plunder someday, so seeing it before that happened was a privilege I would never forget.

A Day in Maxixi

The first thing I noticed about the town of Maxixi (pronounced Ma Sheesh) was that all but one of the streets were made of sand. I felt like I had landed in real Rimbaud country. The wild, young French poet had been a gunrunner in Africa and paid for his adventures with his life in the nineteenth century. His burning, passionate poetry was the major influence on modern poetry afterwards, like Hemingway would be on American novelists a hundred years later. Lines from Rimbaud's "A Season in Hell" kept running through my head. His poetry colored my dreams. *"Where mingle with flowers, the eyes of panther"* – was a line that captured Mozambique for me.

Maxixi was a much more pleasant place than the capital Maputo. Maputo had war torn buildings, shell-shocked people and hadn't seen a drop of paint in the 30-year civil war. Maxixi was just a bit ramshackled. It had never been painted in the first place.

I lay in my tent and watched the magnificent sunrise over the bay in front of us. Suddenly a group of teen boys came running down the road to the beach. Stripping off their shorts and tee shirts, they jumped naked into the water from a dock. They laughed, clowned and splashed each other for about minutes then, just as rapidly as they had arrived, they donned their clothes and ran back into town.

At breakfast Philip said, "We are going to rest up for the day and you are all free to enjoy the town."

I joined forces with a couple of the Dutch women from the group and we set out on a shopping expedition. I needed laundry soap, another needed toothpaste. It appeared all the shops were owned by Indians. A pickup truck loaded with people navigated the sand street. All the people were singing. All over Africa people seemed to form instantaneous choirs. It always made my heart joyous.

I purchased some soap at a shop the size of my closet at home. Then I spotted a dry goods store. I had been admiring the brilliant sarongs the African women wore and finally here was a place that supplied them. The cloths, two meters long, one meter wide were flimsy and unhemmed but gorgeous. And they were only about two dollars each. I quickly selected a half dozen. The Dutch women laughed at my American extravagance. I had noticed they were close pocketed and bargained fiercely over everything.

I asked the Indian lady in the shop, "We saw a ceremony when we arrived at sunset the night last night.. A lot of ladies wearing saris were at the shore throwing flowers on the water."

She explained it was a ceremony to honor the girls who had begun menstruating that year. They were welcomed into womanhood with an all-female ceremony followed by an all-female feast. I was charmed.

We all split up outside the shop and I wandered alone down one of the sand streets. I bought a soft drink and sat on the step outside the shop to drink it. I had been warned by a doctor to drink only carbonated beverages while in Mozambique. While I disliked the sugary quaff at least it was cold and wet. The street was full of busy people.

A group of about half dozen men were at the corner talking animatedly. I saw a boy about fourteen watching them. I was struck by the boy's appearance because of his clothes, or lack of them. I had never seen anyone dressed like that. His upper garment had once been a shirt. I could tell because it still had a collar. The rest of the garment hung in streamers from the collar and blew in the breeze. His shorts had once been a cotton-polyester blend but all the cotton had worn out of the fabric. The pants were now transparent. This boy had no privacy for his privates.

He began sidling up to the group of men. He had almost approached them when one of them noticed him, shouted to the others and began chasing the kid. The other men also shouted at him and waved fists.

The one man gave up the chase after a couple dozen yards. He went back to his friends, and the boy stood at the end of the street brushing dust off himself, for all the world like a cat trying to retrieve its dignity after having been clumsy.

Later around our midday meal at the camp I asked Philip about the scene I had witnessed.

"Probably a child war veteran. No one trusts them, no one likes them," he replied.

In its long war, boys as young as six or seven were taken from their villages and forced to kill their family and neighbors or be killed themselves. It was a conscription of horror. Mozambique has about 100,000 of these boys who are not welcome in their home villages because they are murderers. No one wants them.

Philip warned me not to look for the boy when I expressed a desire to at least give him enough money for some clothes. "They are trained killers and terrorists," he said flatly.

That afternoon we went for a ride on an Arab dhow, the sailboats that have plied the African coast for centuries. I washed clothes and helped fix the evening meal. I kept thinking of the almost naked boy wishing with all my heart I could hand him a t-shirt as my day in Maxixi drew to a close.

Tree Schools

As we drove through Mozambique, I saw something I had never seen before – something I began calling "tree schools". Someone, usually a man, would be sitting on a piece of log under a tree while a group of children sat in the sand in front of him. They would be writing their lessons in the sand.

I learned when Samora Machel came into power after the war for independence from Portugal was over, he demanded literacy for his people. Teachers were sent to places even if there were no buildings to house a school. Thus, the tree schools. There was no budget for school supplies. The only time students saw paper and pencil was when they had to take an annual state exam.

I had already learned teachers had often been targets of terrorists in the civil war so I knew not to take photos of the tree schools as much as I wanted to. But I had brought a bag of school stuff with me, pencils, notebooks, colored pencils, rulers and such. I asked Philip if we could stop so I could give them to the children.

"You'd break a lot of the kids' hearts, Andrea," he explained. "Yes, the kids would be happy to get them at first, but then the teacher would collect them after we left and sell them."

"What? That's terrible."

"Not so terrible. He might use the money so his child could buy a school uniform and go to a better school and learn to become a teacher."

I was chastened. I had so much to learn about this level of survival. I had already seen buildings with windows broken out, just bare shells that were still serving as part time health clinics. A sign with a date and time would be posted outside indicating that a nurse or doctor would be coming. On the chosen day women with young children would line the road for a mile waiting their turn. One thing every Mozambique mother wanted for her children were vaccinations against the many diseases Africa offered.

Once we stopped at a roofed picnic spot. I had a new package of cookies I had bought in Maxixi. A bunch of children descended on us. I began handing out a cookie to each, but one boy refused and although I don't speak Portuguese, I understood when he said "I am not an animal."

I told him, "No, you will one day be the presidente," and handed him the package indicating he should give them to the others, not me. He nodded and gravely accepted the responsibility. He was distributing cookies as we drove off.

I wondered if he had been a student at a tree school. If so, I congratulated his teacher. On our return to Johannesburg I made sure the school supplies got to the young Zulu man, Chris, who struggled to spread education among the illegal immigrants in the "informal settlements." I knew he would know best how to get them where they were needed.

Best Job in Africa

Back in South Africa after visiting Swaziland, we found ourselves in Zululand. We reached a town where fruit vendors lined the road across from a small strip mall. At the last few campgrounds, shops had been closed and we were all eager to buy popsicles so we made Sandy stop the van at the shops. I came out carrying my cherry popsicle triumphantly and as one of the Zulu men was playing wonderful salsa music at his fruit stand, I danced my way to the bus. The Zulus liked that and cheered me on. When I got on the van Ziggy called out and offered to sell me to the vendors for four cows.

We had learned that was the going price for a Zulu bride, and Ziggy had also offered to sell Gretchen to the border guard at Swaziland who was clearly enchanted by the Black Dutch woman.

Sandy told us she was taking us to the living museum that had been established by the Zulus. It was a Zulu village and the government paid the people that were there to demonstrate old Zulu life. We walked up to a crude gate made of crossed branches. It looked simple but it was very important. No one went through it before calling out Sawubona and waiting for the reply Yaybo. Otherwise you could face some serious warriors with big sharp spears.

Once in, people were dressed in traditional garb. Married women wore a short modesty cape that covered their breasts but the maidens went topless. We saw some wild leaping dancing by the young men some wearing leopard skins, the maidens were more sedate when they danced.

We wandered around and then saw an old man with a musical instrument. He was smoking a joint as he played. We all laughed.

"The government pays you to do this?" Ziggy asked.

He smiled and said yes. "Old Zulu custom."

"Nice job," said one of the Dutch women.

"Best job in Africa," the old man grinned and took another toke as he strummed his instrument.

Section 2:
Bali

I went to Bali for the music. When I was eighteen I had gone to a concert put on by the Ethnomusicology Department of a university in southern California led by a man with the charming name of Mantle Hood.

He explained the music we about to hear was stratified. The higher the pitch of the instrument the more rapidly it played the melody. The orchestra or gamelan was made up of all percussion – gongs and xylophones with just one single non-gong, a one-string instrument which set the melody. There was one huge gong that that was just struck from time to time. You felt rather than heard it. It was music unlike any I had ever heard.

I was spellbound. I vowed to someday go to where that haunting music originated. It had taken me a long time, but now in my late fifties, I was here. The flight took two days with an overnight stopover in Japan. Fortunately, Japan Air Lines was very efficient. Before I could think of something to be more comfortable, the flight attendants were already bringing it to me – hot perfumed towels, slippers, you name it. Plus I got to visit Japan, albeit briefly as there was an eight-hour stay going and coming.

I had read much about the romantic island of Bali and most people were lavish in their praise of "paradise". However, I was to discover there are shadows in paradise. Long-time "Bali Hands" learn of them and still love the island. By the end of a month I had learned to love it, too, warts, shadows and all. I also learned on that trip to be discriminating in my choice of travel companions.

Kuta Cowboys

I had been in Bali a few days when I realized I had to acquire a husband, even if an imaginary one. The Balinese asked three questions in the first five minutes "What is your name? Where are you from? Are you married?"

When I replied in the negative to the latter, I got three proposals the first day, all from men in their twenties.

My travel companions Linda and Terri had met a pleasant older "Bali Hand" on the plane the day before. Patrick had advised us about a good hotel and restaurant at Kuta Beach, and had rejoiced at my decision to stay in Ubud. He said it was indeed the center of true Balinese culture unlike the tourist center of Kuta Beach. He accompanied us in a taxi to our hotel before continuing on to his lodgings and returned to meet us for dinner.

Our room at Kuta Beach was lovely, as was the entire pretty hotel. But the Kuta Beach scene was not for me. It was thronged with young Aussie surfers and Javanese massage girls offering the surfers happy endings. It was a tropical seedy Coney Island. Linda and Terri wanted to make use of their bikinis and decided to stay an extra day at the hotel. I left to find us lodgings in Ubud. I took off in a bemo for Despensar the capital, where I hoped to catch another bemo to Ubud. Bemos are a sort of bus made out of a pick-up with a canvas cover and benches in the back.

A teenaged girl got inside with me. Instead of inquiring into my marital state she asked what religion I was. "Humanist," I replied. That made her very thoughtful. Bali is an island of Hindus surrounded by the Muslim islands of the rest of Indonesia and they are curious about religion.

In two walks outside the hotel I had already learned the Balinese were very polite. Approached by vendors, you exchanged names, and even when you refused their wares, they and you would say "another time," to save face for you both.

In Despensar I couldn't find the bemo stop but was approached by a taxi driver. For an hour's ride to Ubud, his offer was so cheap I hopped in. That's when the taxi driver proposed. I laughed thinking he was joking. He was serious. The longer I stayed in Bali and learned about the "Kuta Cowboys' the more I realized just how different life is in Bali.

Just as many Western males have given Thailand a sinister reputation because they go there to successfully hunt for underage girls for sex, so Western women are casting a long shadow over Bali because they have found a place where the young attractive men find them desirable even if their own culture has not for various reasons.

Fat women, ugly women, old women, even diseased women (the Balinese have had to learn about AIDS the hard way); as long as they are women and have Western currency, the Balinese men are willing. They are not direct prostitutes for the most part. The men who have earned the nickname among tourists of "Kuta Cowboys" after the beach town they and the tourists mostly inhabit, don't charge for sex. They just expect the woman to pay for their meals, transportation, maybe lodging, and any entertainment they share in addition to sex.

And they mean it when they ask if the woman will marry them. They assume she will support them and free them from the daily task of trying to earn a living so that they are free to do their much more important temple jobs. When the woman gets fed up and wants to get a divorce, he agrees and immediately goes looking for a new wife so his temple duties will not be neglected. I felt that the marriage to a westerner did not count as real to the Balinese.

The taxi dropped me off in the center of town and I was hungry, so I went into the Lotus Café. It had a large pool full of flowering lotus plants and a rare open view as Ubud sits at a high altitude. I savored the atmosphere of the peaceful setting even more than the spicy chicken and rice I was served. I made my way to the tourist office and asked about *losmans* – family compounds that offer lodgings to visitors. I was given directions to one a few blocks away.

The monarch of the losman was Theodora, a regal, unusually tall woman. While the men own the rice paddies in the family, the woman rules the household, and any money she makes from it is under her control. Theodora's husband Wayan was a laid back, rather lazy fellow and was content to let Theodora make decisions. I was given the key to a small bungalow in a large garden that included a swimming pool with a waterfall and flowering vines at one end. I knew Terri and Linda would really like that pool.

I strolled down to the telephone office and called the hotel to let Terri and Linda know where I was and tell them about the pretty pool. They were delighted and let me know they'd be in Kuta for one more day.

I spotted school kids carrying brooms and buckets on their way to school. I asked about that at the tourist office.

"Every Friday the kids clean their school so it's ready for them the next school week," I was told. I thought that charming. It gave the kids a sense of ownership of their school I felt. They all looked very cheerful.

I learned there was a temple that was performing a dance drama that evening and for a few dollars I bought a ticket that included "transport" as the temple was a few miles away. The transport turned out to be a motorbike and I sat on the back, and while refusing another offer of marriage from the rider, I noticed he had on gloves with long claws. He was one of the dancers as well as a driver. There were rows of folding chairs in the temple.

It was my first chance to see a gamelan, an Indonesia orchestra and a full dance performance. The scene was lit by torches and the music began. My motorbike rider was transformed into a demon. There was a scene when a monkey king is knocked out and he got a four-foot erection while he lay unconscious. Everyone burst into laughter as the soldiers around him were filled with admiration. Laughter was considered an offering to the gods, so every performance had some kind of bawdy scene to provoke it. The monkey king followers were played by the little boys of the *banjar*, a temple congregation, and they tumbled gracefully around the stage/altar. The charming little girls danced behind a princess.

Everyone was gorgeously costumed. As the performance ended, the women carried their elaborate offerings up to be blessed. It was so beautiful and the people so clearly reverent I was moved to tears.

I went over the performance in my mind as the demon, bereft of costume now, took me back to the losman. I was impressed by the strenuous dancing which seemed almost to be a high form of yoga and took a lot of muscles and control. Older people could not do it.

The next day Terri and Linda arrived. I hadn't known them very well before the trip but had been eager to have travel companions. By the end, I never wanted to see Terri again, but Linda and I became close friends and later made more trips together. Theodora moved us into a larger bungalow we settled in..

At Theodora's Losman

I woke up and wandered on to the terrace outside our bungalow at the losman. The garden was a blaze of tropical flowers.

The grandmother of the family had already woven the morning offerings for the family temple. She had made little baskets of banana leaves, filled them with rice and fruit and decorated them with flowers. Those were for the gods. She had made another set which she set outside the gate. Those were for the demons. The Balinese believe in treating the demons well so they will leave you alone. It never took long for the stray dogs to find the offerings. That was all right because the dogs were considered the reincarnation of faithless wives and therefore in the demon category.

The houseboys had made a thermos of tea for us and left it on our table on the terrace. Theodora, our landlady, ran an efficient operation. All the money she earned within the losman was hers to spend. The family rice fields and such belonged to her husband Wayan, and those earnings were his to spend. Theodora had earned enough to give her daughters an excellent education. The family had four children, twice the number of the usual Balinese family. Theodora set a big pot of rice to boil and sautéed a batch of vegetables to go with it. She spent about ten minutes at that task. I had noticed Balinese families did not sit down for meals together. They just helped themselves as individuals from the pots of food throughout the day whenever they felt hungry.

Then Theodora and grandma got down to the task that really mattered. They began making the offerings for their banjar's temple. A banjar is a temple congregation. The elected male head of the banjar controls everything in the congregation's lives even down to birth control. About a hundred families belong to a banjar. When the population grows beyond that they form a new banjar which owes allegiance to the mother banjar.

The women gathered perfect fruits, made various colored rice pastes, took a large basket and began constructing a beautiful tower of shaped rice paste sculptures, integrating the fruits and flowers from the garden. It would take them hours. It would be done before sunset when Theodora would dress up and carry it on her head to offer up at the temple when the kulkul drum that substitutes for a church bell summoned the banjar..After the gods there had eaten their spiritual bellyful, she would retrieve what fruits were still good for the family kitchen and discard the rest until tomorrow when the process started all over again.

I poured some tea and wandered over to look at the women at work and admire what they were doing. We chatted a bit. Then I strolled the garden until the gals woke up. They usually slept later than I did.

A monkey was leashed to a tree near the pool. His name was Sweetie and he was not charming. He leaped out with teeth bared at anyone who came near the tree, only kept from attacking by the length of the leash which would choke him back. He never got discouraged. I learned to give the tree a wide berth. He often just leaped when no one was about, as if he was trying to hang himself. Wayan loved Sweetie. Each day he unhooked the leash and took Sweetie to the pool to swim. Sweetie was a good swimmer and did a lot of laps. His daughters ignored Sweetie, and his son, about three, was terrified of the monkey.

Terri was unhappy because the bed was too hard. We decided to go to the huge outdoor market just down the road and see if we could buy her a piece of foam for her bed. Terri had not traveled much before and on her first trip abroad we had immersed her in a very exotic culture. It wasn't easy for her.

Linda, however, had lived for a few years in Taiwan and had traveled many places. She became our Asia expert. I had read a lot specifically about Bali and had learned some important phrases from a phrase book so I could greet people and ask them vital questions. So the others depended on me for communications.

Terri became excited at the market when she saw a shoe salesman. She tried on shoes while Linda and I shopped, picking up some groceries, and admiring the many handicrafts. Balinese are artistic people because they are constantly making things to offer to the gods. Finally, Terri caught up with us gleefully carrying about six pairs of shoes.

As we located foam pads Linda panicked. She had left her camera and sunglasses at a stand and couldn't remember where. Just as she looked dismayed people around us called her and she saw a woman at a stand trying to get her attention as she held up Linda's camera. Balinese believe so strongly in karma they never steal.

Karma makes them gentle, too. Even pointing is considered a violent act. I never heard anyone shouting angrily there, not even at the pesky stray dogs which they won't kill, but neither do they manage or care for. They might hit them with a stick if they attacked but they didn't want bad karma coming at them. When a Balinese got angry, he pouted, got grumpy and gave the silent treatment. I never saw anyone hit a child. The gentleness is one of the things that makes Bali paradise to many.

Wayans and Monkeys Everywhere

Life got confusing when Theodora asked us if we wanted to hire her driver Wayan. We thought she meant her husband Wayan, but no, it was another Wayan.

There are just four names in use in Bali: Wayan, Made, Nyoman and Ketut. Male or female, the oldest child is Wayan, the next is Made and so on until the names are used up, then they begin again with Wayan. Since most Balinese practice birth control now and generally have just two children, there are a lot of Wayans and Mades on the island. Theodora was the one exception and we never learned how she managed to get her own unique name but after having three daughters then finally a son, it was self-evident why she had exceeded the acceptable number of offspring.

This new Wayan proved to be a problem. We were enjoying the extraordinary landscape of Bali. The mountainous island had many steep valleys that had been sculpted into rice terraces. You only saw the sky in small slices.

Wayan pulled into a wide spot with a nice view. We got out of the car to take some photos of the steep rice paddies when we were attacked by a crowd of vendors. They were aggressive and we had to fight our way through them to get to the car. Linda was trapped and when a policeman came along she called to him for help. Wayan just sat in the car watching.

"We're going to get rid of the driver," she announced when we stopped at a restaurant for lunch. "He just threw us to the wolves. Drivers are supposed to help you."

After lunch he tried to get us to shop in a store of his choosing but we went to another one a few doors away. We saw him signal the store owner and start what seemed an argument with him. He clearly had a deal with the store we ignored and was now trying to set up another. I realized he probably had a deal with the pack of vendors that had swarmed us as well. Once back at the losman we told Theodora we were going to find our own driver. Her Wayan just didn't work out for us.

That evening when I persuaded Linda to come with me to the palace to see the Ramayana danced we ran into another Wayan. He was a young sweet man and he owned a van. We decided to hire him to get around the island.

The palace performance was, as promised by the tourism office, spectacular. It was a rich banjar and so was able to hire the best teachers and musicians to instruct them.

When we returned to the losman we told Terri we had found another Wayan. We set up a schedule for ourselves. One day we would stay in Ubud and sightsee on foot or rest. The next day we would drive around the island with Wayan. We explained that to him when he showed up the next day and he was happy with the plan because he also had another job in a tire repair shop.

"My wife Made is expecting our first baby," he told us.

When the houseboys Theodora hired spotted him and realized he was now our driver, they turned sullen. There was no more smiling "selamat pagi" (good morning) with our tea. I finally sat the chief houseboy also named Wayan down and asked him what was wrong.

"You hired Wayan, but now have someone from another banjar drive for you. You lied."

"No, I did not lie. Wayan did not work out for us. He did not help us."

He still seemed unconvinced, so I explained my friends and I had spent a lot of money to travel to Bali, and we had the right to enjoy our stay even if it meant hiring someone outside his banjar.

"We don't belong to your banjar or our driver's banjar. We are free to choose."

He finally nodded at my reasoning, and good humor was restored to our relief.

I persuaded Terri to come with Linda and I to the Sacred Monkey Forest which was a short walk away. She had steadfastly refused to go to any of the temple dances. She preferred to hang out in her bathing suit at the losman and flirt with the houseboys. She had a fiancé at home, and was missing him, but she was desperate for male attention.

But Terri liked monkeys. She kept trying to befriend Sweetie in vain. It was cool in the shade of the forest. A number of people were strolling the path that ran through it. The people in front of us had some plastic bags. Suddenly they were attacked by a several monkeys who tried to snatch the bags from them. Terri instantly wanted to go to a shop nearby and buy something to feed to the animals. I pointed out the signs that said that was forbidden.

She took a candy bar from her purse and called to the monkeys. To her pleasure some responded, but then the monkeys also jumped Linda and I. Linda began screaming. I helped her dislodge a monkey tangled in her hair and she ran away terrified. Terri just laughed. I was furious with her.

When we got back to the losman we discovered another monkey problem. Sweetie had somehow freed himself and was running wild. Oddly enough he never left the walls of the compound. I thought he'd run off to the forest and join the sacred monkeys.

Instead he ran into the family temple and trashed all the offerings grandma had left in there. He scampered into the trees while everyone tried to lure him down with bananas. Wayan, Theodora's husband tried to call him to the pool. Instead Sweetie, who knew the little boy was scared of him, jumped the boy who promptly started screaming and when his mother came to grab Sweetie, the monkey jumped back in the tree. Finally, the chief houseboy Wayan did a clever thing to lure Sweetie back into captivity. He took a mirror and held it up. Sweetie instantly came out of the tree to get closer to monkey he saw.

The monkey chase had been fun to watch. While Wayan, the husband, tied Sweetie back to his tree, Wayan, the houseboy, came by.

"Who let the monkey loose?" I asked.

He shrugged, "The Monkey God," he replied.

It's handy having a multitude of gods available to take blame.

NABR Network
ML @ Quaf 1941

Pd8 y 2 6 6 F

The Golden Girls Explore

Our driver Wayan and I bonded right away. He was from a distant village and missed his mother, so he adopted me and insisted I take the shotgun seat whenever we set out on an expedition. One day he told me that the neighborhood called us The Golden Girls after the American television show.

I burst out laughing. Linda and Terri were upset when I told them. Though each of them was in her fifties they thought themselves too young to be a Golden Girl. Then they argued over which of them was Dorothy – the smart Golden Girl. Wayan told me because I kept learning more Indonesian while the others didn't bother, I had the honor of being dubbed Dorothy. Terri, with her constant flirting and careless display of her body was the slutty Blanch, and Linda, who was absent-minded and a bubble headed blonde was innocent Rose. I didn't share the details with my companions. They were still grumpy over the whole thing.

I was astonished that the Balinese watched American television, but I saw the family at the losman gathered around a set out in the garden. All the commercials were locally produced with gamelan music and the little girls would get up and practice dance moves during the commercials.

On our Ubud days I always went to another temple dance. Terri never did. Linda came with me a couple times. They were such colorful pageants. At one performance a god suddenly appeared in all his glory. The tall dancer emerged from behind a curtain clad in the most ornate costume I had ever seen outside of films of Carnival in Rio. He stood on one foot on tiptoe in an elaborate pose and to my admiration held the difficult pose for well over a minute and a half. It had to take immense strength and was truly an immense offering to his god.

Granahan*

Another night I made a bus trip to attend a Kecuk dance. This had actually been introduced by western anthropologists who had come to study the unique culture. It required all the males in a village – one hundred of them ideally and instead of being accompanied by gamelan music, the men chanted. It was done by torchlight, the men naked from the waist up. It was impressive but I preferred the dances that involved everyone including the children. I saw many versions of the Ramayana legend danced out.

I also developed a great fondness for the Barong who appeared frequently in dances. This was a friendly demon. Every village had their own Barong. The costume was kept in a special little house and once a year a dancer would become Barong and dance around frightening the children and blessing every house in the village. If you have a friendly demon, it frightens away all the unfriendly ones.

Wayan clued me into not revealing I was a widow. A widow is considered to have such bad karma that anything can be done to her with impunity. Widows can even be raped without incurring any bad karma. Suttee, widow self-immolation on her husband's pyre, was still legal in Bali long after it was outlawed in India. The last Balinese suttee had been in the 1960s, long after India had given up the practice.

I also realized elderly Balinese were not venerated, and barely respected. I saw elderly women given difficult jobs to do such as hauling rocks. I saw a pickup truck loading up a bunch of young men, some teens, and an elderly grandmother. The males filled the cab and made granny sit in the truck bed with a load of rocks. Grandpas and grannies had the jobs of tending the shops of family businesses and babysitting young children so as to free those of the age of strength to prepare the constant offerings. The old folks weren't strong enough to perform the demanding dances; youth and strength mattered, not age and wisdom.

On our non-Ubud days we checked out the rest of the island or had adventures. One adventure was we went on a river rafting expedition.

The river crew said they'd pick us up at 6 a.m. – before sunrise. Linda laughed and said "It's Asia. They run on Asia time. We'll be lucky if they are here by seven."

She hadn't reckoned on Balinese temple duties that would need the young men later. They showed up at 5:55 a.m. We hastily threw on clothes and stumbled after them to their van which headed for the highest mountain peak outside of Ubud.

We were on the steep slopes of a volcano. Life jackets, oars and helmets were handed out, then we were given a brief lesson.

We learned the Indonesian for right and left and then were taught the word "Bong!" for lowering our heads as we were about to collide with something. Then we shoved off.

For the first fifteen minutes or more I thought I had made the biggest mistake of my life and my children would have to fly to Bali to claim my corpse. We went through a violent steep stretch of water and every few seconds I heard "Bong!" as we bounced from rock to rock, from cliff to cliff and all three of us screamed our way down the mountain. During the fracas I accidentally hit Terri's knee, bruising it with my oar; she never let me forget it the rest of our stay. She blamed me for injuring her at least once an hour when we were together despite all my commiserations and first aid efforts, even after the bruise faded.

Suddenly we entered a river valley and the water flattened out. We had been delivered to a paradise. Jungle and flowers cascaded down the mountain, farmers worked oxen as they plowed fields. Every bend in the river opened to another postcard view. We paddled leisurely enjoying the sights. Tropical birds flew overhead. Monkeys swung on vines.

Eventually the boat crew pulled up to the shore. They gestured we were to climb up the mountainside on a flight of gigantic steps. Each stone step was about three feet high, and there were a lot of them. We levered ourselves up. Before long it became a struggle as we wearied. Our crew cheered us on. At last, we reached the top.

There, sarong-clad young women with flowers in their hair awaited us with tropical drinks made with "brim" a homemade liquor decorated with orchids. Terri immediately cheered up. The girls fussed about us with towels, tucking flowers in our hair and seating us at a table under a thatched roof for lunch. It was an elegant lunch and afterwards we learned the river crew van was right outside to take us back to the losman.

We were all quite proud of ourselves and I was relieved my children wouldn't have to come to Bali to claim a coffin after all.

The Mother Temple

I persuaded Linda we should seek out the Mother Temple of Bali, the largest, oldest one on the highest peak. Wayan knew all about it and thought it a worthwhile adventure. An entire village had formed below the impressive mountaintop walled shrine. A lot of steps climbed from the village to the peak. Visitors from all over the island were paying homage to the temple that had begun the whole Balinese culture in the twelfth century.

Wayan drove to the parking lot and met with a bunch of other drivers that he knew. Linda and I climbed slowly to the top enjoying the unusual open view.

When we walked through the gates we were met by a pushy loud man who told us he was in charge and said we should give him money. Never in all the temples I had visited had I been accosted like that. Tickets were sold, very inexpensively when a dance-play was going to be shown. It was considered a donation and the money went to buying more elaborate costumes or new dance teachers, never into private pockets. The money belonged to the gods, not to private individuals.

"Then you can't come in here unless you want to pray," he insisted.

"We have come to pray," I told him. I treated all temples with reverence and prayed quietly in my own way, giving thanks for the care and beauty that had gone into creating the temples. Linda agreed. I moved off to admire the amazing architecture of the main Balinese temple grounds and didn't notice Linda had gone in a different direction.

The man again appeared at my side. "You are not praying," he demanded.

"I pray in my way, you pray in yours. Stop interfering. Leave me alone," I told him. He backed off.

In a while I left the temple and descended the stairs. At the foot of the stairs I found Linda sitting on the lowest step sobbing while a whole bunch of village women stood nearby very concerned. I instantly sat with her and put my arms around her.

"What's the matter, hon?"

"He wouldn't let me pray. He said I wasn't good enough to pray in the temple," she wept. I knew Linda was having some marital problems and she had confessed she had taken the trip to give herself and her husband some distance so they could hopefully appreciate each other again. Her self-esteem was at a low. The rude man had stirred up some troubled waters.

"He is not worth a single tear. He was a cheap conman, that's all," I consoled her. I told the villagers there was a rude man who had bullied my friend.

"She just wanted a chance to pray at the temple, and he wouldn't let her." By the time we reached the parking lot the entire village was concerned and Linda's tears became a matter of general alarm.

Wayan was very angry when he learned what had happened. "A bad banjar," was his conclusion, but his anger did not stop there. He stopped next to a police kiosk, talked, pointing to the Mother Temple. The cop looked shocked and got on a phone. We drove off.

"Bad banjar, bad banjar," Wayan kept muttering. The banjars elected their leaders regularly. He disapproved of the new leadership if it permitted visitors to be treated badly.

I realized how much depended on banjar leadership. If a banjar leader allowed Kuta Cowboys to flourish, if it allowed visitors to be treated badly, it was bad banjar and according to the Balinese screwed up everyone's karma.

To the Beach &
Love and Marriage in Bali

After our success river rafting, Linda, Terri and I decided to go to a beach for a couple days. I refused to go back to Kuta Beach. I'd had my fill of Aussie surfers, Indonesian massage girls, and the seedy atmosphere. We opted for a beach resort on the other side of the island. It was a long drive and Wayan and I chatted about lots of things.

He told me about his courtship and marriage. The Balinese are fun loving people and the young people freely mingle at school and at the unending temple festivities. They choose their own mates and marry for love, but the ceremony is very different from ours.

Wayan and Made had fallen in love, but to get married officially is very expensive and only aristocratic families who are very caste conscious or wealthy business people can afford to go through the business of going to each other's families three times and entertaining the entire banjar with hired musicians, storytellers, cooks and delicacies and such. Most Balinese, including our Wayan and Made, use another method: the man kidnaps his bride to be. It's a carefully arranged kidnapping. Her clothes and special offerings are artfully conveyed to a pre-arranged place, in their case, a friend's house.

Wayan took his van (carless men rent one for the occasion) and outside of town, where Made was walking with her girlfriends, he and his buddies pretended to spirit her away. The Balinese love theater. Their entire culture is based on dance dramas. So, the young people make a great show of the mock kidnappings.

Made pretended to kick and bite, Wayan pretended to overpower her. The parents get into the spirit of the thing, too, apparently. They pretend to search diligently for the young people but always manage to avoid finding them.

Wayan and Made had to consummate the marriage before the offerings wilted. That made them married in the eyes of the gods. Then they were free to go on a honeymoon trip. They went to the Water Temple – a beautiful place on a high mountain lake and water-skied. After a week of bliss they returned home.

When they came home their parents had to accept the marriage and threw a party at their temple. Made dressed up and the two publicly fed each other something and from then on, they could set up housekeeping together.

Mind you, if there was ever a real kidnapping in Bali, the police would be called in and the entire island would help locate the culprit who would likely be put to death. But the mock kidnappings are very practical, saving the couple lots of badly needed money even if it means the honeymoon precedes the public marriage.

On our to the beach way we ran into a heavy rain.

"The people are angry at the gods because of the rain," Wayan said.

"Why is that?"

"This is the time for wedding parties and festivals. The rain is supposed to be gone by now. All the people have made offerings, but the gods didn't take the rain away this year."

Our resort was very nice with a large pool and a bar in the middle of it. Our rooms were nice but it was a little too far from a beach for me. So we decided to stay overnight and get a taxi to another resort right on the water the following day. When I went to tell the man at the desk, he laughingly called me Dorothy. Our reputation as Golden Girls had preceded us. Later swimming in the pool, I paddled over to the bar to discover to my horror Terri had yanked down her bathing suit to show the bartender her breast tattoo. I got a beer and swam over to Linda to tell her what I had just seen.

"Oh, my God," Linda exclaimed. "I am embarrassed to even be here."

The next morning we left early. The new resort was perfect. It offered us small cottage with mosquito net draped beds. There was small restaurant next to it offering fresh seafood. The beach, alas, was not sand, it was rocks. Out in the flat calm waters I saw fishermen with nets standing on long poles. I also saw small craft fishing in the sea. I saw no one swimming.

Wayan had told me most Balinese can't swim despite living on an island because they don't like the sea. They prefer mountain tops which is why most of their temples are on the mountains. When someone dies they are buried until it is time to cremate them, then the ashes are dumped into the sea, so it is seen as the abode of the dead. Typhoons come out of the sea also making it a scary place.

We swam and enjoyed a lazy day and then went to the restaurant. There the proprietors offered a free glass of homemade brim before and after the meal. Then they sold us a bottle of brim. Brim is sneaky, like tequila. We joked and drank in our bungalow. Linda went to the bathroom and a moment later screamed. Terri and I ran in and there on the wall was the biggest gheko we had seen. We were used to the cute lizards and they ate pesty bugs so were considered a blessing. Their mating call was their name. "Gheko, gheko" they'd repeat until a female responded. This one suddenly called and startled us all with its too loud cry. I took a book and tried to chase it. It finally fled out a window which we promptly closed.

The next day Wayan came to pick us up and take us back to our losman. It rained again. Naughty gods!

Blind Date

In preparation for the Bali trip I had joined an online forum. There a man named Ted described himself as an old Bali Hand. He had gone there regularly while stationed in the Philippines as a serviceman. He was about to buy a retirement home there. He told me he was meeting his daughter and a friend in Bali while I was there. He proposed we meet.

On the chosen day Linda and Terri were thrilled I had a date and played Cinderella's fairy godmother as they dressed me up.

I went to the Lotus Café that afternoon. There were three young Balinese women there whom I had befriended. I told them I was to meet a man I had not seen before. They excitedly asked if he were younger.

"No, my age."

"Oh, American?" They were disappointed I hadn't chosen a Balinese man, a Kuta Cowboy.

"If he is handsome you can tell him I am here. If he is ugly, tell him I'm not here," I told them and they were delighted at the game.

Not long afterwards I heard them giggling and calling my name as one of them led Ted to my table. He wasn't bad looking and we sat and chatted. He was a talker and bit on the boastful side, but not unpleasant company. He asked where I was staying and asked if he could come by that evening and have a drink with me and my companions after his appointment with a realtor.

He liked having three women pay attention to him and hung out with us for a couple hours. He told us about the baths in Bali. They were a combination spa and salon and offered various services. His daughter was eager to try them when she flew in the next day and he had picked up brochures for her. He gave us one. He became more loquacious after a brim cocktail and began boasting about his extensive travels in the area.

He invited us to join him and his daughter and her girlfriend the following evening at a restaurant. As soon as he left Linda and Terri began their assessment. Terri had flirted with him, but I was relieved she hadn't decided to show him her breast tattoo. We decided he seemed nice enough but I was still a bit wary.

The next day we went to the baths. I had a flower bath and a wonderful massage. Linda had a spice bath and a facial. Terri bathed and decided to spend the afternoon having her hair corn-rowed. That evening we all dolled up or as Linda said "tarted up." Some thunder began rumbling and we looked at the sky apprehensively. We took umbrellas with us as we set off downtown.

We hadn't gone a block when the skies opened up with a tropical monsoon. Damn gods! We instantly used our umbrellas but they did no good. The rain came down with such force it bounced off the stone streets and up under the umbrellas. In a matter of moments we were totally drenched, our hair dripping, clothes beyond sodden. I thought it comical and began singing "Singing in the Rain". The gals got into it with me and we merrily began dancing and splashing. As we sang. Balinese huddling under shop overhangs laughed and cheered us on.

We arrived at the restaurant laughing and shaking the water out of our umbrellas. We saw Ted and he did not look amused. We sat and explained we had been caught in the downpour as Ted introduced us to his daughter. He had not waited for us to order his dinner, and proceeded to eat without asking us if we'd like a drink or some tea. In fact, he was quite boorish. His daughter was a lovely young woman who kept the conversation going as her father shoveled his food. She and her girlfriend were served their meals. But they waited to eat until we ordered something.

"Please, go ahead," I said as the drinks we had ordered were served. Ted got up to use the restroom and as soon as he was out of sight, his daughter began apologizing for her father's behavior. Linda, Terri and I finished our meals as Ted returned and devoured his dessert.

He asked if I was free the next day to have lunch with him.

"No, I am planning on visiting some temples tomorrow. In fact, I'll be gone a couple days," I told him. "You'll enjoy the baths," I told his daughter and practically ran for the door.

"Who'd have guessed he'd be such a jerk, and cheap, too," Linda exclaimed. Ted had paid only for his own meal, not even including his daughter's.

"Well, that was the international blind date," I laughed. "Big whoop. But at least we got to dance in the rain."

Departure

Before we left Bali Wayan wanted us to come to his house for dinner. I was determined to buy baby gifts for his and Made's coming child. I explained to Linda and Terri that giving gifts to a Balinese involved a different etiquette. One pretended that one had brought something by accident, and simply put it in a corner as if the giver had forgotten it for them to open later in privacy.

Getting local etiquette across to Terri was not easy. She kept pointing to people even though I explained it was considered not just rude, but almost violent. She continually patted children on the head despite me telling her Balinese thought children were closer to the gods and that patting their heads was interfering with the highest chakra.

As things transpired, I got Bali belly after eating an elaborate duck meal with Linda. I had a fever and was too sick to make it to Wayan and Made's dinner. I lay in bed groaning instead.

The next day Linda told me Terri had made the visit a misery. The couple had been very sad I couldn't make it.

"You are obviously Wayan's favorite," Linda said. "Terri was awful."

The couple did not sit and eat with their guests. Instead they served them many courses of food that had clearly taken an effort to prepare. Terri treated Made as if she were a servant. Then she had insisted on making a production of giving them each gift, acting as if they were all from her, not all three of us. She had been loud, demanding and had too much to drink. I groaned and not from Bali belly which had ended.

The next day when Wayan showed up to drive us to airport he had Made with him. I had heard all about her but had not met her before.

"She came to meet you because you could not come last night," Wayan said. She and I embraced. At the airport Linda and I were paying Wayan and he teared up as we embraced in farewell.

"I need your passports," Terri interrupted. She didn't bother to say farewell to Wayan and Made as Linda and I were doing. When the couple had left and we joined the line to board I discovered what Terri had been up to. I had reserved a comfortable exit aisle seat for myself for the long flight. While we were emotionally engaged with Made and Wayan, she had changed our seats and taken mine. She smiled smugly when I realized what she had done.

That last flight was the last we saw of Terri. Linda and I were not interested in seeing her again.

A few months later someone I knew went to Bali. I sent along some money for the baby, a girl named Wayan of course, and a card to Wayan and Made.

Section 3:
Italy

When the Unspeakable Happens

I had planned my trip to Italy carefully. I would be traveling alone for a month. I was excited and my son had dropped me off at the airport shuttle stop very early that morning. I was at the gate, in line waiting to board the airplane, when blaring emergency signals went off. Everyone looked around. I figured somebody opened a wrong door, one intended for staff with key cards or something like that.

The man in line behind me was on his phone. "Someone flew a plane into the World Trade Center," he told his travel companion.

I was annoyed. Didn't he know you weren't supposed to make jokes like that at an airport? Then his companion got off his phone and replied, "Two planes." Good God, this was carrying a joke too far.

The emergency signals still blared. The airline attendant ahead of me in line answered her ringing phone, "No Daddy, I'm all right. Daddy, Daddy, calm down. Don't worry, Daddy. Just tell me was one of them one of ours?"

I was flying American Airlines. "It was? Daddy, I'm going to be very busy so I won't be able to talk to you until much later, but I'm okay. Don't worry."

As she hung up I asked "Did planes really fly into the World Trade Center?"

"I'm afraid so."

At that time Oakland Airport did not have television monitors but someone ran by and yelled to the cluster of people still hoping to get on a plane, "There's a television in the sports bar down there," gesturing at the end of the terminal. We promptly stampeded in that direction. We got there just in time to see the second tower fall. A collective gasp filled the room. The television announcer when he could speak was obviously crying.

A woman in the bar started screaming, "Let me at 'em. I'll kill 'em. I'll kill 'em all!"

"Kill who?" I asked. At that time no one had any idea who was responsible.

"Middle Easterners. Anybody. Just give me a gun and I'll kill 'em all. I'll kill'em! I'll kill 'em!"

People stepped away casting wary glances at her. She subsided. Cell phones weren't as common then and I did not have one although my kids did and were nagging me to get one. The television newsman had said all flights were being cancelled and those in the air directed to land. One plane was still out there under control of hijackers. I got in line to use a pay phone. I reached my son, who like the newscaster was in tears.

"Mom, I just saw hundreds of people get murdered." He didn't believe they could hold up air traffic for more than a day and advised me to get a hotel room. I tried while I had the pay phone. No hotel would even bother to answer the phones. Just then a loudspeaker demanded we leave the airport. Those with checked baggage were advised to line up in one designated spot. As I made my way out of the airport to the shuttle stop, I was glad I had just a carry-on. The baggage line was very long and beginning to spread out the door into the parking lots.

I found a group of us from up north waiting for the shuttle.

"Does anyone know if the bridges are open?" I asked. Everyone suddenly looked alarmed. One man spotted a Highway Patrolman on a motorcycle and flagged him down to ask. The patrolman got on his radio to find out.

"There are guards on the bridges, but they are open. Your shuttle can get you out of here," he reassured us.

On the shuttle headed north I looked across the bay. A country girl, the city intimidated me usually, especially on San Francisco's steep hills when I was driving. Instead, that morning I felt it was so fragile, I felt a great surge of affection for San Francisco and a yearning desire to protect it. The feeling was familiar and I realized I had felt it once before when the moon astronauts brought back a picture of the full Earth. I had realized when I first saw it, that everything I loved, that had value for me was on that fragile bubble in space.

The next week as I waited for planes to fly again was a nightmare of horror for me as well as the rest of the nation. My children used every bit of emotional blackmail they could to try to persuade me not to go on my trip.

"Do you realize how hard it will be to tell the grandchildren that they've lost their grandmother so soon after losing their grandfather?" My daughter said. I told her that was a lot of assumptions and their grandfather had been dead two years now so was distant in their memories.

"I am speaking for Dad right now," said my youngest son. "He would want you to stay home."

Even my oldest son who was always the most encouraging about my traveling told me I should reconsider the trip. I knew his brother and sister had put him up to it.

Finally, they were reconciled to the fact that I was going to Italy and made me promise to email home daily. I dutifully agreed.

It took a week before planes could take to the air again. American Airlines followed the example of all the others and did not charge fees for readjusting my ticket. At the airport I was dismayed by a line so long I realized even having showed up three hours early as instructed, I might miss my plane. But as we shuffled slowly along when the three hours were coming to an end an official came by calling out the number of my flight. I raised my hand and he pulled me out of the line and led me to a gate.

At length I was in my seat, buckled up and on my way to Italy, well to Heathrow in London anyway. I had a four-hour layover at that airport and looked forward to getting a good cup of British tea.

No such luck. Heathrow was mad pandemonium. Oddly enough, in the middle of the throngs I saw an Indian family sit down, light an alcohol burner and make themselves a pot of tea. I longed to join them but was being bustled, shoved and yelled at to move my luggage, here, there, stand in this line, in that one. Four hours vanished and once again I was concerned I'd miss my plane until I realized the flight crew was getting no special treatment and was in line with the passengers directly in front of me.

The plane was late leaving for Italy, but so was the crew. Yes, I thought happily as I buckled up again, this time for a short flight, I am finally going to Italy.

Angels Made Me Do It

After all the security I had gone through at Heathrow en-route to Milan, I was startled that there was no customs check when I entered Italy. I simply bought a subway ticket right at the airport.

I got out and mounted an escalator expecting to see busy sidewalks, taxis, street traffic as it was sunset and would be rush hour. The escalator rose right next to one of Italy's loveliest cathedrals. It is covered with angels. The angel faces, glowing in the setting sun looked down at me beatifically. As I gazed straight up awe stricken, I missed the top of the escalator and fell ass over teakettle.

A Japanese couple rushed to my side, helping and inquiring if I was all right. I was more embarrassed than anything, thanked them, grabbed my suitcase and hurried away toward my hotel.

As I reached the steps of the hotel I realized I was not all right. Something had happened to my foot and ankle. When I reached the desk and they dealt with my being a week late by the owner giving up his room for me, I asked for ice.

The solicitous owner instead came up with ice spray and removed my shoe from my swelling foot icing it. He provided me with a bag of ice. At 3 a.m. pain woke me. The ice was melted. I wasn't sure I could walk. I cried and thought my trip was ruined before it started. I took aspirin and ibuprofen. Then I realized I could use my wheeled carry-on as a crutch. I also saw there was a pharmacy across the street from the hotel entrance. I had luckily packed toe-strap flat sandals that accommodated my swollen foot.

In the morning I hobbled leaning on my carry-on. I showed the pharmacist my foot. He gestured for me to wait then went down into his basement. He came back up with a box of envelopes. He then explained I was to open an envelope and put the powder in it in orange juice every day. It was very inexpensive. He also told me each afternoon to put my foot up for an hour.

I wondered what the magic white powder was but realized after my first dose, it was going to save my trip. I was able to take a taxi to the train station to Lake Como and ride the ferry to Menaggio where I had reservations at a hostel. There I met an American nurse who bandaged my foot with an Ace bandage. From now I was to wear socks and keep the foot warm. Neither of us could decipher the medical Italian on the medicine. It would prove to be a steroid.

A week later I came back to Milan to see the remarkable cathedral that had done me in. You can even tour its amazing marble roof "shingled" with thick slabs of marble and covered with gargoyles. An exterior elevator whisked me to the top. Inside the building its many pillars reached up like a redwood forest.

My favorite view was to sit at a café across the piazza and see all those hundreds of angels light up in the setting sun. I watched a commuter cross the piazza one night in his business suit on a scooter, a briefcase strapped to his back. At dark, the golden angel Gabriel with his trumpet that crowns the duomo would be lit, and he would begin his nightly job of protecting the people of Milano.

It was an exciting city. It is the home of high fashion. But the favorite garment I discovered was a rain poncho. Like most Italian cities, Milano was infested with Vespas. But at the first sign of rain the many young men riding their noisy steeds would don the rain ponchos that flowed out behind them as sped through the narrow streets of the medieval part of town. They reminded me of knights with their capes streaming in the wind.

My last night in Milano was a dry one. I grabbed a seat in my favorite café and waited for Gabriel to make his golden appearance and offered thanks for all Milano had given me – especially that precious powder from the pharmacist. I idly wondered if his name had been Gabriel.

Switzerland for Lunch

I was staying in the small town of Menaggio in Italy on Lake Como. It was a beautiful place. The place where I was staying doubled as a gourmet cooking school, and each evening, for a pittance, we guests were able to buy a three-course dinner complete with local wine.

One day, my landlady told me there was a bus from Menaggio to St. Moritz in Switzerland, which left each morning and returned in the afternoon. I strolled down to the tourist office and purchased a ticket for the next day. It was sunset, so I went to a lakeside café and ordered a glass of prosecco, served in miniature flutes, while I enjoyed the view. Some of the local townsfolk greeted me as I sat there and the café proprietor came and joined me for a while.

The next morning instead of looking at the Alps, I was climbing them. The road wound tightly up the hairpin curves. The fences were horizontal rather than vertical. I wasn't sure if that was to block snow slides in winter or to keep the cows from falling on the road in the summer – perhaps both. I've seen a lot of mountains, but none so steep as an Alp.

The weather got chillier with every kilometer. We got to the Swiss border, or what remained of it in the European Union. No one stopped us at the abandoned checkpoint. Italian architecture gave way to Swiss chalets. Old mountaintop fortresses instead of elegant palaces began to decorate the landscape. Despite the lack of border formality, I definitely knew I had changed countries.

The villages were pretty, with painted window boxes on the houses, and antiseptically clean. The Italian villages around the lake were also clean, but weathered. These places looked positively scrubbed. Eventually we pulled into St. Moritz. My first impression was of being overwhelmed by hotels. Because they were built up the mountainside they seemed to be stacked on one another.

A cold wind was blowing as I wandered through the streets, admiring the upscale shops and restaurants. For some reason everything was closed. It must have been a local holiday, though I saw no merrymakers, just very cold occasional tourists, huddled in down jackets. That surprised me because it was still a warm September in Italy and lots of Swiss had found their way to Menaggio – I had run into a whole rowing club, and lots of hikers carrying their steel-tipped staffs. Perhaps the Swiss desert their country with the first winds of autumn, I mused.

I was getting hungry by this time. A small shopping mall had a couple open shops. I was not at all interested in buying a cuckoo clock so I just window-shopped. Then I found a small sports bar and grill open. The Swiss staff was efficient but not very friendly. But at last, I was warm and there was food to be had. I ordered a hamburger and coffee and nearly choked when I realized my bill would be about $30.

After some more strolling, I went to meet the bus. It was parked by the railway station and the Italian driver was nowhere in sight. I went into the railway café where I found him chatting with friends. I ordered a glass of local wine from a grouchy old man while I waited. It was expensive and as sour as the expression of the old guy who served it.

Finally, a number of us passengers boarded the bus for the three-hour drive down the mountains back to another world. I realized, with satisfaction, that I'd be back in time for another lovely, gourmet Italian dinner at my lodgings.

As I disembarked someone on the bus surreptitiously patted my fanny. Yes, I was back in Italy, all right.

Later that night, full of a lovely risotto, I e-mailed my kids. "Today, I went to Switzerland for lunch, but I came back to Italy for dinner. The food is much better."

Bellagio

I plied Lake Como using their convenient ferries. The architecture around the lake was stunning. The Italian palaces and villas graced the shores and up on mountain peaks churches welcomed the adventurous. One church looked accessible only to mountain climbers as it perched on an inaccessible cliff halfway up the mountain.

I saw villages that could only be reached by funicular they were so high up the slopes. I decided to visit the island of Bellagio.

A cold Alpine wind began blowing and I went into a café as I waited for the ferry.

I saw a couple workmen come in and one ordered a "café coretto" – strong coffee, made strong by adding alcohol. A drizzly rain had begun to fall, and suddenly it seemed like a great idea.

The waitress brought me my espresso with grappa and it warmed me to my toes as my fingers warmed wrapped around the cup. The ferry arrived and I boarded.

Bellagio was famous for its fashionable shops. Living out of a carry-on bag I was not interested in shopping, but had come to see the architecture and art. Holding an umbrella I wandered the streets. The rain which had increased kept almost everyone indoors so I had the colorful town to myself.

One of the streets was so narrow that when a car turned down it, the handful of us on it had to back against the walls and lift our umbrellas high to let it pass. In a garden I spied a piece of ancient sculpture mounted on a stone wall. It was a young woman's face.

Swept away by the beauty of the town and its lovely gardens, I began to feel chilled again. I spotted a small restaurant on a back street. I went in and an attentive waiter came to tell me what was on offer that day. They had a bean soup.

That bowl of aromatic bean soup served with fresh crusty bread and a glass of chianti was one of best meals I had ever tasted. Hours later as I rode the ferry back to my room at Menaggio I felt I had been thoroughly nourished: my body by the simple superb meal and my soul by rainy, wet beauty of a lovely place.

The Fat Cats of Vernazza

The sun was bright in the small harbor, but the small colorfully painted boats were all on the beach because the seas were still high from a windstorm. The rulers of the village of Vernazza didn't mind. There were five of them asleep in a heap on a canvas boat cover. One, a tabby, woke, stretched, and hopped off the boat to stroll to the fish shop. She deigned to stop and let me pet her on the way.

The fat cats of Vernazza have become famous. They even sell signs there that say "Beware of the Cat" in Italian in all the shops.

The cats were everywhere. They were all well fed and healthy. Some people had household cats, but the vast majority belonged to everyone.

I asked Rosa, the lady who had rented me my studio apartment. "Are there kittens?"

"Si, she answered. "Two litters, one by the cemetery, one at the tower."

The tower was named The Tower of the Screaming Voice. In the bad old days the fellow with the loudest voice was made lookout and lived at the tower watching for pirates so he could warn the villagers.

I asked Pietro at the fish market about sick cats.

"There is an animal doctor in the next village," he told me.

There were no "scaredy cats", no mangy strays. They were all friendly and all pampered. When the people found out I was photographing their beloved cats, they'd pull me off the street into their homes to meet their personal cats. Each restaurant or cafe had its own group of cats. The cats tolerated the local dogs, who treated their feline bosses with great respect. Visiting dogs quickly learned to do the same.

Vernazza is one of the five villages that make up the Cinque Terre on the Italian Riviera. There are no highways linking them. Each is nestled in an impossibly steep canyon by the sea. They were tucked into their inaccessible locations to avoid the pirates that terrorized the Mediterranean in medieval times. The Cinque Terre, unlike nearby ritzy Portofino and San Remo, is a down-to-earth place. Trains tunnel through the mountains to reach the villages, and some challenging hiking trails link them. In good weather small ferry boats also travel back and forth. The villages were so picturesque I had to thank the pirates for their influence on architecture.

To get to my room I had to climb seven stories from the harbor. There is only one street that is not a flight of stairs in the entire village, and it is on a steep hill. Some streets are not only stairs but tunnels that wind through the mountains. I watched the locals haul their groceries and children up and down as they got their aerobic and strength exercises. I wondered how (and why) the older folks did it.

There is constant construction and repair work going on - old villages need a lot of maintenance. The workers used small barrow cement mixers and hoisted their concrete up with flexible rubber buckets and clever slings. The man working on the roof next door to me always sang opera as he worked. His black and white cat kept him company and sometimes "sang" with him or objected to his arias; it was hard to tell.

The hills around the town are so steep even donkeys can't handle them, and a tiny monorail has been built to haul down the grapes from the mountain climber-built terraces. I watched the driver take off one morning singing as he climbed, the soles of his shoes facing the sky. His cat refused to accompany him but waited at the piazza below.

The villagers make a wine, sciachetra, only found in Vernazza, not even in neighboring villages. At sunset I'd go to a cafe by the sea that had yellow umbrellas to enjoy a glass of it as I watched the sun go down and the cafe patrons take on a glow from the light and the bright umbrellas (and maybe the sciachetra). Cats would curl up among the patrons, purring, or sun themselves on the beach.

On Friday evening the church which also served as a breakwater for the harbor, was tolling its bells. In storms waves came through its windows. When the bells stopped, grandmothers and mothers streamed out of it and sat on the benches outside or joined their men at the cafes while the children played tag in the small piazza. The golden light settled over everyone. Conversation and children's laughter filled the harbor. The sea was finally calm.

And I realized why no one minded the difficulties of getting around Vernazza. Golden moments like that were worth any number of stairs. The calico at my feet resettled herself more comfortably and purred as she agreed.

Unprepared for Beauty

I thought I was prepared for Venice. I had seen films, read books – especially those of Jan Morris who wrote powerful love stories to the city – I had read novels set in Venice, seen movies set in Venice. I took the train from Genoa and prepared my itinerary for the city, including a day in Murano and a visit to the gondola workshop. I had booked a room that I was told was a two-minute walk from the train depot.

Dragging my one small bag I walked out of the station and promptly collapsed on the steps of the depot that overlooked the Grand Canal. I couldn't move. I just sat there stunned.

"This is impossible. They can't do this. They did this. How could they do this?" the thoughts wheeled uncontrollably in my mind. After my first slap in the face by impossible beauty, I was finally able to stand up and I walked out on to the bridge outside the station to look up and down the Grand Canal. The same thoughts wheeled in my head again.

The two minute walk turned into two hours. I kept stopping to look at the beautiful drowned city, marveling that`mere humans had created such a thing.

If you look at a map of Venice you will notice it is the shape of a fish with an open mouth. The mouth is swallowing the railway station. It is a perfect metaphor for what happened to me on my arrival. Venice simply swallowed me as efficiently as the whale did Jonah.

I dumped my bags in my room and dashed out to board a vaparetto, the water buses of Venice. I felt my itinerary in my pocket and threw it away. I reached Piazza San Marco and sat at a table outside one of the cafes, just drinking in the marvel. The bell tower, the golden domed basilica decorated with the four large horses stolen from Constantinople, the Doges Palace all dazzled me. The immense piazza was lined with cafes that each had its own orchestra. I sipped a glass of prosecco – the price of admission for a seat – and let the beauty wash over me.

"Other cities get tourists, Venice gets lovers" was one of the popular sayings about this magic place, and now I realized why.

After two days of dazed wandering I finally bought a ticket to Murano. I failed to make a connection to another boat and as I sailed back to the city my heart rejoiced. I didn't want to go to Murano. I just wanted to stay in Venice so I was pleased to have missed the connecting boat.

I woke at dawn each morning to watch the worker boats. I saw concrete boats churning away as they went about the important business of patching things up in a city trying to self destruct. I saw delivery boats ferrying vegetables, meat and fish to the market. I saw garbage boats collecting the waste at regular stops where the collectors had carried the bags of trach Venetians had carefully hung on their door handles the evening before.

One day on a vaparetto, we had to pull over and let the ambulance boat, with its screaming siren and flashing lights go by. We passed the fire station with its fire boats at the dock. As we sailed by, I saw they had a sliding pole just like all other fire stations.

I noticed some of the buildings were made of cloth. Whenever a building undergoes repairs or renovations that require scaffolds, the owners were required to hang great life-sized canvas murals of the finished building outside so Venice would look the same despite the construction work. The murals were excellently executed and you only noticed what they were if the wind blew them too hard.

One afternoon I saw what I believe were the only wheels in the city. They were on a plastic wheeled toy ridden by a three-year-old. It was his birthday gift from his grandparents. We were sitting in a tiny piazza. The boy could only go in circles in the piazza. There are too many canals and the bridges that cross them all have steps making wheels not just impractical but outright silly in Venice. Instead everyone walks everywhere they don't sail to.

I loved the market and wished I had a kitchen so I could cook some of the wonderful things I saw. The major market housed the stalls under a roof with red draperies all around it. The traghetti gondolas that crossed the canals back and forth with everyone standing in them as part of the public transportation system, took people to and from the market. It was a busy place.

One day "*aqua alta*" claimed the city – that is a higher tide than usual. What I had thought were picnic tables stacked up everywhere suddenly revealed their real purpose. They were our boardwalks. Piazza San Marco was underwater. The worshippers in the basilica had to splash through six inches of water to receive communion. Fortunately, the tide receded and things dried out.

I kept noticing signs that said Stop Moto Ondosso. Some of the signs were homemade on sheets hung from house windows. Being a journalist I first suspected they had something to do with politics, but I dug out my pocket dictionary and had to laugh at myself. The signs meant Don't Make Waves. Residents were just trying to keep their homes dry and protect them from the wake of boats moving too fast. The only boats allowed to speed were the ambulance and police boats, and the latter only in a major emergency.

Alone in Venice

One morning I had left my very tiny room overlooking a laundry-filled courtyard to find the closest café for my morning cappuccino. It had been overcast for three days, but today the rising sun lit the canal.

I had fallen into the reverie that afflicts so many people who come to Venice, especially us romantics. I sprang for the extra lire it took to sit down in the café – you always pay for a seat in Italy or you stand as you eat or drink. As I wrote the date down in my journal, my heart gave a lurch. It would have been mine and my late husband's anniversary.

This romantic city suddenly seemed to be a very lonely place. Even in public young lovers did everything they could with their clothes on, and I had seen an elderly couple, so frail they leaned on each other for support while they walked, but they were lovingly holding hands. A pang of envy had shot through me.

But I rallied and decided to treat myself to a celebration that day. I'd eat at the restaurant under the Rialto Bridge I had been eying up, and I'd find a concert to attend that evening.

I hopped a vaporetto, the ubiquitous water bus, and stopped at the fish market on the Grand Canal. Where else but in Venice would you find a busy fish market that sported long red drapes in the arches of the palatial building that sheltered it? I had no way of cooking anything, but I imagined the meals I could prepare if I did and settled for buying an apple from a fruit monger.

I was at the doors of the tourist office on San Marco piazza when it opened. I told the young woman it was a special day and I wanted the best music Venice had to offer. Her eyes lit up at the challenge. She got on her computer, then looked up at me grinning. "I have found it, signora. Vivaldi, the best Venetian composer at San

Bartolomeo, the church with the best acoustics in Venice. It is fortunate you are here early. This will be sold out very quickly."

I then tried to deal with some practicalities. There had been some kind of bank mix-up that hadn't let me get cash a few days before. I had e-mailed my daughter who had assured the bank it was indeed me trying to get my money, and lo and behold the ATM worked. I was so jubilant, I stopped at an internet café to e-mail my thanks, then went shopping, buying cameos for the females in the family for Christmas at a San Marcos jeweler. Cameos like blown glass seemed so very Venetian.

Along the Grand Canal I came upon a small outdoor market run by Gypsy women. One was selling gorgeous velvet brocade scarves for fifteen dollars. As I was choosing some, an Asian-American lady began eyeing them. "So reasonable, and so elegant," I talked up the scarves on behalf of the girl running the stand who was watching me, grinning. The lady bought quite a few.

"Now, since I am such a good saleswoman, do I get a discount?" I asked her. She laughed, gave me a quantity discount and gave me handful of blown glass mock candies. I was delighted knowing my grandkids would love them.

I went to my favorite "sombre" for lunch – a nickname, "shadow", for the little bars in the shady alleys of Venice. I always met interesting people there, and this was no exception. There was a young man trying to impress his lady friend. We were all crammed together in the tiny place and I noticed he had the perfect piato misto – mixed plate of Venetian treats. He explained you had to order the items separately, not just order a piato misto, and he then proceeded to offer me samples and explain how each was made. I was duly impressed with his culinary knowledge, as was his date, who looked at him with new interest.

Then we talked about Venice and my favorite Venetian painter, Canaletto. I was dismayed to learn there were few of his paintings in Venice; most were in London.

I strolled off to see the Academia art museum even if they were sadly lacking in Canelettos. I enjoyed the Tintorettos but most of the other art bored me – I was heartily sick of the mutilated saints Venetians loved so much. I had injured my foot when I had first got to Italy and had been advised to rest it elevated each day so I caught a vaporetto back to my room. On the street outside my room someone was selling a Canaletto calendar. I contented myself with it and gloated over all my fine purchases and then spent an hour or so reading a mystery set in Venice.

Before long I was up and out again. I did not want to miss sunset at San Marcos. I strolled the huge piazza – the largest in Europe in the heart of space-starved Venice. It was circled by orchestras playing outside the restaurants. I chose one with music I liked, ordered a prosecco and settled in to watch the setting sun glitter on the golden basilica. I was waiting for the bells. While the piazza was big enough that each of the orchestras could play and not interfere with each other, when the bells of the clock tower rang at sundown they drowned out everything.

Sure enough, all the orchestras looked like someone hit the mute button – they kept playing but no one could hear them and the pigeons took to the air as the melodious but clamorous bells reverberated.

As the skies darkened I made my way to the Rialto Bridge. The tide was coming in and the water was up to the top step. Shopkeepers were hurriedly laying down the boardwalks that I had mistaken for picnic tables until my first high tide. They were stacked all along the canals.

I sat at the water's edge and looked up at the bridge and down the canal at the lights and reflections as I ate my meal. The gondolas began poling by. The gondoliers of Venice pride themselves on their flirting. When they spotted me alone at my table they poled near and sang to me. I laughed and waved as they went by. One fellow ignored his passengers and sang an entire aria for me. He had a good voice and I applauded him. So did his passengers.

Finally, I got on a vaporetto for San Bartolomeo. While in line to be seated, an older British couple chatted with me. They were charmed this was my first visit to Venice.

"She is a Venice virgin," exclaimed the woman to her husband. "Remember our first time?"

He smiled at her fondly. They came every year – another couple of Venice's "lovers". I told them I loved the city but was disappointed there were so few Canalettos. We discussed how things were in places they shouldn't be. He was upset that Samuel Pepys diaries of medieval London were at Harvard. I said the Elgin marbles belonged in Greece. I said I'd battle for the return of Pepys when the Greeks got the missing pieces of the Parthenon back. It was all good-natured.

I was relieved to see this church was full of angels – not a bleeding martyr in sight. Two huge marble angels flanked the dais where the musicians performed as if they were listening to the music. A young, long-haired, passionate violin-cellist capped the evening with a stunning Vivaldi concerto. I could have sworn the angels bent in closer to listen.

My heart was singing as I bid good night to my new British friends and boarded the vaporetto back to my room. The Grand Canal glittered with all the lights of the city. I was alone but no longer lonely. All the magic of the day could only have happened in this magic place.

I murmured as if my husband could hear me as I went to sleep, "There, honey, I enjoyed it for both of us."

Night Train to Naples

I was in Bologna. I was very sleepy but afraid to drift off because I could see the sleazy man in the corner eyeing my belongings. I chose a seat next to an equally uneasy family with two sleeping children on the bench beside them. This station seemed to be thronged with thieves.

I clutched a paper cup full of coffee. The Gypsy woman had followed me to the coffee stand, rudely besieging me. I pretended not to understand her Italian demands for money as I fished out change for the coffee. A man had leered at me as I walked the underground passages to the track and followed me until I spotted a cop and followed him. I was glad for the security alert that had put Italian police on the streets and in the depots in great numbers.

I clutched a "cucetta" ticket entitling me to a protected berth on the night train to Naples, but the train was intolerably late.

"Where's Mussolini when you need him?" I muttered to myself recalling the Italian Fascist dictator who had bragged of making the trains run on time, since there was nothing like a firing squad for a work incentive.

I looped my arm through my purse straps and put my feet on my bag. I started to nod off but jerked awake more than once. It was 2 a.m. I had been awake since before dawn. I always woke early in Venice. I couldn't bear to miss a moment there, especially on my last day. I wanted to feast my eyes on the Grand Canal one last time. Even the garbage and sewage boats fascinated me as they plied the canals at first light. So, I had stayed as long as possible in my favorite city catching a late train to Bologna.

I was paying the price now. At three the train finally arrived. Weary travelers mobbed it. A conductor spotted me waving the cucetta ticket and literally lifted me and my bag up the steps to his car.

He hurried me down the narrow aisles unlocking compartment after compartment, but they were all filled. In one, a man was sleeping with a clothespin on his nose. I spotted an empty bunk in one and tried to claim it. Shocked because a young man was sleeping on another bunk, he yanked me back.

Instead he shoved me into a closet sized compartment that housed five other women and all their luggage. He pointed to an empty upper bunk. I couldn't even reach the ladder to get to it for all the luggage piled around it. He hastily shoved it aside and pushed me in. I was too tired to argue but felt like I had been shoved into a crowded coffin. In my bunk I gratefully realized what looked like a wall was a window shade. I opened it enough to feel less claustrophobic and dropped off to a sleep that lasted just a couple hours.

I woke at daybreak while my cucetta mates still snored. I had to figure a way to extract myself and my bag from the huge jumble of stuff between the narrow bunks. I stepped out of the compartment into a choking fog of cigarette smoke.

The narrow aisle was blocked by hordes of men smoking. I found not only had I been locked in my compartment, I was now locked in the train car with the smokers and out of the compartment I had just left.

I struggled past each male with my wheeled bag until I finally reached the conductor's cubicle and told him I wanted out and I wanted a bathroom. He opened the car door and pointed the way.

I discovered Italian male smokers need their morning toke desperately. The aisles of the coach car were just as smoke laden as the cucetta car. The compartments, much roomier than the cucetta, were filled with sleeping people. I finally perched on my bag next to the outside door, which I illegally opened in order to breathe.

And so I arrived in Naples, which would prove to be my least favorite Italian city, longing to be back in Venice and vowing to never book a cucetta bunk again.

The Old Man and the Museum

I loved Italy. Everyone loves Italy, but I was absolutely fed up with Italian state workers. Tim Parks had described the phenomenon in one of his books about Italy. There are people who work for private companies, people who are self-employed and the real plum is a job working for the state. Then you do the least you can possibly do and use your freed-up time on the job to establish your own business on the side and use government supplies to run it.

Inevitably, at train stations or other public places the elevators or an escalator would be marked "Non Funziona" – out of order. They weren't really out of order. I saw the people in charge use them. They just didn't want to be bothered to clean them. Street sweepers gave a few pushes with a broom and left the mess behind. Everyone from ticket sales people to security guards ignored the public they were supposed to serve to have long phone conversations with friends or set up orders for their own side businesses.

Naples was so traffic ridden that the only safe way to cross a street was to wait for a young mother with a baby stroller. They had total faith in the braking systems of the ubiquitous Fiats. I didn't, so followed docilely in their footsteps. I took the metro to the museum.

The museum in Naples is a must. It is where the treasures of Pompeii are kept. Various ancient finds from Pompeii launched the Renaissance in Europe. Michaelangelo had restored some of the broken ancient Roman pieces. It's all stashed in that fabulous museum.

It was a grand building with a great marble staircase leading to the main galleries. The only railing on the staircase was the balustrade that was so wide a human hand couldn't grasp it to keep from falling.

There was an old man with a crutch standing in the hall. He was wizened and shaky. He was wearing old patched clothes and he stank. He was looking at that staircase helplessly. I looked for an elevator and cursed all Italian civil servants when I saw the only elevator had a "Non Funziona" sign on it. The old man had lived in Naples all his life. Before he died, he wanted to see the treasures his city was famous for.

His eyes teared up as he looked at the grand staircase and said, "I can't."

The museum guards just sneered at him.

"You can do it," I said as I took his arm and led him to the stairs.

Inch by inch, step by step, I got him upstairs. I was almost nauseous from the smell by the time I found a bench upstairs where he could sit and look at all the wonders. He clutched at my arm, but I had to leave him. I had booked a special tour   of the "Secret Cabinet" of Pompeii's bordello art. I promised I'd be back to help him downstairs after I had looked at the art.

"Grazie, grazie bella" he said.

I looked for him after a couple hours but he was gone, so I went back to gaze at ancient art some more. I hope some kind-hearted soul had helped him, or just maybe he managed to get a guard to let him in the elevator after all.

When I finally headed back to my room, my head full the wonders I had seen, I remembered the poor old fellow and muttered to myself, "Non funziona, non funziona, my foot. The only thing that is non funziona are the damn employees."

The First Days of Pompeii

If you haven't read Bulwer Lytton's purple prose novel "The Last Days of Pompeii" (he of "It was a dark and stormy night" fame) or seen the old black and white movie, you are definitely missing out on a treat. Because I had read it as a youngster, I decided I could not go to Italy without seeing Pompeii – the city buried by a volcano in 79 A.D.

I have seen a lot of ruins so thought I knew what to expect, but what happened to Pompeii defies belief. Imagine a city of more than 70,000 people buried in a matter of hours. Add to that the age of the city at the time it was destroyed. It was already a power to be reckoned with in 424 BCE. That makes it twice as old than any city in the US today back in 79 AD.

I got off the train from Naples and reached the gates of the city. The first thing that hit me was its vastness. Not only is it a large city, but it has been steadily excavated for over 400 years. They give you a city map with your admission. I usually dislike audio tours but the one in Pompeii is a necessity. Still people get lost and tourists constantly ask for directions to various intersections. The government has conveniently put up street signs – they got tired of hunting down lost tourists. It would take days to really see it all.

I wandered down a street. The sidewalks were high with stepping stones at intersections. The street acted as drainage for the city in ancient times. At a house there was a mosaic that said Beware of the Dog in Latin. A dog was sleeping on it. I chuckled and when the dog woke patted it. Wherever I wandered I met more dogs.

They are everywhere. No one owns them, but they are well-fed, well-behaved, and no mangy curs among them. They roamed the ruins freely and lay down in the streets in the sun to sleep. It was as if the catastrophe had just happened and the dogs were expecting their masters to return at any moment. It made the sadness of loss more immediate and unavoidable as I roamed the ruins. One dog followed me to a café when I stopped for lunch and I shared my sandwich with him.

I went into an ancient shop which the audio guide told me had been a fast food shop. The circular holes in marble counter had held pots of hot food that people would buy to take home.

I entered what was clearly an affluent home. A phallus stood outside the main entrance. Ancient visitors would touch it to bring prosperity to the household as they went in. Just inside the door was an opening to the sky and a small pool that caught the rain where guests could wash their hands. There was an opening to a courtyard to help light the house. All rooms opened on to the courtyard except the sex room which offered more privacy. Big houses had "sex rooms" for the slaves. Since married slave couples lived in dormitory conditions, it made sense if a family wanted another generation of slaves to provide a venue for procreation. The audio told me the name of the family that had lived here. I felt like I knew them.

I wandered into their homes, their temples, their bakeries, and, yes, their brothels. Most of the brothel art has been taken to the museum in Naples and you must go on an "adult tour" to see it.

They were an earthy, lusty people with a strong zest for life. Sex was not shameful. A phallus was good luck. Babies' cradles were hung with small winged phalluses to bring the baby health and fertility. (My kids were startled to find them in their Christmas stockings later that year. They sell replicas in the gift shop). Don't take a prurient mind to Pompeii.

I had the feeling when I saw the Villa of Mysteries that I could have lived happily in that spacious, comfortable seaside home (the sea is far away now, after Vesuvius has had its way). The name comes from one room that was used for worship by the women of the household. Wouldn't you expect that the first time a man isn't allowed in he dubs what's inside a mystery?

Pompeii had given me intimacy with the ancients. Time dissolved as I realized how they lived their lives. It also gave me sorrow.

The volcano was kind to the art even as it was cruel to the inhabitants. Even the wall paintings are superb. But the plaster casts of the actual bodies are chilling to behold. They were discovered by one of the early archaeologists who had the presence of mind to pour plaster into the hollows the diggers found. I was especially struck by a young boy named "The Muleteer" because his mule was found beside him. He is upright but in a fetal position shielding his face from the horrible fumes that killed so many. It brought me to tears. The probing with poles for hollows to unearth as statues of the once living continues today.

I also went to Heraclium, a smaller fishing and shipping village nearby, wiped out by the gases then buried under mud. Archaeologists thought at first the people escaped in boats. The sea is a mile away now and a deep manmade gorge only recently unearthed the waterfront warehouses where the people had tried in vain to flee and their remains were found. It was interesting but spooky and for me didn't hold the same sense of intimacy that Pompeii offered; maybe because there were no dogs there to bring it all down to human scale.

Vesuvius looms over both towns and over Naples. The government holds regular evacuation drills for the populace in case Vesuvius gets frisky again. It would be hopeless. I can't imagine getting over a million people out fast enough. I felt a sense of relief when I finally boarded the train to Rome and left the murderous mountain behind me. Again, I felt a pang of sorrow for the lost souls of that lovely city.

A Castle in Tuscany – With the Gonfolieres

It was the night of the October full moon – the Hunter's Moon. We had all gathered on the wide marble terrazzo of the castle and were sharing some prosecco, Italy's lovely sparkling wine, as we waited for the moonrise.

Across the broad Tuscan valley we could see the silhouette of another castle on the opposite peak. The moon rose, fat and warm in the fragrant night beyond the cypress trees. We raised our glasses in salute and watched happily as the light filled the vineyards.

"Viva!" said the Belgian nobleman lifting his glass. We returned the toast.

"And what are your plans for tomorrow?" Marta, a German tourist traveling with her husband Kurt, asked me.

"I think I will go to Umbria," I told her.

"To Umbria," said one of the American school teachers who had rented an outbuilding with a group of her colleagues, raising her glass.

It was a perfect night at Castello Montegufoni where I had a spacious apartment to myself.

My bedroom had been the "gonfoliere's" – a sort of governor. Frescos of each of the many gonfolieres that had ruled from Montegufoni circled the walls beneath the twenty-foot ceiling over my bed. The oldest one was dated 1224. I always bid goodnight to my gonfolieres before I drifted off to sleep on my huge, gilded bed because I felt like they stood guard over me.

In my living room, in addition to ceiling murals there was a very old and much mended tapestry depicting a hunt. I imagined a gonfoliere had killed the strange looking animal shown in the tapestry. I think it was supposed to be a dragon but looked like a cross between and alligator and a rabbit.

I had the choice of privacy on my own balcony, or company on the terrazzo in the evenings.

There was a small kitchen tucked into an armoire, and I liked sitting at the huge slab wood table in the main room. I had immediately purchased fruit and flowers for it at the tiny village that clustered at the foot of the castle. That old table deserved no less. And once with the German couple, who were as impressed with the table as I was, in my tiny kitchenette, we cooked a meal fit for a gonfoliere that we gleefully spread it on the noble table.

In 1154 the castle had been sacked and rebuilt. Dante stayed there once, got angry at the then owner, and consigned him to one of his circles of hell in The Inferno. Never underestimate the staying power of a writer's revenge!

Not all the gonfolieres had met happy ends. At the foot of my bed under inches and centuries of wax, was a great dark stain in the ancient bricks. Reading the castle history, I learned, sure enough, one of my bedroom companions had met an unenviable fate. It was his blood when his throat was slit that decorated the floor.

There were whole warrens of rooms, a huge watchtower that dominated the valley, a fragrant lemonaria below my balcony, gardens everywhere. The huge reception hall that led to the terrazzo and my rooms was a lovely, immense space with another magnificent table running its length and light magically filling the cavernous space. The modern pool was artistically hidden behind a ring of cypress trees. A wildly rococo grotto under the terrazzo was being restored. The castle had had many owners but the families that lived around its walls had been there since time out of mind. Pietro, the castle guard, became my buddy and told me many tales. After the Allied invasion of Italy in World War II the Allies had hidden all the art from the Uffizi Museum in nearby Florence in the castle.

"Where did they put it all?" I asked.

"Everywhere, crated up. In the tower, in the rooms, the dungeons."

Usually I drove off after breakfast to explore the hill towns of Tuscany and Umbria. But one day I chose to simply enjoy the castle.

I took a book, a watercolor pad and paints and my lunch to the terrazzo. I had it to myself so kicked off my sandals and greedily drank in the view. Pietro came upon me and was surprised.

"Ah, today, you are the contessa."

"Without shoes," I answered in Italian, pointing to my bare feet. He roared with laughter, taught me the word for barefoot, and after that I was "the barefoot contessa".

Twice a week, a gourmet cook was brought into the castle and we could reserve a place at the table for a multi-course dinner. The first time I was asked if I preferred red wine or white. I answered red, and immediately an entire bottle of chianti was set at my plate. The food was wonderful, and it took hours to get through all the courses (and much of the wine).

"This is excellent food," my Belgian neighbor groaned in pleasure.

"She gives cooking lessons," Marta said. "I think I will sign up for one."

When my week at Castello Montegufone ended, I was sorry to go. I knew I probably would rarely if ever enjoy such elegant and history-laden surroundings. Before I turned in my two-pound bronze key I went on the balcony to look over the valley one last time, then I went to my bedroom and blew each of my gonfolieres a kiss, thanking them for the good company.

Tuscan Towers of San Gimigiano

I was staying in a castle in Tuscany, Castello Montegufoni. The week's lodging also included a tiny Fiat so I could explore all the backroads and ancient villages of Tuscany and Umbria.

Pietro, the faithful security guard at the castle, saw me to my car inquiring where I was going that day. He enjoyed a chance to flirt a bit.

"San Gimignano," I told him.

"Molte bene, very good," he smiled.

It was a drizzly morning. None of the roads in Italy seemed to have names or numbers, but at every intersection there would be a signpost with lists of all the towns any direction might lead you. Trying to read all the Italian names, and find the one I wanted so I'd know which way to turn, sometimes led to honking and angry shouts if there was anyone behind me. Italians, polite everywhere else, make up for it by being very rude behind the wheel. Even a moment's hesitation riled them. I spent a lot of time being happily lost rather than endure the honking.

Today, on a narrow back road we were all slowed down by an APE – a three-wheeled motorbike cart. No one was honking this time. Even the most rushed Italian accepted the presence of APEs. They are the only way to get goods up the narrow ancient streets of the walled cities and towns. On the highways, the APE drivers always pull over when they can, but there is seldom a place to do that along the raised narrow Tuscan roads.

Eventually I crept my way to San Gimignano. I could see it in the distance. It looked like the New York City skyline rising out of the vineyards. San Gimignano dates back to Etruscan days. Tuscany wasn't always as peaceful as it is now. During medieval times the city built its walls and seventy-two soaring towers for defense. I was told fourteen remain. In its day, it must have been very threatening when it had all its towers because it is still intimidating today.

I parked in the car park outside the walls and walked into the dramatic little city. The drizzle had lightened somewhat. I roamed the cobble-stoned, hilly lanes. I found one shop that sold nothing but game meat. There was a special on boar and pheasant that day.

I came to the duomo, cathedral, of the town. By this time, I was worn out by elaborate Renaissance art. But this duomo was different – it was a simple brick medieval building. No stained-glass windows, no statuary, just elegant lines from a simpler time. I had read the frescoes were worth seeing, so I bought a ticket to enter it.

Because of the frescoes, the building is monitored for humidity so that all the heavy breathing modern humans won't ruin the work of their ancestors. Because of the damp day, the humidity was higher than usual, and so the line of visitors was moving very slowly. I sat on a bench out of the rain in the courtyard while I awaited my turn.

On a bench across the courtyard a harpist had taken refuge under an awning with his instrument. He began playing Bach's *Jesu Joy of Man's Desiring*. The liquid notes of the beautiful melody filled the courtyard. Everyone stopped chattering and just listened, rapt. The guard beckoned to me just as the harpist plucked his last notes. I felt sublimely happy.

As I stepped through the doorway into the building, I had a totally different sort of aesthetic experience. I felt like I had fallen into the Sunday funnies. The walls simply exploded with color.

The frescoes were intended to teach the illiterate worshippers their Bible stories. They were executed in pure, bright pigments and arranged in panels from floor to ceiling just like comic strips. The art was the simple, non-perspective drawing of early medieval times. Three walls depicted scenes from the Old Testament and the fourth wall showed the story of Christ. No photos were allowed. The San

Gimignanians are determined to preserve their brilliant treasure and flashes might fade it.

No one rushed me and I could wander at will, taking it all in. I was aware of the others outside who were waiting for their chance. Even so, I must have lost track of time. When I went out at last I found the rain had stopped and the sun was rapidly drying everything.

I had planned to find a café for lunch, but discovered a quiet, lovely garden on a hilltop behind the duomo. I bought picnic makings and sat up there admiring the beautiful towers. I spent most of the afternoon roaming the streets.

I finally set out for the castle where I liked to enjoy a glass of wine on the marble terrace that offered a spectacular sunset view. As I drove up Pietro greeted me and asked about my day.

"Bene?"

I smiled at him my head still full of harps and cartoons, "Si, molte bene, Pietro, molte, molte bene."

Umbria

As I left the famous rolling, fertile hills of Tuscany and entered Umbria, I felt like I had suddenly entered the Dakota Badlands. Umbria was starkly eroded. Its walled cities were built atop sharp-sided mesas from rock of the same golden color. They looked fiercely impregnable.

At Orvieto, the mesa was so steep, a funicular carried people up to the city from the train station and parking lot below. A special one-seat-wide bus that could navigate the medieval streets also took people to town. I rode it and was impressed by the driver's ability to navigate the town with just a few inches to spare on either side. I was charmed by Orvieto's striped duomo and piazza full of statues waiting to be tucked back into a place undergoing restoration. A kindergarten class came by led by their teacher and stopped to wish me good morning.

I had heard of an Umbrian town called Civita de Bagnoregio that carried its walled isolation to a ridiculous extreme. A newer town, just called Bagnoregio had been built below the mesa. Getting there meant a long winding drive on back roads.

Like the environment that spawned them, the Umbrians seemed inhospitable, even surly, perhaps from living next door to their richer, snobbier Tuscan neighbors. I reached Bagnoregio during the long siesta time and only one place in town was open where the proprietor grumpily agreed to sell me a panini and pointed the way to Civita telling me I'd have to walk because the buses didn't run during the mid-day break.

It was a long, hot walk up a steep hill. I found myself at the foot of a long, narrow footbridge that seemed to soar into space up to a lost city. Civita de Bagnoregio looked like Oz.

I have a ridiculous fear of heights. I can't go beyond the third rung of a ladder and I have never been on my own roof. The thought of crossing that bridge was daunting, but I *had* to reach Oz. I kept my eyes on my steadily moving feet with just a few stops to gape and gasp at the stupendous views.

I thought about what I had managed to learn about Civita. The Etruscans first built it 2500 years ago. It had been a stronghold throughout the Middle Ages because of its location. Up until modern times, an earthen causeway linked the mesa to the rest of the world. Gravity and storms wore that away isolating the townspeople until the government built the new bridge. For a long time just a handful of residents remained in the old town.

But as word has spread and tourists have begun trickling in, those who moved out are moving back. There are still very few permanent residents, but now some spend their days on their property above and their nights in their homes below the mesa. A few wealthy Italians have begun buying homes for summer villas.

I reached the end of the bridge – short of breath from the climb and gasping once again at the ever-unfolding views.

A cart pulled by a motorcycle putt-putted up behind me as I roamed the narrow streets. I dodged into a doorway and the driver called his thanks. It was the town's only vehicle.

I stepped into the church and a lady hobbled over to me smiling. I followed her explanation of the church's history as best I could with my phrase-book Italian and bought a candle from her. She patted my hand kindly and blessed me. I lit the candle and continued my stroll.

Another older lady was sitting on a bench in the sun. I greeted her and she told me her name was Rosa, and asked me if I liked the town. I smiled, said yes, and gestured at the view, "Bellisima!" I said.

Rosa stood and gestured for me to come through an arch into her home. She led me through a simple room out through a back door into a courtyard.

Rosa had an outdoor kitchen that looked as if it could date back to Etruscan times, with a fireplace, a few shelves and handmade pottery. She kept grinning and gesturing for me to keep following her. A path led above a terrace where her husband was tending some fruit trees. He waved. These folks were a lot friendlier than their fellow Umbrians I decided. The stone walls came to a point where she spread her arms and said, *"This* is bellisima!"

Indeed, it was. The entire mesa came to a sharp point at that peak out over a great eroded canyon. My guide was still grinning. Rosa knew I was properly impressed. It was like her personal Grand Canyon. I was a little uneasy. With all that evidence of violent erosion I wondered how safe that precarious point of land was. On my walk I had seen a metal staircase that went to nowhere, all the land below it having washed away.

Rosa walked me around her property and in one direction pointed to a town across that deep chasm. It was close enough that people could call across to each other but she explained it took hours to get there because of the impossibly steep canyon.

I gave her a little money, "for the church", to thank her for her time, and she, like the lady in the church, patted and blessed me.

Siesta time was over when I made my way to the only piazza in Civita. I found a shop with old photos of the town for sale. There was no one tending the shop. A small café had opened offering snacks and wine. I asked the landlady about the shop and she assured me I could pay her for anything I wanted and she'd get the money to the owner.

The lady was in her fifties and with the exception of the motorcycle driver, was the youngest person I had met in town. That abruptly changed as an art class that had made the trek descended upon the piazza. They made drawings as they kept the landlady busy serving them, wine and coffee and their teacher went from one to another critiquing their efforts.

I chose my souvenirs and enjoyed a glass of wine and a pastry as I watched the young artists at work.

Finally, knowing I had a long walk and drive ahead of me, I bid farewell to Civita de Bagnoregio and its handful of aging, friendly residents.

For me, Umbria will always be epitomized by that town clinging stubbornly to its peak, an ancient little Oz.

Il Professore

An Italian friend of mine had asked me to contact his uncle, a history professor in Rome who knew English. He said he would let his uncle know about me. I was in Rome two days before I called the professor because I thought he might be some stuffy fellow and didn't want to be stuck with him the entire time I was in Rome. I spent my first two days using a hop-on-hop-off bus tour and wandering the forum, Coliseum and the heart of ancient Rome. The professor decided to wait to contact me because he didn't want to be stuck with a crude American. Then we finally met. It was friendship at first sight.

"Come let me show you my city," said Il Professore. He told me he had taught in London for some years and that's why his English was so very good. He had taught one semester in Boston and couldn't understand why his nephew had settled in California. He now taught English and history at a Roman university.

As we strolled, we came across a marble plaque set into a brick wall. Il Professore pointed to it. "That is a decree from a pope in the sixteenth century. It's says, 'Don't litter'."

We both laughed. There was a pile of litter below it.

We walked by the Spanish Steps and he pointed to a building. "That's where Keats lived. Do you know who Keats is?"

"Of course," I replied.

Then he quoted the opening lines of a famous Keats poem, "She walks in beauty like the night."

I chimed in with the rest of the line, "Of cloudless climes and starry skies." He stopped dead and looked at me as if I were a dog that had suddenly talked.

"An American with an education. Who would have thought? I am honored to have met you," he said.

"Some of us do go to school," I laughed. "Even in California." But I was dismayed to learn that's how low Europeans' opinion of us was.

Il Professore wanted me to see the usual wonderful sights of Rome that I hadn't yet visited but he also showed me a Rome I could not have seen without him. In the Piazza Navoa he took me into small dark church and made me stand in one spot. He then inserted a coin in a machine. Lights came on as Il Professore gave me sweeping bow and I gazed on Carravagio's masterpiece of St. Matthew receiving an angelic message. I stood there rapt until after about ten minutes the lights went out.

Il Professore used his bow to introduce me to such delights as the Trevi Fountain and the Pantheon. He would make me stop then move beyond me and bow. Then I knew I was about to step to another wonderful piece of beauty. Whenever he started telling me about the history of something a crowd formed around us because the Romans wanted to hear what he had to say. Not only did I learn something, Il Professore educated the locals.

Another day he took me on what I called The Assassins Walk. I learned that Caesar was not assassinated at the Forum, but down the road from it in another ruin inhabited by feral cats that an old woman was feeding. There was a donation box for neutering the cats, where we deposited coins, figuring we owed it to the assassins of the dictator. Then Il Professore and I walked a long way to a street where he pointed out the very spot where Aldo Moro's body was found in the trunk of a car after he was assassinated by the Red Brigade in 1978. I marveled that the president of Italy could have been kidnapped and held for ransom.

"That was the end of the Communist Party in Italy. It still exists but has no teeth, very few voters. Of course, that meant the end of the Christian Democrats, too. Once their enemy diminished so did they," Il Professore explained.

While we were on the subject of politics he suddenly announced he was going to take me to a communist coffee shop. As we walked to it, he told me he and the owner coached a boys' soccer team together and tried to avoid talking about politics.

His friend wasn't there but his beautiful daughter was there to make coffee for us. I was fascinated by the tiny shop. A huge plaster bust of Lenin dominated the space. Behind it hung the old hammer and sickle red flag. There were other Soviet decorations but there was no picture of Stalin. I wondered vaguely if Il Professore's friend was a Trotskyite.

"I am sorry you didn't get to meet my friend, but there is another friend I want you to meet. I know he will enjoy meeting you."

We strolled on until we came to small church. Inside the church there was a fancy wooden box about the size of a telephone booth. Il Professore knocked on it, and it unfolded. The sides folded down to reveal a priest that looked like he was ninety years old.

"And who is the beautiful young lady you have brought to me, my friend," he said.

He opened a panel that served as a gate and came out of the box to be introduced.

He bowed over my hand as he kissed it. It seemed like he would never let go of my hand, so I was relieved when Il Professore told him we had to go. He sighed but went back into his box and began reconstructing it. It was a portable confessional that he brought to that church once a week because the church was too small to have one of its own. I thought the box offered the priest a lot of privacy but none to whomever was the confessee, but perhaps it had a handy curtain attached.

Il Professore and I hopped a bus to go to the outskirts where he wanted to show me gardens and statuary, many of which were missing their heads. He explained that in Rome's turbulent past, some religious fanatics had beheaded the pagan art. I mulled over that whenever religious fanatics couldn't attack people they picked on art. Il Professore agreed.

The next day he had appointments to keep. He asked my plans and I told him I was going to St. Peter and the Vatican. He told me some special things to look for and we said our arrivedercis to each other.

"You are my favorite American," he told me.

"And you are my favorite Roman," I said as we air kissed each other's cheeks in farewells.

When in Rome, Do as the Catholics Do

My room in Rome was comical. It had been advertised as a room with a private bath. When the landlord opened the door, I saw the bed, a twin in a room the size of my bathroom at home with a sink in one corner.

"The bath?" I asked.

He gestured for me to move farther into the room so I could look behind the door. There was a glass cubicle with a toilet in it. You sat on the toilet and turned on the spigot beside it to shower. I burst into laughter. My landlord was embarrassed at his having over-hyped his room, but I had reserved it and for the five days I was in town I could live with it as I would mostly be out anyway.

I left my mini-room before daylight when I went to the Vatican. I thought St. Peter's Square which faced east would be a perfect place to see a sunrise. A streetlight showed a gate where Swiss Guards were huddled talking. I walked up to the gate thinking they'd move out of the way. Instead they all stood erect and pointed their halberds at me.

I know Swiss Guards wear funny clothes, but there's nothing comical about those men. They must have a height requirement because I never saw one under 6'5". And when all those big men are pointing those sharp spear heads at you it is beyond intimidating. I jumped back. One of them told me I had to use a different gate and gestured in a different direction. He said the Vatican wasn't open yet. Not open? An entire independent country "closed"?

I obediently found the right gate, and before too much time had passed, someone came out of a building and unlocked it. It was just getting light. I would get my sunrise after all. I went up on the portico of St. Peter's to wait for it. There was a marble plaque that I could just make out in the dawn light. It told me that was the very spot where the Emperor Constantine knelt when he accepted his mother Helena's new religion, Christianity, and made it the official religion of Rome, banishing the panoply of ancient gods to oblivion. The year had been 313 AD, long before St. Peter's church had been built, but the spot had been marked.

As I waited for the sun to rise a very disheveled man with a backpack came walking up. He had an unkempt beard and was none too clean. I thought he was an outdated vagabond hippie until I saw him enter the church and prostrate himself. He was real pilgrim. This was the ultimate goal for a Catholic pilgrim.

The sun rose and it was beautiful to see early morning light shining in the empty piazza. I went into the church and giving the pilgrim wide berth, so he had his privacy for this important moment in his life, I quietly moved up close to Michaelangelo's La Pieta. The magnificent piece was protected behind glass, alas, since a religious fanatic had attacked it a few years before. Once again, religious fanatics, when not attacking other people, seem to like attacking statues.

I wandered around admiring more statuary. I was especially impressed by one of St. Andrew who looked like he was hauling a telephone pole on his shoulder. I knew St. Andrew was the patron saint of Scotland and the name means strong. I wondered if this statue gave rise to the Scottish sport of caber tossing or if it was the other way around and St. Andrew had been the original champion caber tosser. There was also a striking statue of a young female saint who looked like she was caught in a hurricane.

A small group of people came in and walked to a flight of stairs leading underground. I tailed along and a priest smiled and gestured me down the stairs as well. I thought it might lead to more beautiful art, but instead I found a funeral going on. I discreetly made my way back up the stairs.

St. Peter's is a huge place and its grandness swallowed me. The pilgrim was still praying, his head bowed to the floor, but others were arriving. The vastness of the space caused everyone to speak in hushed tones. I saw a group of African nuns arrive and fall to their knees. I felt I was intruding on someone else's faith and went outside to buy tickets to see the Sistine Chapel from a vendor who had set up shop. The Vatican is not just a religious center, it is a religious shop where serious money is made.

My chapel tour wasn't until an hour later, so I had breakfast at a café before lining up at a designated spot. The tour guide could have taken us directly to the chapel, but the rules required he walk us through boring halls for a mile or so, once in while pointing to a painting or piece of furniture, but mostly just herding the group. It took him over an hour to actually get us to the chapel.

The chapel was packed with people. It is overpowering. I just wanted to drink in the sight, and did, despite an annoying security guard who kept unnecessarily shouting at people to be quiet. The crowd was very hushed. An infant in arms began to cry and even as his parents tried to comfort and quiet him the guard became frenzied in his shouts for quiet. I thought he might have an apoplectic fit. They gave us about a sparse fifteen minutes or so to take in the masterpiece and then began moving us out to make room for the next batch of tour groups who were arriving.

After all that piety, I was ready to leave the Vatican. I stopped outside again to admire the view of St. Peter's columns wrapping around the sides of the piazza. I felt a great surge of gratitude for Michaelangelo. Before leaving the Vatican I bought a reproduction of the ceiling at the Vatican gift shop.

I took a silly shower in my silly bathroom and packed to leave magical Rome.

Intimidation *vs* the Unspeakable

Getting out of Italy was a lot harder than getting in when I just walked out of the plane and on to train in Milan. There was a line outside the terminal at Fiumicino Airport. They were letting people in one by one or in family groups.

When it was my turn, I was startled to see a mezzanine above the vast lobby filled with soldiers pointing mounted machine guns at me. The guns followed me as I walked to a man in uniform beckoning me to him. He inspected my passport and directed me to a long line. The next person entered, and the soldiers pointed the guns at him.

In the line we were all talking about the intimidating security.

"Do you think there has been a special alert?" asked one man.

"I remember this was the airport where there were hostages and a shootout a few years ago," said a woman.

"This is unbelievable. I'm going to make a video," said a man as he took out a camera.

He was instantly surrounded by a dozen soldiers with automatic weapons aimed at him. They seized his camera, confiscated his film cartridge and marched him off to a room for questioning. He returned visibly shaken.

"Don't take photos of their security," he warned newcomers.

At length there was a security check of our luggage. When a man lifted my roll-on, carry-on he found it heavy and looked at me suspiciously.

It's full of a lot of books," I explained.

They opened it. Art books were beautiful and cheap in Italy. I had gradually discarded clothes and toiletries and replaced them with books. Before my flight home I only had what I was wearing, even sacrificing my pajamas to squeeze in a few more volumes.

"It's all books," the disgusted guard said, disappointed he hadn't caught a terrorist, just a bookworm.

Then we were led up to another level where we were lined up and told we would be randomly searched.

I am convinced that Italy chooses their police by their looks. The men and women were all young and stunningly gorgeous. I figured when they became middle-aged, they were put to work behind the scenes. The cops working the airport security were no exception. All the women in line looked at the very handsome fellow doing the searching and smiled.

It was random done by various counts and the cop pulled a middle-aged matron out of line and into a room.

She came out a few minutes later grinning from ear to ear and with her thumbs pointed up. She did a little dance step and declared, "I got the lucky number!" We all laughed.

We had to go up one more level for a second passport check. Finally, we were pointed towards down escalators that they said led to the gates.

It was a three-story escalator, the longest I had ever seen. I stepped on dragging my book-laden carry-on. It slipped out of my grasp and began tumbling down. There was man farther down and I began shouting in panic to him but he didn't hear me. Finally, people at the bottom shouted and pointed. He looked back and began running in a frantic race with the merrily bouncing valise.

I watched in frozen horror. Was my book greed about to kill an innocent Italian?

He was young, agile and fast. He leaped to safety just as my luggage hit bottom. Onlookers applauded. I did, too. He laughed, relieved and set my carry-on upright for me.

I apologized profusely as he handed me my luggage.

I wondered why there were no soldiers with guns at the gate to arrest me, and was grateful there weren't.

Little Neros and Caligulas

Surprisingly, Catholic Italy has the lowest birth rate in Europe. It is now 1.35 children per woman. I think that is because it has become so expensive to raise an Italian child. It means those 1.35 children become the total focus of their parents and grandparents and are being spoiled rotten.

They become adults feeling so privileged and entitled I believe the Italians are bringing up a generation of little Emperor Neros and Caligulas.

I saw a ten-year-old boy outside a church one Sunday morning yelling, screaming and beating his father. The father's response was to plead, "What do you want? Want do you want? Tell me."

"He wants some limits and some discipline, you idiot. He wants a father, not a servant," I thought but did not say aloud.

While I was staying in a small seaside village at a café one afternoon an older man and I were sharing a cup of coffee at a café while he waited for his wife to get out of church. We were deep in conversation about fishing, and his six-year-old granddaughter came up and imperiously demanded, "I want a gelato."

The old man explained he hadn't finished his coffee and was having a conversation so she should wait a little.

She looked at him with disdain, "No, I want it now!"

The old man nodded his apology to me and abandoned his coffee to go to the gelato stand.

While in a castle in Tuscany I woke one Sunday morning to discover the windows in the bathroom sixteen feet up had been left open and a torrential rainstorm had left the sunken bathroom floor in four inches of water. I had to take off my shoes and wade to the toilet. I went to the office where a very young woman was chatting with a friend. She was the weekend help in charge. I explained we needed a maintenance man because there was a flood in the bathroom. She reached in a drawer and handed me a rag.

I explained it was serious and showed her how deep the water was. "You need to fetch maintenance people. This is a serious flood."

"It's your problem," she answered haughtily.

I demanded to speak to the owners. She looked at me horror-struck and refused. I told her if she didn't, I would contact the travel company that had booked my stay and have them call the owners.

"I have paid to stay here, and I am not responsible for the maintenance. This is YOUR problem not mine. I am going out and expect to find a dry floor in the bathroom on my return. So, I suggest you call the owners or the maintenance people," I told her firmly. She was not used to any authority and sat open mouthed as I left. Later that day I returned to find the flood cleared away. The rest of my stay I only dealt with the older generation that worked on weekdays.

I ran into a similar situation when I returned home on the then state-owned airlines. The young pretty attendants ignored the passengers. When it was time to serve a meal they just shoved a packet of food at us all. They all sat in the galley of the plane chatting and flirting with one another and when a passenger tried to ring for service, the call was ignored. At one point I needed water to take medication and I rang and was also ignored. I went back into the galley where they were drinking and chatting, and they looked annoyed at me for walking in on their party. I asked for water and one of them just pointed to a large bottle of water in the corner and they all went back to their conversation. I managed to pour a glass of water from the outsized awkward bottle.

State employees generally were bad, but the flight attendants took it to a new degree. The state sold the airline to a private company a while later and I chuckled wondering if those young people could still be as smug about their employment.

Not long after my return I was listening to the radio and heard a report about a forty-four year old Italian man suing his father for support because he hadn't yet decided what to do to earn a living and he had won the case. Daddy had to support him.

No wonder the Italians had so few children if their responsibility extended into middle-age. I know there's a phenomenon of Italian men not marrying, just staying at home so Mama will do their laundry and cook their meals. They just have girlfriends for sex and laze away their lives. That forty-four-year-old had just taken it public.

I loved the older Italians I was privileged to meet, but they are doing a rotten job raising their kids. Sorry, but it's true.

An Evening to Remember in Venice with a Surprise Ending

(This story was told to me by the late Lucille Gonnella, another widow. It is too funny not to share and long ago Lucille told me to do whatever I wanted with it, so here it is for you.)

In 1997 I went to Venice with my son and his family, including my two grand-children about twelve and thirteen years old. After landing we took a water-taxi to our hotel, The Metropole, which was supposed to be a very nice place.

The water-taxi driver, dropped us off on a small dock, unloaded our luggage then sped away down the canal. We were a bit concerned. There we were on this small dock, surrounded by water and no one to greet us. I kept knocking on the glass door in front of us but no one inside paid any attention to us.

Finally, a very scantily clad waitress came to the door and unlocked it. She was carrying a tray full of dishes, glasses and silverware. As she turned around she spilled all of it on the floor in front of us.

We walked through the mess and I went to the registration desk to get our room keys. The man at the desk said he didn't have our reservations and since it was Saturday night there were no rooms available. I showed him my pre-paid reservation form but he simply said, "Sorry, no rooms for you." This is a disaster in summer in Venice when it's at the height of the tourist season and rooms are impossible to find.

I started pleading with him that we had two children with us and we were all tired from our journey and needed a room. As I was arguing with him a bride in her dress and veil ran down the stairs and up to the desk and threw her room key down. She cried hysterically that she was not going to spend the night in the room with her new bridegroom. She ranted and raved about how terrible he and what he expected of her was, and ran out the front door of the hotel. I looked at her startled.

Just then a man in full chef's white uniform came running into the lobby carrying a real, dead, plucked, whole chicken, head and all. Holding it by the neck, he slammed it on the desk between me and the desk clerk and declared at the top of his lungs that he was not being treated with proper respect. He shouted if he couldn't be given better chickens he was quitting. Then he ripped open his chef's jacket and pinned on his undergarments were at least 100 different medals that he insisted he had won all over Europe. Then he stormed out of the lobby.

By this time, I was on the verge of tears and demanded to speak to the manager. My grandchildren sat there wide-eyed. They were scared and wondered where we'd spend the night. My son didn't know whether to laugh or cry.

As the clerk went to get the manager, I noticed a small crowd gathering around the desk. The manager came out and I was just about to give him some choice words when he took my hand, kissed it, and said, "Smile, madam, you are on Candid Camera."

It was true. Italy also has a Candid Camera show. That night they showed the film of my arrival to all the hotel guests in the lobby. They treated us to a lovely dinner and we enjoyed the rest of our stay in beautiful Venice. I love Venice and would return there any time, but I doubt that anyone else has ever been welcomed there in the same way!

Section 4:
Road Trips

Are We There Yet?

I can think of nothing more American than a road trip. I dearly love a good road trip. As a kid we made an annual trek from New York to the family farm in Alabama. Us kids loved it although we could seldom get our parents to stop at the unending Stuckey's Pecans stands that peppered the Southern roads. Our parents usually made one stop at a Howard Johnson along the turnpikes of the north east so we could all eat fried clam strips – a family favorite.

My first cross country trip was with my first husband. It was a long trip with many visits to his family in Pittsburg and Cleveland, then with visits to my family in the South before we turned west to California – having to cross a whole lot of Texas to get there.

Later I made an epic road trip across country. My late husband and I once took over a month to cross the country moving west with our then two children. We were limited to back roads because our car was so loaded with our possessions we couldn't go over thirty-five miles per hour.

As a widow I have always been on the lookout for good road trip companions. That is the critical factor on a road trip – you need a good-natured companion who looks on inconvenience as adventure.

My mother and I traveled well together, so did she and my stepdad when we all joined forces.

To begin, I step back in time in my first cross-country road trip tale to when I was a teenaged bride married to my first husband.

The Hills of Alabama and the Importance of Corn Flakes

I was seventeen and we were newlyweds. We had bought a new car with my husband's last paycheck when he left the Air Force. It was a totally different kind of vehicle back then in 1959, a Volkswagen bus. I had sewn curtains for its many windows, and we had packed it up for an epic journey from New York to Alabama, then to California where we planned to settle down. I didn't realize until we were underway how exotic we seemed.

The mini-bus attracted attention whenever we stopped for gas or food. Gas station attendants (remember those?) would look in bewilderment when my husband handed them the metal handle that opened the gas tank. He had to continually demonstrate how it worked. Again and again we gave "tours" of the mini-bus to satisfy strangers' curiosity.

Since it was so new a model, there were still some kinks to be worked out. We were in the wilds of northern Alabama en-route to Birmingham where I had relatives who were expecting us, when at the top of a hill, the engine gave a cough and sputter, then conked out. In the fast fading daylight we could see a filling station at the foot of the hill. We coasted into it. It was closed.

We sat in the silence for moment. We looked at our map. We were miles from any city. We looked in the Volkswagen book and found the nearest dealer was in Birmingham, still over sixty miles ahead of us. There was nothing for it but to spend the night in the car. It was late fall and getting very chilly.

Just then we heard a lot of barking, and striding over the hill in back of the filling station, we saw man carrying a rifle, surrounded by dogs. He and the dogs took an immediate interest in the mini-bus. He greeted us.

"Whatch'all doin' here?" he asked politely in his soft Southern drawl.

"Our car broke down."

"This here is a car?" he wondered.

We explained it was a new model and we had to get it to the dealer in the morning and were hoping when the station opened in the morning, we could use a phone. He asked where we were going to spend the night.

"Here, in the car."

"Now, y'all can't do that. It's cold. Come with me. Me and the missus have a room y'all can use."

Despite, or maybe because of the rifle, we obediently followed him. We crossed the road surrounded by his curious dogs. He had been coon hunting he explained. Off the highway about a quarter mile we came to a log cabin. It was the real thing, not a modern imitation. Kerosene lamps lit it with a soft glow.

When we went inside, we found the missus in a rocking chair beside a potbellied stove. She was chewing snuff and spitting into a bucket. She was immediately very solicitous.

"Y'all came from New York? My, my. I'll show you our extra room. I hope it's all right with you folks. We don't have much here."

I was embarrassed that she was so apologetic when we were the intruders into her life. The room she showed us to was beautiful. A painted iron bedstead was covered with a beautiful handmade quilt. Everything was spotlessly clean. I admired the quilt explaining that my grandmother was also a quilter and I asked about the relatives whose pictures hung on the walls. She beamed at me.

The mister was pleased I had made his wife happy. He explained to us that since the children had grown and left, and he had retired, he had insisted his wife retire, too. Instead of her cooking dinner, each evening they drove to the nearest town called Arab (pronounced A rab) for supper at the café. We were welcome to join them, and there was even a pay phone we could use. We jumped at the chance.

In Arab we called my Birmingham relatives who said they'd drive up to get us and tow us to the dealer in the morning.

We all ordered hamburgers and fries, except the missus. She ordered a bowl of cornflakes and was slightly embarrassed by it. The mister chuckled and said it was what she had for dinner every night.

I had learned that cornflakes were such a novelty and so expensive in poor rural areas a whole generation grew up dreaming of eating them. My mother said as a little girl when the leaves fell in the fall, she'd close her eyes and crunch them as she walked saying to herself, "Cornflakes, cornflakes, cornflakes." My late father-in-law recalled vividly the first time he had ever eaten a bowl of them at a rich relative's house. "I thought it the most delicious thing I had ever tasted."

And now we watched the missus eat hers, her face rapt with the bliss of it.

Back at the house she offered to let us have the slop bucket for the night, but I declined. Instead, I took a flashlight and made my way to the outhouse, surrounded by barking, obnoxious hounds. It was spooky and spidery. I got back to the house as fast as I could.

In the morning, the mister went to the filling station to show all his friends our strange vehicle and alert the owner as to what was happening.

The missus came out of retirement for breakfast. She insisted on cooking us sausage, bacon, grits, eggs, potatoes and flapjacks. We tried to give her money for having put us up.

"Oh, no. The mister would be right put out."

She compromised on taking some money to cover the cost of our food. She gleefully tucked her unexpected "egg" money in her apron pocket

The cabin had no phone, electricity or indoor plumbing. But it did have running water with a bit of work. A pump handle was by the sink in the kitchen. I helped with dishes.

My kin arrived and a whole community of people had materialized out of the hills to look at the mini-bus and see us off. Everyone helped hitch us up. My aunt who lived in a Birmingham suburb commented, "They must be nice people. I wouldn't take in strangers off the road and put them up in my house like that."

I thought my aunt and uncle were also very nice for being willing to tow us over sixty miles but simply said, "Yes, they are very, very nice," as I waved farewell to our hospitable new friends.

Keys to Fun and Chickens

I talked Mom into a mother-daughter road trip to Key West, a place I always wanted to see – the USA tropics. We were supposed to meet at the Tampa airport.

Somewhere on the East coast there was snowstorm although there was no snow in San Francisco, where I started from, Tampa or in St. Louis where I was to change planes. Nevertheless, I was told we would be delayed in California by several hours. It was pre-cell phone days. I tried calling Mom at her home before she set off for Tampa, but she was gone.

Once on board I learned there would be no flight from St. Louis to Tampa because we'd be arriving so late the airport would be closed there. I was assured the airline would have arranged a hotel room for me. That was a big fat lie. At 11 p.m. I tried calling hotels from the airport – all were full and the personnel just laughed at me. I also tried to call Mom again at our Tampa hotel, but I was told they did not put through calls that late at night.

The airport in St. Louis wants to discourage homeless people, like passengers abandoned by their airlines, from sleeping there. All the seats are hard plastic with built in armrests. They also play very loud heavy metal music all night, even in the restrooms. It was a very uncomfortable night and in the morning after catching a short nap with my head resting on my roll-on suitcase, I discovered one of my favorite earrings had fallen off somewhere, never to be found, and I was awfully grouchy for the short flight to Tampa

I managed to call Mom just before we left. The hotel had never delivered my messages to her, so she was relieved to hear from me and was cheerfully waiting for me at the airport with a cooler packed with lunch. We decided to head for the first part of the Everglades – the part they call 10,000 islands. We got there just in time to book a sunset cruise, so not stopping to book a room or eat dinner, we hopped on board.

That part of the Everglades is made up of mangrove islands. The remarkable trees send out floating seeds that have already germinated. The traveling seeds send down roots surviving salt water and wave action. Once its roots get to the sandy bottom the tree flourishes and traps sand, eventually forming forested islands of tangled roots, catching more floating seeds so the islands grow. Only birds, fish and floating creatures can use the islands. There is no solid land to stand on.

Our boat was accompanied by a school of dolphins that played in the bow wave as the beautiful sunset lit up a world of graceful egrets, lovely islands and a flat calm sea. Mom and I smiled at each other while she tried to get photos of the dolphins in action.

Once back on land, we were famished and went to the only restaurant in the small port to eat dinner.

We perused the menu. There were very few items listed.

"Fried alligator, frog legs and conch?"

"Yes, ma'am. That's the house special," the waitress said.

We asked the waitress about lodgings when she delivered our novel meal. "Ain't none here, ma'am. You have to head east or north," she told my mother.

Mom and I headed east, confident we'd find a motel along the way.

It was dark and the two-lane highway had no lights. We were in a canyon of impenetrable bushes as we drove. I was very, very tired because of my night in the hospitable St. Louis airport. An hour passed and there was not one sign of life. A few times we saw a panther crossing sign and hopefully looked, but there are just a handful of the critters left, so no luck. I began getting sleepy behind the wheel by the second hour of darkness with not even a wide spot to pull over and nap.

"Mom, I don't care what kind of place it is, I have got to sleep so the first place with a bed, we'll stop," I told her.

She agreed. A couple hours later I saw Motel on a neon sign. The M had burnt out so it actually read "otel". Mom was uneasy. There were no cars there. We went into the office where a polite young Seminole man told us the motel belonged to the reservation and he could only take cash, not credit cards. A room was forty dollars.

"Oh, we'll have to keep driving," Mom said quickly, but I hauled out two twenties to her chagrin.

The room was very simple but clean. The old iron bedstead held a freshly laundered hand-made quilt. A simple outdoorsy print hung on the wall. There was no air conditioning, but the night air was pleasant. The bathroom was old but spotless.

I unpacked pajamas and told Mom "I can't wait to shower off airplane and airports."

"You sure you want to do that?" she asked.

"Unless you want to shower first."

"No!" she said sharply.

I took a long time showering and the hot water lasted. I came out and found Mom was in her nightgown and that she had propped a chair under the doorknob and stacked all our luggage against the door.

"What's this about?" I asked puzzled.

"Didn't you ever see Psycho?" she asked, and I burst out laughing.

"No, I didn't. So many of my friends were afraid to shower for months I had no interest in seeing a movie that would do that to me. But Mom, that movie was like forty plus years ago."

"Doesn't matter – motel in the middle of nowhere, a young man at the counter…"

"A very nice young Indian man," I said as I crawled into bed. I didn't point out to Mom that while she had efficiently barricaded the door, the window in the room was wide open with just a screen and a curtain between us and Anthony Perkins if he was lurking outside.

In the morning I saw the motel had filled up. We packed up and drove off in search of breakfast. Just fifteen minutes down the road we reached a major intersection with Highway 1, the route to the Keys.

"You see, if we had just kept driving we could have stayed at one of these nice places," Mom admonished gesturing towards the bland roadside hotels, motels and restaurants that Henry Miller had called "air conditioned nightmares". I had preferred our simple but clean and comfortable Native American lodging. Well, comfortable for me, not Mom, who it turned out had nervously lay awake much of the night, wary of Anthony Perkins and his knife.

We began the drive to Key West where I had made reservations at a youth hostel. Mom and I had a small budget, and in addition, I had discovered hostels were great for women traveling alone because of the security. I explained that to Mom who still had misgivings.

Key Largo was a big disappointment. I expected something isolated like in the old Bogart movie, but it was covered with air-conditioned nightmares instead. But after that the drive was spectacular. The highway became a causeway over the sea, a brilliant turquoise sea. We saw sections of the old railroad built by Flagler a century before and the abandoned highway that got eaten by hurricanes many decades before. I labelled then "ghost bridges" Some sections were so long I wondered why they hadn't become party venues for boaters. Mom and I discussed how a fund-raiser might be organized on the longest ghost bridge about seven miles long. As we crossed keys, I watched diligently for a sight of the miniature Key West deer that are supposed to inhabit the archipelago. I never did see one.

Finally, we reached Key West. I saw a large K-Mart looming ahead of us.

"Oh, God, Mom. I think we are thirty years too late."

But on the Caribbean side of the island (one side is Gulf of Mexico, the other the Caribbean Sea, locals told us) we got into the old town. Wary of falling coconuts under the wind tossed palms we located the hostel. To my dismay it appeared it was an old, neglected looking motel with a number of older men in the courtyard drinking cans of something in paper bags.

"I can't have my mother stay here," I thought, and hoped that without reservations we could find a hotel room. Then the cheerful woman at the desk pointed out a newer building next to the motel. "That's the women's dorms," she told us.

We went to check it out and as Mom saw the security rules posted, she breathed a sigh of relief. In the four-bed dorm we found two compatible roommates. Both were older women. One was moaning as she lay in bed. It turned out she had been a passenger on an Amtrak train that had derailed the day before. We had heard about the wreck on the car radio. The Amtrak people had simply handed her a bottle of painkillers and hired a taxi to take her to Key West, her destination.

Mom promptly started nursing her and finally told her she was in shock and had better go to the hospital and get in touch with an attorney as well as a doctor. We talked to the woman running the hostel and she sent for an ambulance. That left us with Peggy, a woman in her sixties who was very healthy. She told us she was from Mississippi and had recently buried her mother after nursing her for several years, and decided on a vacation.

We strolled into town, bought trolley passes and settled ourselves into laid back tropical life. One of the first things that caught our attention were the chickens. They were everywhere and didn't seem to belong to anyone. There was horrific traffic and it seemed no one stopped for pedestrians, but whenever a chicken hopped off a curb all vehicles came to a dead stop until it was safely across. We learned to watch the hens when we wanted to cross ourselves and docilely followed them.

We found a place with a patio for lunch and the chickens were busy in the patio, eating crumbs although once in a while a waitperson would shoo them. We went back to the hostel so Mom could rest a bit before we went out for a sundowner at Mallory Square.

As soon as Mom sat in the courtyard at the hostel a gentleman handed her a paper bag holding a cold can of beer.

"Thought you and your daughter might like one," he said as he handed me one, too. "Not supposed to have alcohol in a youth hostel, but us grown-ups bend the rules a little," he grinned.

Mom grinned right back and started a conversation. He was there to fish and it turned out a whole group of elderly anglers had met there. Mom, an avid angler all her life, began describing some of methods she used. She became the center of attention. Word spread about her knowledge and more men came and offered us another cloaked beer. Finally, Mom begged off to take a quick nap to their disappointment.

Later, Mom, a petite blonde, dressed for the sunset in a cute little outfit she had made herself topped with a straw hat. We were early and found a terraced bar overlooking the action. We ordered an umbrella topped rum drink and sat back to watch a circus unfold.

A steel drum band was playing in the distance, then some bagpipers began marching around. One man was juggling three active chainsaws, another flaming batons. Someone was doing magic tricks while costumed stilt-walkers were prowling the crowd. The act that captured our interest was a man with trained domestic cats who performed all sorts of charming tricks. Since getting an ordinary cat to come when you call it is not easy, Mom and I were very impressed.

In the middle of all the colorful chaos a wedding was happening right between the bagpipers and chainsaw juggler. The photographer was taking pictures of the happy couple using the sea as a backdrop. Their album would show a peaceful setting, not the increasing madness around them. Fire dancers came to perform dangerously, various bands set up to compete with the steel drums and bagpipes.

"I have got to see those cats," announced Mom after one of them wheeled another around in a doll baby carriage.

We immersed ourselves in Mallory Square Madness. There were about eight or so of the trained cats quietly sitting along a walkway with a sign and basket asking for donations. The cats were so mellow they looked high and I sneakily wondered if the trainer had fed them some special catnip, but we donated since we had been so happily entertained. We stroked the comfortable felines and earned purrs as a reward.

Then Mom found a man making hats from what looked like palm frond strips. Mom was immediately ecstatic, saying she had worn one out gardening, and needed a new one. The man agreed to make one to fit her for just $15 after some bargaining. It was clear he found Mom as charming as the fishermen had. We strolled for an hour and sure enough Mom had her new hat, and some palm roses he had fashioned for her as well. He presented the latter with a bow.

Mom handed me her straw hat and donned her new palm one as we walked into town to watch the action in the growing dark. I was feeling somewhat disappointed in Key West – so much traffic, so many tourists despite it being off season. We walked away from the tourist area to where the working fishing boats were moored, and there we found what I had been looking for, something real. This was blue collar Key West. There was a six-foot wood fence with a knot hole in it. I glanced and saw a patio with tables. We had found the entrance to the Hole in the Wall Bar.

This was not the glam part of town. People wore real worn denim, not designer torn jeans that cost a week's pay check. Mom and I felt at home. Of course, a conversation sprang up about fishing, this time commercial fishing. We had a lot to learn.

We became habitues of The Hole as its regulars called it, for the next few days we were in the Keys.

One night, taking Peggy with us, we went hunting for a place on Big Pine Key a neighbor of Mom's had told her about. It was perfect. The raw wood shack of place was on a dock. There were a few oil-cloth covered picnic tables inside but more outside. It was a balmy evening so we ordered a beer we were given right away and placed our order for the seafood chalked on a blackboard menu then went outside to wait until our number was called.

This was the Florida I had come to see: the sound of a calm sea lapping the shore, a warm night, fresh sea food, palm trees decorating a clear night sky.

Mom and Peggy praised youth hostels. Every day there were events posted on the bulletin board, and people shared food they had cooked. Mom was excited to have discovered older people populated them.

"Mom, it's ex-hippies. They traveled the world in their youth staying in them and they recapture those days by staying in them now."

She asked me to fetch the hostel directory I had brought with me from the car to see if there any more on our planned route home. There weren't to her disappointment.

The next day Mom and I left, glad no coconuts had fallen on her car, and blowing farewell kisses to the chickens who ignored us. We stopped a few times to let them cross the road as we headed north. We agreed, the Keys had been kind to us.

Alligators Everywhere

My mother and I were on a road trip in southern Florida. Neither of us was interested in Miami. I had been there and found it an unsavory mixture of pretentiousness and the seedy. Thank goodness there was a lot more to Florida than that despoiled part of it. Places like the Everglades. After a lovely few days in Key West, that's where we were going now. We wanted to see alligators.

We had come to the right place. Everglades National Park was established in 1947.

"The park service did a census of alligators in the park when it was first established," said the naturalist guide driving the van of people we had joined. "They found four. Everybody hunted them then. Now there are over 200,000 of them in the Everglades alone."

In 1967 a law was passed protecting the gators, but poaching was a problem. An elder in Mom's church in northern Florida shamefacedly admitted to poaching them when he was young, and he even served time when he was caught once. "Then I got religion, found the Lord and left the gators alone," he had told me. I guess old time religion can serve a worthy purpose sometimes.

Actually, it was the Endangered Species Act in the 70s that put real teeth into the laws that brought the population back.

Alligators are essential to the ecology of that unique "River of Grass" as the Native Americans called it. It's a river almost a hundred miles wide and just inches deep filled with sawgrass interrupted only by "hummocks", small islands that rise a few feet above the water level where ancient people made their home. Once a hummock became too polluted with their waste, the people would move to another one while the first one cleansed itself in time. The gators roll around and around in the mud and grass, and create small pools of water that attract the many birds that populate the Everglades.

Once in a while a gator will eat one of the birds but for the most part the scenes at the alligator ponds were peaceful. Many birds waded, eating fish and other juicy things while the alligators seemed to be asleep.

The grass was punctuated here and there by an alligator nest. In the spring the male alligators bellow to attract mates, then the females build three to five foot tall nests to keep their eggs warm and dry. The temperature determines the sex of the baby. Hotter eggs produce males. Alligator moms are very attentive we were told. They guard the nest until they hear the babies begin to hatch, then mom breaks open the nest and lovingly carries her newborns down to the water in her mouth. She fiercely guards them for a year or more.

"Don't go picking up a baby alligator thinking it's cute," a ranger warned us. "It'll squeal and then you will have to contend with an angry mother."

An alligator's worst enemy is another alligator, somewhat like people in that regard. Every alligator lives in fear of another alligator jumping on his back and killing him.

Some areas of the Everglades had pools large enough to support waterlilies with giant pads. Mom and I spotted a Purple Gallinule, a bird that hops from lily pad to lily pad as it hunts. It seemed a fairytale life – letting lily pad after lily pad provide one with food and a resting spot.

In the middle of the Everglades an oil company wanted to drill but was stopped when it was declared a park. Before the company left, however they had constructed a ramped tower and a very large pond. Our guide took us out there as it has become a popular alligator viewing spot. From the top of the tower we could look over the idyllic scene below us where scores of alligators and hundreds of wading birds shared the rich waters.

We got out of our van often to walk around and view the alligators but we marveled to see brave people actually riding bicycles among the fierce looking creatures.

"You can rent bikes at the park entrance and they tell you how to protect yourself and not interfere with the gators, but I wouldn't do it," our guide said.

Then he told of an incident the week before. A Brazilian family, the parents and a young son, had rented bikes and gone riding. The boy somehow fell off his bike right next to an alligator pool. He fell on to the gator.

The poor alligator assumed he was being attacked by another gator, and quickly turned to grab the boy. The mother who had been behind the boy quickly jumped into action, hopped on the gator and began punching it in its snout. It let go of the boy to turn on the mother, but she had grabbed her son and jumped back on the road. The father just stood there dumbstruck by the astounding scene. Someone summoned help and boy was taken to the hospital where he needed a few stitches.

"But the mother didn't look very pleased with her do-nothing husband, and she was so upset we all wondered just how long that marriage was going to last."

Mom and I agreed afterwards that alligators were dangerous in ways we had never thought of.

The Jeweled Clasps
of the Pearl Necklace

I hadn't been camping for a few years and was longing for a bit of roughing it in the wild. Camping was one thing I wouldn't do alone as a woman. I tried to talk some of my women friends into coming with me but was met with laughter.

"My idea of camping is ordering room service," one friend told me.

But Doris who had worked for my newspaper in the past was willing. I wanted to research and photograph the Conde McCullough bridges of the Oregon coast for an article. My husband and I had discovered them on a camping trip years before and I was enamored of the poet of bridge building.

McCullough called his extraordinarily lovely bridges linking Oregon's beautiful beaches "the jeweled clasps in a wonderful string of matched pearls." He tried to fight scam-artist engineers who submitted plans for bridges that often failed in months, accusing them of "busily ruining this fair earth and taking all the romance out of it." He used reinforced concrete for his bridges, a new concept allowing him to design soaring arches, and had his beautiful bridges come in with low bids so governments could feel good about hiring him.

Doris and I mapped out our trip. I invested in some new camping equipment and figured between the two of us we could handle the work of camping. We would also use youth hostels as I had discovered they offered better security for women alone than most hotels or motels.

Our adventure was set. Unfortunately, Doris had failed to disclose that she had some health problems until the first day when we had to set up camp. She could not help with any of the labor because her hips hurt. I put up tents, set up a camp kitchen, cooked, and washed up while she got stoned. I don't smoke anything be it tobacco, marijuana or herbs. Nothing goes in my lungs but air if I can help it. So, after all was done and I was exhausted, having also done all the driving that day, I poured myself a generous glass of wine before bedtime.

The next day I cooked breakfast, broke down camp and asked her to drive.

We were rewarded the second day with our first McCullough bridge – the one over the Rogue River at Gold Beach, Oregon. After the discovery of King Tut's tomb in 1922 the world went Egyptian mad. It influenced the whole Art Deco movement, including Conde McCullough's work. At least that's my opinion.. The huge stone bridge has been sometimes called "Caveman's Bridge". I have been under it in a boat a few times and get the reference since the stone arches made of massive stones exude the safety and protection of a cave.

Later driving through a town, Doris was regaling me with wild stories of her love life. After years of being Mrs. Goody Two Shoes as a Catholic wife, bearing five children to a physically abusive husband, she had opted out and did so with an explosion of daring. Her sexual exploits left me gaped-jawed.

But as she did this she drove right through a red light.

I yelped, "Doris you just drove through a red light. If we get a ticket you pay for it."

She just laughed. Suddenly she squealed to a sharp stop turning my seat belt into a straight jacket. We were at a green light and the car behind us honked.

"What are you doing?" I demanded.

"I am making up for the red light I didn't stop at," she said innocently. I demanded she pull over.

"Honestly, Doris. You can't help with camping, and I won't let you drive again. Here's the maps. Be my navigator."

The Suislaw Bridge at Florence, Oregon stopped us in our tracks. It is the most Egyptian looking of all the bridges and is a stunning entrance to a lovely town. We camped in the Oregon Dunes nearby after dinner in town. If I was doing all the work, we were going to eat out more.

At Waldport I stopped because I had learned this was the only McCullough bridge that had ever failed after 51 years of service and there was museum at the base of it dedicated to him. It failed because the contractor had used salt infused sand. Salt intrusion had eroded the rebar.

The failure put the state into a frenzy. They had to save the rest of their beautiful bridges. Declaring the bridges a state treasure, with some help from the California Department of Transportation the state launched a massive restoration program.

The bridges, once any gross repairs have been made, are coated with a 20,000th of an inch thick layer of zinc. A low voltage direct current is then applied which has the effect of driving salt intrusion that threatens the metal rebar towards the zinc instead. It works something like a rechargeable battery. The "cathodic protection" has been studied by the road departments from places as far away as Sweden, and Finland. It will double the life of the bridges.

The locals demanded when the bridge at Waldport was rebuilt, that original design pieces be incorporated into it. The Alsea Bridge, as it is called is a true tribute to the original builder.

By the time we reached Newport and the Yaquina Bay Bridge I realized that Doris was also lousy at reading maps.

"I'm dyslexic and have never been able to do it," she explained.

I began laughing. "You can't help camp, you can't drive and you can't navigate. What am I going to do with you?"

"Well, I can change the weather."

I snorted. "Okay, I am sick of all the fog. Give me some sun," I retorted.

"Give me ten quiet minutes and I'll do it," she promised. Ten minutes later the fog was gone and we were driving in sunshine. I was impressed.

"Okay, from here on out you are in charge of the weather," I told her.

We got to the Depoe Bay Bridge. I insisted on us "bridge crawling" whenever it was possible – getting underneath the bridges to look at the structure below. At Depoe Bay Gothic arches held up the roadbed. There was a small empty freighter parked on the waterway and the crew invited us on board. We shared a cup of coffee with them and declined their invitation to spend the night and headed on our way.

The bridge over Coos Bay was spectacular. Once again the understructure was worth a detour. It was like the ramparts of a massive castle, but with graceful sweeps of wall. The longest and toughest to build when McCullough suddenly died at 58 of a brain aneurysm, it was renamed Conde McCullough Memorial Bridge. Frank Nelson, a retired head of the Oregon Bridge Division said, "Driving over that bridge is like entering a cathedral."

I had a heyday photographing it. Then I tried to get a distant view and drove down a public road to park and use the camera only to have an irate householder emerge demanding we leave. Apparently, that spot was so regularly used by bridge tourists we had become a nuisance.

Doris and I settled into a family room at a charming hostel on the outskirts of Portland. Our room came complete with a sunflower mural, a balcony, and pet bunnies on the lawn below. We still had Ashland and the Shakespeare Festival ahead of us on the trip. I could take it easy as only hostels, no more single-handed camping lay before us. And I do have to say in addition to racy tales, Doris provided excellent weather for the whole trip home.

A Lucy and Ethel
Road Trip Moment

Mom and I met at St. Augustine, Florida. It's one of the oldest cities in the USA dating back to the 1500s, and a very pretty place. We were there before the newest tourist boom made it overpopulated while it still had its small-town charm. It's the oldest continuously inhabited city in the continental US, founded by a Spanish conquistador in 1565 (San Juan is even older). Ponce de Leon found his fountain of youth here according to legend.

I had flown into Fort Lauderdale to visit my dad and rented a car. Mom had left her farm on the Florida panhandle. We planned to meet at the tiny St. Augustine airport where I could return the rental. Much to our surprise and delight we arrived just two minutes apart. I turned in my car and joined Mom in hers.

We found a lovely B&B facing the harbor. Our room came with a two-person Jacuzzi tub. We enjoyed luscious breakfasts, then sherry and cheese at cocktail time on the veranda. We prowled the town which is built for pedestrians with its narrow brick-paved streets. It was easy to imagine the place under attack by pirates. Sir Frances Drake pillaged and sacked it in the 1500s once. Then other pirates did the same. It was a big drag for locals who would be taken hostage and if not ransomed, sold into slavery.

So locals built a fort, Castillo de San Marcos and used a peculiar building material – coquina which is a stone formed by millions of shells from tiny shellfish. The stuff, cut from a beach hardens when exposed to air. Those who attacked the fort would lob cannonballs during the day leaving gaping holes. During the night those in the fort would secretly cut fresh coquina and patch the holes. The peculiar self-healing fort got a reputation for being haunted. Mom and I had a great time exploring the lovely battlement.

We also enjoyed traipsing everywhere looking at the Tiffany glass windows that developer and oil man Henry Flagler brought in. Flagler claimed St. Augustine for himself, building massive hotels and capitalizing on the fountain of youth legend. He also built a railroad to the Keys farther south that got blown apart by hurricanes.

At the end of the day Mom and I were footsore and worn out. That's when we remembered our Jacuzzi tub. I am very fond of bubble baths and have learned to use shampoo in a tub for really lasting bubbles. Mom thought bubbles sounded like a good idea.

I grabbed a bottle of what looked like shampoo but proved to be body washing gel instead. Apparently, gel does not act like shampoo as we learned.

Mom and I poured ourselves a glass of chardonnay as waited for the tub to fill, and we chatted about the sights we had seen that day. We opened the door to the bathroom and a wall of bubbles poured out. Panicked, we tried to find our way to the tub through the bubbles to shut off the Jacuzzi jets. We carried armloads of bubbles to our balcony and dumped them.

But the bubbles kept coming. We were finally able to shut off the jets. We tried flushing armloads of bubbles down the toilet. They didn't flush. We tried washing some down the sink. They just floated. There was veranda overlooking the parking lot behind us. We carried armloads there and dumped them.

We finally abandoned the bathroom, closing the door. We went out to dinner and came back a few hours later and to our relief the bubbles had finally evaporated.

We had a good laugh in relief. There was a delicate film over the bathroom floor and up high just below the ceiling was a bathtub ring on the walls. So, we left our chambermaid a big tip when we left in the morning giggling like naughty schoolgirls.

Anasazi Country

There are some places where time seems to vanish. There's a blending of man and landscape in such a perfect way that a thousand years doesn't seem like such a long time. The Anasazi country of the Southwest is like that. Anasazi means Old Ones. That is the name the Pueblo Indians call the ancient cliff dwellers in the Southwest.

The Indians lived there so long no one is quite sure how long – nor does it seem to matter. The Anasazi picked up and left at one point. One theory is that their numbers had grown too much for the environment to support them and they had to move on.

They have left behind traces of their lives that look just like today's pueblos. At Mesa Verde there is a kiva, the sacred round underground places of worship. The modern Pueblos still build and use kivas.

The Navajos moved in on the Hopi and other pueblo tribes at one point. They were really nomadic Apaches but stole sheep. Once you have livestock you have got to take care of them, so the nomadic people settled down and learned to build hogans. Be careful how you choose your enemy is the moral there – you will become him.

One of the most moving places I visited was the Canyon de Chelly (pronounced de shay). It is in the Navajo Nation and is a Navajo National Park. We camped nearby and then went to Spider Woman Rock, a sharp, high pinnacle, to look for the trail down into the canyon.

It was dry desert above. The desert smelled wonderful – like sage and other herbs but was dessicatingly arid. We made our way down the hairpin trail, moving between the great rocks until we reached bottom.

There around a bend I saw an arched rock and through the arch I saw a simple hogan and some corn growing beside it. It was poignantly beautiful in its simplicity, and in the midst of the dry barren surroundings seemed lushly bountiful.

The river wound through the bottom of the canyon turning things verdant and it was fragrant with wildflowers. Enchanted we began walking beside it gazing in awe at the dramatic cliffs soaring above us.

Then I saw it. There perched in a niche in the cliff like a lovely bird was the White House, a famous Anasazi ruin. It looked over that lovely canyon and looked like it was the abode of gods. The massive cliffs, striped with weathering rose above it making it seem small. I tried to photograph it but no photo could capture that sense of man and nature welded together through the ages.

Before we left that canyon, I plucked a handful of herbs and flowers. I thrust my nose deep into them inhaling the special smell of the desert and that verdant canyon meeting one another. Maybe no photo could capture the moment, but that scent could. I put the fragrant handful into a tiny handmade Acoma pot I had bought so whenever I needed to, I could once again let the aroma carry me back.

East to the West

Mom and my stepdad Harry were among my favorite fellow travelers. Harry had rarely been out of his hometown area in panhandle Florida and southern panhandle Alabama until he married Mom, so he was always thrilled when he saw something for the first time.

This time we were traveling from my home on the California coast through Yosemite east to the Southwest. I had found us lodgings at the Wawona, not the huge lodge in the valley, but the original place higher up where John Muir worked as a stable hand and learned to love Yosemite. Our room could accommodate three and had a shared bathroom down the veranda. It got a little chilly during the night if you had to answer a call of nature.

Harry saw his first white water at Yosemite. In his homeland rivers slowly meandered and formed swamps and bayous. They might rise, but they never formed rapids and waterfalls. It had been a wet winter, and as it was May the melting snows had created magnificent waterfalls where I had never seen them before. Harry was as enthralled as a young child at the rushing river near the Wawona. He was also impressed when we stopped in at the big lodge, The Ahwahnee, to have a drink and he discovered the fireplace was so large he could stand in it, another first for him.

He spotted snow high up in the Sierra – his first glimpse of snow in real life.

"That is so pretty," he drawled. "Ya'll get to see this a lot?"

"Whenever we're willing to make the drive to the mountains, Dad," I replied.

After enjoying waterfalls, magnificent vistas that never fail to take one's breath away, and big trees I turned up the road leading to the

Tioga Pass. I had hoped to cross the Tioga Pass so I could show them the ghost town of Bodie and then spend the night in or near Death Valley. But the pass was still closed.

"Oh, no! We are going to get Barstowed!" I exclaimed.

I told them I am always getting skunked by Tioga Pass. I originally entered Yosemite coming from the east over the Tioga Pass, but I have never made it heading west. Once in June I called making sure it was open and drove up there just as rangers were barricading it because of a freak out-of-season snow storm.

Instead I got Barstowed. That's what I learned to call it when I was forced to take the highway south through the Central Valley from Yosemite instead of the Tioga Pass. Barstow is a remarkably uncharming town. The only worse one is Kingman, Arizona which is just a truck stop on steroids instead of a real town.

The landscape seemed very dull after the beauty of Yosemite as we resigned ourselves to our new destination. We endured a relatively cheap motel and pizza dinner in Barstow. Mom and Harry didn't mind. It was all an adventure to them. Harry even appreciated the Mojave Desert as we traveled east to see The West. The Mojave is not my favorite desert. It was his first desert.

The next stop was Las Vegas, again a city I detest. It just doesn't belong where it is, using all that water so recklessly just for recreation while subsistence farmers on the Colorado in Mexico don't have enough water to grow their beans. I don't gamble, so it holds no attraction to me. Mom and Harry enjoyed the spectacle but wanted to leave. The playground for adults held no attraction for them either, so we hit the road after just a couple hours of watching a ship artificially sink in an artificial sea, and artificial fountains in artificial lakes.

We headed for the Grand Canyon. I knew Mom and Harry would be overwhelmed. That enormous gash in the earth never fails to impress everyone. I feel like it reveals the bones of the earth. It lays bare all of time if one only knows how to read its geology. None of us wanted to descend to the canyon floor. It was too hot. The hike would have been impossible for Mom and Harry and the thought of riding on mule back down the steep hairpin trail made me dizzy. I offered to pay for a helicopter tour but Mom vetoed it.

"No way. Too dangerous," she said emphatically. I agreed because I had an easier canyon in mind that I knew they'd love – the Canyon de Chelly (pronounced de Shay).

Flagstaff was next. It's a place I love. I often thought if there was just some way to capture the scent of the mountains above Flagstaff in the spring someone would make a fortune because it's a perfume everyone would want. I'd buy it by the gallon.

The city itself is lovely, with mountains behind it, Old West character, and friendly people. But we left it behind for the Navajo Nation and spent the night at Chinle.

While Navajos inhabit it now, we were entering Anasazi country.

I learned the area open to the general public via the White House Ruin path was closed because it was flooded. That meant I wouldn't be able to see Spider Rock or the White House – beloved places I had seen before. But another part called Canyon del Muerto was open. Canyon de Chelly is actually a network of canyons. In order to see what was open we would have to hire a Navajo guide. I insisted on splurging because it was Mother's Day, and Mom had to acquiesce.

Outside the elegant Navajo Lodge we boarded a battered old truck with very large tires. To get on the back of the truck we climbed a ladder and found some benches. Another half dozen people joined us. Our driver, an unsmiling, poker-faced Navajo, introduced himself as George.

George told us we had made the right decision to go with a guide because drivers who tried to go on their own often got stuck in the frequent quicksand areas.

"We used to charge them $20 to pull them out, but then a couple fancy cars got damaged and owners sued us. Now if you get stuck we charge $2,000 to pull you out."

We drove off towards the river called Chinle Wash. We thought we would turn on to a riverside road but instead George abruptly drove us right into the river with a big splash. Everyone screamed wondering if we were at the mercy of a kamikaze driver. The truck stopped and George got out of the cab just above water level with a big grin on his face.

"Scared you, huh? Not to worry. The road is underwater. I know where it is. You are in no trouble," he said. "You won't get any wetter than you are."

We laughed, a few passengers a little nervously. We set off downstream moving slowly. The desert above us was desiccated, but at the bottom of the canyon it was a lovely Eden with trees and occasional crops like corn growing. Wildflowers scented the air. Chinle Wash was melodic and it sang watery lullabies to us.

"Now, ain't this something," Harry exclaimed. Mom agreed and was busy filming everything with her camcorder.

Every so often George would stop and explain what we were seeing. We passed some hogans, and at one point some children waded out to the truck to offer us seed pod necklaces for sale. Mom and I happily bought some.

"What will you use the money for?" I asked a little girl.

"School clothes," she promptly answered. She and her brother and sister returned to the shore where their parents were tending a corn field.

At the Antelope House, an Anasazi ruin, we made a lunch stop. A Navajo family was selling delicious freshly made fry bread. The cook was using a smoking hot frying pan full of lard over a camp stove.

144

"It's a good thing they don't have this where we live or I'd get fat," Mom said happily chewing.

"You're a good cook. Do you think you could learn to make some?" asked Harry.

"No way," declared Mom.

I roamed the Anasazi ruins feeling pulled not back in time, but to a timeless place, present, past and future all seamlessly joined together. It's a gift the Anasazi left behind that is maintained by the Navajo and Pueblo.

The rocks were vividly streaked by past and present moisture. We drove under overhanging ledges at times, at other places we were in the open, or dodging tree branches. Petroglyphs decorated the canyon walls in places. George stopped at one that told the story of Massacre Cave.

"The people hid in the cave when the Spanish conquistadores came. One little girl saw the Spanish murder her family. When she saw the soldiers again, she got very angry and ran from the cave to scream at them and curse them. So, they found the cave of people and killed them."

My blood ran cold. George spoke of it as if it happened just a few days ago instead of the 1500s. That is one negative side to the timelessness of Anasazi country – memories are always fresh, even of outrages.

A new site of outrage awaited us. At the junction of two canyons was a wide area that held a high narrow mesa, Fortress Rock. George stopped to tell us the story.

Kit Carson who at first tried to treat the Navajo with some humanity was ordered by his general to follow a scorched earth policy – kill all you find who don't surrender, including women and children, and destroy their homes, livestock and crops. Remaining Navajo, escaping the army, stockpiled food and water on top of Fortress

Rock, destroying ladders, and climbing holds as they made their way to the top.

The siege lasted and lasted. Some braves at night made their way down precariously using some hidden climbing holds to bring water back up. Some were captured. Many weary of the lack of food, water and ways to get rid of waste surrendered, but several hundred simply starved to death. It is protected today. The last footholds were chipped out so no one can climb the rock. Even the airspace above it is protected so no helicopter can fly over it, much less land on it. It is the most sacred spot to the Navajo. We felt privileged to just be able to behold it. George clearly revered it. We were all quiet as we reboarded the truck and turned around to head back up the canyon to Chinle.

The beautiful canyon unfolded new views of itself as we reversed our direction. At one point we spotted the family with the seed necklaces climbing out of the canyon via a steep path. George told us many of the families that farmed the canyon left it when the harvest was in, so the children could attend school up above where roads existed.

"Now that was something," exclaimed Harry as we drove away from Chinle. It was first for all of us: underwater roads, lard fry bread, Navajo mourning.

Mariachis and Radar

I had been on a road trip with my mother and stepfather Harry in the Southwest. I combined our trip with a writer's conference in the Santa Fe - Albuquerque area. I bid the folks farewell at the airport in Albuquerque and returned to our hotel.

I had been invited to visit Los Alamos before the conference began and a van was to pick me and some other writers up at the hotel where I was permitted to leave my car. After the conference I intended to drive through Indian Country. I had been invited to Moenkapi by a doctor who worked at the clinic there and looked forward to it.

All went well and we began driving up to mountains where we were to have dinner at ski lodge and meet Los Alamos notables. I was looking forward to visiting the museum dedicated to the atom bomb development and reading Einstein's famous letter warning the government about what it might unleash on humanity. On the way, I got a call from my daughter.

My Siamese cat, Radar, had been wounded by some kind of forest wildlife. He was badly injured, and she had taken him to the emergency vet hospital.

I gave her my credit card number and told her to keep me posted. At the lodge the only place I could get a cell phone signal was outside in a cold biting wind and unexpected snow flurries. The vet said surgery was necessary for Radar. I okayed the expense.

Our hosts took us to a hotel. Early in the morning I got the word Radar would not eat. Unless he would take nourishment the vet wasn't sure he would make it and even if he did, he could possibly lose a leg. I knew I could get him to eat. I needed to get home and fast.

I asked if someone could get me to Albuquerque where I had left my car. The van driver told me she could get me to Santa Fe where I could catch the airport shuttle to Albuquerque. I knew there was a hotel shuttle from the airport to the hotel where I had left my car. We set off. Complicated but doable.

I saw the lovely Santa Fe Hilton where I had paid to stay and where the conference was due to begin the next day. I realized what I would be missing and muttered some curses in Radar's direction as I waited for the airport bus. All the way to the airport I kept thinking alternately of what poor Radar was going through and what I was leaving behind.

At the airport I went to look for the shuttle depot and couldn't find it. I went inside to ask. A six-piece mariachi band dressed up in red, black and silver with big sombreros saw me, ran up and began to play. I wondered if they did this for all tourists and spotted a sign showing the way downstairs to the hotel shuttles. I started to head for the stairs. The mariachi band followed me, never missing a note.

Worried about Radar, I was frantic to get going and thought the band would leave when I got on an escalator, but they determinedly followed me. They were a noisy distraction and wouldn't leave me. Clearly, they had mistaken me for someone else. I dodged into a ladies' room. When I emerged a few minutes later the band was still there and struck up another song as soon as I opened the door. I just could not shake them.

I spotted the right hotel shuttle and got on board just before the doors closed hoping the band couldn't follow me. I looked back. The mariachis looked at each other puzzled and watched my bus drive off with long, sad faces.

At the hotel it took me just a matter of minutes to hop in my car and set off for the interstate highway. I stopped only long enough to consult my road atlas and find the shortest way back home. I called my daughter to tell her I was on the way. Radar was still apathetic. I knew that he would perk up when he saw me.

The highway bore through the desert straight as an arrow. I passed semis doing 80. I ate up the miles, stopping only for gas, and grabbing service station junk food and coffee to keep going.

As it got dark, I realized as I entered Kingman, Arizona that the driving was getting dangerous. I pulled into a motel. The entire town seemed to be just eateries and motels – a truck stop on steroids as I have always called it. I grabbed a room and slept for about four hours. I woke as I saw the sky just beginning to lighten a bit. I got coffee and hit the road again.

I kept talking to Radar as if he were in the car with me, telling him to hang in there, I would be there soon. After crossing the Tehachapis, I hit Interstate Highway 5 and headed north. I needed just one more stop for gas. When I reached the Bay Area I had to slow down for the traffic but never before did such daring driving as I did that day, wildly weaving my way through traffic.

My tank was almost on empty, and I was dead tired but I had made the trip in less than tenty-seven hours even with my four-hour stop. Just as I drove up, my daughter drove up behind me bringing Radar home from the vet hospital.

I held him in my arms, listening to him purr despite the plastic collar around his neck. I learned what I had to do to take care of his wounded leg and took his collar off long enough for him to eat and drink something. I held him in my lap and just before we both dozed off, I thought of Santa Fe and my missed conference.

"Radar, you are going to get well, and you are going to keep that leg, or I will kill you," I told him. He listened and did both.

Harry Behind the Wheel

Mom, my stepdad Harry and I agreed on driving arrangements when we began our road trip. Mom would drive in traffic in towns, Harry would handle highways, and I would drive in the mountains. We seldom kept that agreement because once behind the wheel, whoever was driving didn't want to relinquish it.

So it was that we got to a town and Harry was driving. We were in the high plains heading for Yellowstone. It had been a long day and we were hungry. We had seen a sign advertising a buffet restaurant and were looking for it.

Harry was a sweet man who lived on a farm in northern Florida and seldom drove in any town with a population of more than 10,000, while Mom who had been trained as a stock car racer in Talladega in her youth, learned to handle New York City traffic. Thus, the rule that she would handle traffic.

Mom was looking one way, I was looking another for the restaurant. I said go left, Mom said go right, when I suddenly spotted the place and called out "It's right there."

Harry trying to please us both turned into a parking lot, cutting off a police car as he did so. The cop's lights began flashing, and he briefly sounded his siren.

"Uh, oh. I told you to pull over and let me drive Harry," Mom said as the policeman walked over to our car and Harry lowered his window.

"May I see your license and registration, sir?" the policeman said politely.

"You should give my mother and me the ticket," I told him. "We were both shouting at him to go different ways."

"No, you should give her the ticket," Mom piped up. "Harry should have listened to me, not you," she turned to me.

"But I spotted the restaurant," I argued.

"We would have got to it," Mom pouted.

"Neither one of us should have been shouting at him," I responded.

"I wasn't shouting," Mom retorted.

"Yes, you were, and so was I."

The policeman looked at Harry's license. "Sir your plates are from Florida, but this license is from Alabama."

"Oh, here's my Florida and Alabama license. We live right near the state line," Harry explained. "We are allowed to have both down there."

In the meantime, Mom turned to me, "It's all your fault Harry is getting a ticket."

"It is your fault, too. It just isn't Harry's fault," I told her.

At that the cop grinned and handed over Harry's licenses, "I am not giving you a ticket, sir. I think you have enough problems," he said and he returned to his car.

Mom and I burst out laughing. "I guess we took care of that," I said.

Mom, still laughing, said, "But I don't get a new dress."

"A new dress?" I asked puzzled.

"Before we left I bet Harry he would get a ticket before this trip was over because he is such a bad driver," Mom told me. Harry was laughing as we got out of car and headed to the restaurant.

"Well, the trip ain't over yet,' he said. "You might still get that new dress."

Safari to Yellowstone

I took Amtrak to Denver where I planned to meet Mom and Harry who were driving out from Florida. My train was late. Amtrak is *always* late. This time we were seven hours late and arrived in the wee morning hours. I caught a shuttle bus to the Denver Youth Hostel where I crawled into a dormitory bunk, exhausted.

In the morning I booked a family room and discovered the family rooms were in a lovely Victorian house next door to the dorms. It appeared no one else was staying there. Mom and Harry drove up late in the afternoon and were astonished to discover the inexpensive lodgings were an entire house with its own lovely garden and patio. We explored the city but discovered most places were closed including the botanical garden we had looked forward to exploring.

"Well, let's just relax and enjoy this here garden," Harry proposed in his Southern accent.

I discovered despite its lovely location, Denver has a very boring skyline. None of its skyscrapers seem to be finished. Apparently, no architects were inspired by the towering mountains beside the city. When they reached the height they wanted, they just quit building. Almost all the rooftops are flat as if the builders are expecting to add more stories.

Mom and Harry lived on a farm in the country and I live in a forest near the California coast. We didn't have such conveniences as food delivery.

"Let's send out for a pizza," Mom suggested. We all rejoiced in the wonderful luxury of having a meal delivered to our door. We ate on the patio marveling at having such a service available.

"This what I call living in the lap of luxury," Harry said. Mom and I agreed.

In the morning we headed out for lovely Rocky Mountain National Park driving through the beautiful town of Estes Park. The next day we headed north for Wyoming.

"Will you look at that," Harry marveled at the snow covered mountains.

"I told you when you married me there would be a lot of firsts, Harry, and this is one of them," Mom said smugly.

The Grand Tetons rise right out of the flat plains that lead up to them making them gloriously spectacular because of the dramatic change. It was spring and the plains and mountain meadows were in bloom.

"Now, I wonder who planted all these flowers,' Harry said regarding the riotous colors in awe.

"Dad, they are wildflowers. Nobody planted them," I replied.

"I reckon God must have planted them. A real good gardener," he told me.

Harry had worked as a farmer and as a firefighter, but was always an unpaid minister whatever other job he held. His congregation adored him because he was both kind and humble. He always considered any advice he gave very carefully, and never judged his parishioners. He just urged them to pray and do better. He had an innocent sense of humor.

We shared expenses on our road trip but he insisted they pay two thirds, not half the cost because there were two of them.

"We share a room with two beds and you two just use one," I countered. "Because two of you are in the car it doesn't cost any more for gas."

"Your mama and I won't sleep well unless we do it our way," he insisted.

Sharing a room was not a hardship, except Harry and Mom sometimes bickered a bit. They liked to speak in what I called "adspeak" – phrases they picked up from television commercials that amused them. There was a cat litter commercial in which an elder cat lectures kittens explaining the shining stuff in their litter removes odors and it is not gems. "Whatever," replies one kitten, then as the kittens walk away one pipes up "I still say they're diamonds."

That's how Mom and Harry would end any argument. One would say "Whatever." And the other would say "I still say they're diamonds." And we'd all laugh.

Harry also liked to tell us corny Bible jokes.

"What car did Adam and Eve use to leave Eden?" he'd ask me and when I didn't know he'd laugh loudly as he replied, "They left in a Fury."

Another time he asked me what car Jesus and disciples used and I was stumped. "They traveled in one Accord."

"Thirteen in one compact, must have been cozy," I replied and he laughed even louder than he had at his punchline.

We'd eat a large meal at lunch time and at dinner time I'd leave them alone in our room to give them privacy as I went out to explore whatever town we were in and find a place to have dinner. They preferred snacks and their "happies" in the evening. Their happies were cocktails, and on my return they'd insist on mixing me one as I told them what I had seen, whom I met or even interviewed for an article, and Harry would have more jokes for me. I absolutely loved traveling with them.

We stayed a couple nights at Jackson Hole so as to enjoy the Grand Tetons more. It was a very ritzy town since film festivals began showing up. I believe it was Robert Redford who first put it on the map at the start of his Sundance Film Festival. The plaza at the town center is famous. At each corner it has a large entrance arch made of entangled elk antlers. The elk roam the national park and once a year when they shed them, some non-profits like the Boy Scouts are allowed to collect and sell them before insects and rodents eat them.

But as much as we liked to window shop there, Jackson Hole would have eaten up our budget before we ever got to Yellowstone, so we moved on.

Yellowstone is a huge caldera. It last erupted about 600,000 years ago and scientists say it is ripe to blow again but they don't know when. They do closely monitor things like Yellowstone Lake levels. The cone is apparently at the lake bottom. It is scary to think of that as you enter the park until its beauty overwhelms you. You are reminded of its violent nature when you see what I thought of as the ugly-truth parts of the park where poisonous gases and violently colored liquids pour from deep in the earth and leave barren landscapes behind. The last time Yellowstone blew it sent rocks hurtling all the way to Texas.

But the rest of the park is beautiful meadows and woods with snowy displays of the peaks that make up the edge of the caldera. And, of course, the animals.

Harry sang "Buffalo Gal" as we drove through miles of bison. One large buffalo bull took over the road in the distance for a few minutes while he danced in circles and leaped up. Then he sedately strolled into a meadow to nibble grass. Another bull was convinced a large white pickup was challenging him and caused a long traffic jam as he rammed the grill with his head. The terrified driver had just braked. We drove by in the opposite lane.

"Harry, stop, I want to get his picture," Mom called out.

No way!" replied Harry. "He just might come after *us*."

The elk were everywhere as well, some in huge herds. The males still had velvet fur on their newly grown antlers that were so huge they looked like the animals were carrying dead Christmas trees on their heads.

I had managed to get press rates for a simple room for several nights so we could thoroughly explore the park. We settled in and discovered the soap provided by housekeeping services came in the shape of bear cubs.

We went to look for grizzly bears at a certain meadow overlook. Crowds had quietly gathered there. Off in the distance we could see herd after herd of elk gathering for the night. They were running through high grass and looked like a graceful wave. Then they lay down and vanished until another wave joined them and they all stood to run again. It was a spellbinding sight and we watched until dark.

Yellowstone Lake feeds the Yellowstone River creating Yellowstone Falls, a stunning sight. We did our stint at the Old Faithful Geyser, but a more spectacular geyser, Crystal, was in full spate, spewing water unendingly up 100 feet or more. We visited the lovely old lodge that at first impression inside appears to be made of branches.

We tried to see wolves, but while we heard them we did not spot them. We left the park to visit a town in Montana. We sang a lot of cowboy songs like "I Ride an Old Paint.' But we re-entered the park to head back to our room. I had left a large tip and asked if I could get a few more bear cub soaps to bring home for my grandchildren. We found a candle "bonfire" surrounded by a dozen cubs on our coffee table which made us all laugh.

At the end of our stay, we left at dawn heading back to Yellowstone Lake where the river begins. We could tell something was happening because a young woman clutching a large camera was very excited.

"Grizzly," she told us in a German accident. "Just there." She pointed to a trembling bush just across the road. "Coyotes just chased it away."

Sure enough, there were two coyotes restlessly circling what was obviously their den. It seemed almost impossible a grizzly would have been cowed by them, but the girl insisted that was exactly what had happened. The bear did not reappear and we moved off a bit to give mom and pop coyote some peace of mind.

We were struck by the loveliness of the morning mist lit up like gold from the rising sun. A herd of bison were in the meadows beside the lake. Suddenly a bull made a racket, while normally the bison were quiet beasts. It plunged into the river and began swimming to the other side. Suddenly all the buffalo began lining up single file to follow him. Mothers with young calves swam alongside their little ones keeping their heads above water, all the others staying in a queue that would make any Englishman proud. Buffalo were running to the river from the hills around. A good 200 or more crossed the river in that golden morning mist leaving us in awe as we left the park.

We headed for Idaho and then my home. As we drove away Harry had one more Bible joke, "Why couldn't they play cards on the ark?"

"Because Noah stood on the deck," he whooped and laughed. Mom and I looked at each other shaking our heads.

Stump Knockers and Humpy Suckers on the Choctawhatchee

When my folks weren't able to come to California for a road trip, I flew to northern Florida to explore it with them. The trips were always fun.

My mother loved and lived to fish. Not content to enjoy it herself, she was always trying to convince me to take it up as well. I prefer to have other people kill my food as rule, but I do love a river, and any day on the water is a good day as far as I'm concerned. So, I got a visitor's license and spent three days drowning worms on the Choctawhatchee near their home.

The folks had a flat bottom, sweet little river craft with a top-of-the-line motor, a "live well" to hold the living critters until you are ready to kill them, and carpeting.

"Carpeting, Mom?"

"It's washable, I just hose it down when I clean the boat," Mom replied.

We started early and clutching coffee mugs and cans of big, fat earthworms; we launched the craft and set off. Caryville, the name of the place where the farm is, is the "Worm Fiddling Capital of the World" according to the sign on the limits of what can't really be called a town anymore since most of it washed away in a flood. (The Choctawhatchee doesn't always behave.)

Harry explained that worm fiddling is sticking one end of a saw in the ground and bowing the saw teeth to make awful sounds that drive the worms to the surface where they can be easily collected as bait. He had fiddled for our can of worms. The Choctawhatchee (choc-taw-hat-chee, a satisfying word to say – sort of fills your mouth) is ever so lovely. Harry knew each tree by its first name and pointed out tupelo, cypress, various kinds of oak and the ever-present willows. We made our way downriver past small sand beaches, streams filled with fallen trees (Harry could tell me which storm knocked down which tree) egrets and herons, and turtles sunning themselves.

Every so often we'd come on a small houseboat that some clever fishermen had built himself to lock his gear from the thieves but keep it close to the water. Once in a while we'd pass another angler who'd always wave.

I admit I was squeamish and did not bait my own hook, but they didn't mind. Mom was hoping I'd land a mess of Shell Crackers and get as hooked as the fish. Shell Crackers are very sweet eating indeed. Harry told me Stump Knockers were even tastier though smaller. That did it; I was determined to get a Stump Knocker. Who could bypass a fish with such a charming name?

Then I found out there were also very tasty Chinkypins and Humpy Suckers. The Choctawhatchee teemed with strangely named critters. We decided what spot looked fishy, tied up to a willow or anchored and then sat back and watched the river flow by as we kept a sharp eye on our corks.

I landed a large ugly fish called a Grennell, which we freed because Harry said they tasted of mud. The same was true of a large Mud Cat I hooked and gave me a good fight. Harry learned his river from his Native American grandfather, so what he says goes. I also landed a cute little thing called a Channel Cat, which was good eating but too small to keep. One Chinkypin eventually made itself at home in the live well, but got returned to his home when we couldn't get enough of his brethren to make a meal.

As the day progressed sometimes we'd chat, eat a sandwich or sip some beer or soda from the cooler and enjoy the scenery. I mused on Florida's strange qualities – crooked politicians, bad drivers, thieves, beautiful rivers and charming fish.

Once a sleepy sounding, droning small plane flew overhead.

Harry glanced at it. "It's just a paper cup," he said.

He was a little hard of hearing and once when Mom identified an overhead plane as a Piper Cub, he heard it as Paper Cup. We all had such a good laugh that we all called small planes Paper Cups afterwards.

The plane left and the only sounds were the quiet lapping of the river and the songbirds that provided entertainment.

"Now you listen to that one," Harry said as a bird called out. "It's talkin' about your mama. Listen it says 'Pretty, pretty, pretty."

Mom slapped at him and they both grinned. They both knew the bird spoke truth.

Once an alligator swam into sight. He and we left each other alone although I got nervous when he suddenly disappeared so was relieved when we decided to try another spot and putt-putted downstream. Once as we tied up to a branch Harry spotted a snake sleeping on it. Fortunately, it was an oak snake, non-poisonous, instead of a water moccasin, lethal.

I think I must have jinxed the folks because we got skunked all three days on the Choctawhatchee much to Mom's frustration. Harry landed the only Stump Knocker, which looked too lonely in the live well, so we set him free, too. I didn't mind that we didn't catch anything. I was just totally content to watch the scenery and let the Stump Knockers, Humpy Suckers, Chinkypins and Shell Crackers, and their brethren swim by me in the pretty Choctawhatchee. But, yes, I told Mom, I loved fishing.

Section 5:
The Auld Sod

Ireland

With a name like Granahan, it was inevitable that sooner or later I'd have to get to Ireland and I finally did. My friend Marlene and I had availed ourselves of an annual Irish travel package that included round trip air, ten days of Bed and Breakfast Inn vouchers and a rental car for less than a thousand dollars. The catch is that it is off season when it may be rainy – although my Erinophile friends who go there often told me that is true of all times of year, especially in the west of Ireland which we intended to explore.

Being a thorough romantic and having steeped myself in Irish literature, I had a few missions in mind to accomplish while I was on the "auld sod": buy a copy of Yeats' poetry in his native land, find wild shamrocks so I could press them in the Yeats volume, hear traditional Celtic music, eat colcanon and Irish stew (native dishes), and smell a peat fire.

Marlene, a redhead of Scottish descent, was perfectly at home in Ireland since it (and Scotland) apparently keep the world supplied with redheads, judging from the vast numbers of carrot-topped children I met. I figure it's thanks to invading blond Vikings coming into contact with the dark-haired Celts.

Our first task after clearing customs was to collect our rental car and find our hotel. The car was a tiny Nissan Micro, not much wider than two airline seats. We couldn't even fit a purse between the two front seats but considering the narrow roads of Ireland, it was still too wide. Of course, it was left hand drive.

A Rainy Day in Ennis

After twenty hours in crowded planes and bewildering airports, we drove in our micro-mini-car to a hotel near the Shannon airport with lodging vouchers in hand. Marlene collapsed in her bed without a word.

But my adrenalin was rising, overcoming fatigue. I was in Ireland and I hadn't come to see the airport. A young woman at the front desk wore a name badge that said "Coemthe". I asked her how to pronounce her name.

"Kiva," she replied. Gaelic spelling would forever remain a remarkable mystery to me.

"Is there a town nearby I could visit?"

"The nearest is Ennis. Look there's the bus coming," Coemthe said.

I pelted out to catch the bus realizing as I boarded it that I had left my umbrella behind, a terrible thing to do in Ireland. I found a handy newspaper that had been left behind to keep my head dry instead.

The bus drove through suburbs and then suddenly past a castle. It was in ruins on the banks of a river. We rolled through a bit of country and I saw some charming traditional Irish farmhouses – small rectangles with chimneys built in flush with both end walls.

The bus radio broadcast the news and there was a bizarre report of an Albanian man killing an Albanian woman who had been dealing drugs, then hijacking a car driven by yet another Albanian wanted for burglary at knife point, but the killer had been apprehended when the Albanian hostage signaled for help at a petrol stop.

From the bus stop in Ennis I walked through a shopping center to the main street – a charming, if wet and narrow, thoroughfare. I found a small but nicely done museum that educated me about the high king

Brian Boru. That was all well and good, but I was damp (the newspaper had melted), chilled, and hadn't had anything to eat in a long time. I asked the kind ladies running the museum, "Is there a place where a cold and hungry person might find something warm and comforting?"

"Most places are closed about now, it being' between lunch and dinner," said one lady.

"Oh, but that Brandon's down the street should be open," said her colleague.

"Oh, aye. They'll have something for ye."

Brandon's was my first Irish pub. Beamed and wood paneled, I found I was the only patron in it. The Brandon family was busy in the kitchen, but the mother and father said they could accommodate me. They went in back and their young son Collin served me up a hot and tasty bowl of potato leek soup and a grilled ham and cheese sandwich. Then he sat beside me to chat me up while I ate. He was intensely curious about California and redwoods.

"And are they as tall as I've been hearin'?" I assured him they were. He told me about his school.

Collin's parents joined the conversation and told of the difficulties of raising children in the electronic era (and I thought – keeping them safe with all those lawbreaking Albanians about). They said I should bring my friend around that evening and return for supper because they were cooking lots of good things. It certainly smelled like they were.

I stopped at a supermarket to buy some sherry and tea cakes as a treat for my tired friend. On the way back the bus radio played a public service announcement that asked people not to be prejudiced against Eastern European immigrants. I took it to heart, realizing there are good and bad Albanians, after all, although the next report was about another Albanian arrested for armed robbery.

Marlene was still sleepy on my return. I went to the front desk to inquire about internet connections and ran into a tourist who had a handful of Irish coffee coupons he would not have time to use before his plane left.

"I have time for one. Would you care to join me in the hotel pub?" The pub was cozy with a fireplace place and the coffee was lovely. He gave me a couple more coupons and left to catch his plane. I went back and woke Marlene with the good news that she need not venture forth in the rain to enjoy a nice meal in a cozy pub since there was one just down the hall, and I had two more Irish coffee coupons.

She was thrilled. We found comfy seats next to the fire and the barmaid chatted us up, introduced us to some local truck drivers eating their dinner after delivering goods to the airport. They told us what sights not to miss and filled us in on road conditions. They asked about American politics.

We settled in. I found Yeats' poem "An Irish Airman Foresees His Death" on my placemat, one of my favorites, and read it to Marlene. The fire crackled. Another bowl of tasty soup had filled my tummy. The Irish coffee had at last dissolved the last of my adrenalin and I was ready for a long sleep to dissolve the jet lag.

"We're going to like Ireland," Marlene said, contentedly warming her hands at the fire.

"As long as we avoid the Albanians," I yawned sleepily.

"Albanians?" she asked puzzled.

Yeats and Shamrocks

Up on the cliffs, the wind whipped around us. It blew our umbrellas inside out. The rain was blown sideways soaking us through. Looking hundreds of feet below the cliff edge we could see waves that had traveled the north Atlantic crashing against the rocks. Flocks of white birds wheeled around below us. We could hear their calls over the thunderous waves.

A tall, thin young man wearing a hooded rain poncho was playing a penny whistle. The wind tore at his flapping poncho and carried the plaintive notes of the ancient song *Over the Hills and Far Away* over the field. I had not sung the song in years but the words easily slipped into my mind.

"Over the hills and faraway

A dreaming of myself and you

And the many, many years since first we met,

And all that we've been through.."

I suddenly missed my husband deeply, and tears mixed with the rain. The desolation of the Cliffs of Moher was complete. The ancients felt it was the end of the world – this dramatic end of a continent. It certainly felt like it. We left, shaking the raindrops from our umbrellas, wiping away teardrops and raindrops from our faces, and huddled in our mini-car turning the heater full on.

We were winding our way through The Burren. I made Marlene stop at a few fields so I could search for shamrocks I was determined to press and bring home. All I found was clover.

We stopped at one of the ubiquitous "wool mill" leprechaun shops that cater to visitors. The lady there told us that shamrocks were almost extinct because of the fertilizers on the fields. Farther down

165

the road at another shop I bemoaned the fate of the shamrocks and the shopkeeper laughed at me.

"And who was tellin' ye such a thing? Ye must be looking on the walls and in cracks between stones. Ye'll be findin' plenty o' them there," she said. "Try the bridge just down the road a wee bit."

She was right and I gleefully collected my shamrocks. I was having a harder time finding a used volume of the complete works of Yeats in which to press my shamrocks. Whenever we spotted a bookstore I went in to ask but discovered the Irish are highly regional about their writers.

"For him ye must go to Sligo, He was born there." I was told again and again and then offered a volume of work by a local bard.

When we got to the town of Listowel I saw a sign pointing out a writers' museum. "They'll be bound to have it," I exclaimed happily as we entered the small building. But no, it specialized in the writers of County Kerry. "Ye must go to Sligo," they said.

We left disappointed but then spotted something just as desirable, a thrift shop. Mrs. Quinn's Charity Shop For The Irish Blind proved to be a godsend. In it we found warm sweaters, socks and ponchos, all at a reasonable price so we could discard them before we left for home since we had little room in our carry-ons. We happily thanked Mrs. Quinn as we donned the layers and finally felt warm.

We made our way to Dingle, a lovely fishing port. The shops were all brightly painted and gleamed in the rain. Irish college students had begun to frequent the town so it had such conveniences as an internet café and a used bookstore. We went in the bookstore and found an older man ran it.

"I was hoping to find a used copy of the Complete Works of Yeats, but I suppose you will tell me I must go to Sligo," I said.

"And why would I be tellin' ye that when I have what ye want right here?" he replied as he reached to the shelf behind him.

"You have no idea how happy you have made me," I gleefully told him.

He grinned as I paid him. "When ye need Yeats, naught else will do," he said, nodding his head of gray hair wisely.

We settled into our B&B which was actually more of a hostel, but we had a private bath for our room. The landlady disappeared before we could ask her how to work the intricate, enigmatic shower. We never figured it out.

We had begun learning the customs of Irish pubs. One would inevitably have "Trad", traditional Irish music. You just had to ask "after the Trad" at any local shop. The musicians would gather to jam after nine p.m. after the families had taken their children home for bedtime. There was no smoking inside. Health warnings about second-hand smoke had led the families to demand outdoor smoking areas only. In Dingle the Trad was at *An Doicead Beag* "The green and yellow pub by the bridge."

At the internet café there was an announcement about a Mexican restaurant opening in the near future. There was description of a taco since Ireland was new to the treat.

"A flat maize cake rolled around spicy meat, cheese, lettuce and tomato."

The Irish were going to love tacos I thought. Their only seasonings available were salt, pepper and once in a while some thyme or parsley. I had wisely brought a small vial of tabasco sauce that I carried in my purse. But compared to England, Irish food was good. Things that were supposed to be hot were hot; things that were supposed to be cold like a salad were cold; things that were supposed to be crisp were crisp; things that were supposed to be tender were tender. Eating was satisfying. None of that was true in England.

It was raining when I left the internet café but the sun was shining. Marlene was walking down the street to meet me.

"Marlene, look over your shoulder. You are walking out from a rainbow," I called to her. She turned to see it.

"That is worth the rain," she beamed.

Sometimes a pub would have a sign outside bragging that it had good crack. That did not mean drugs, it meant good conversation. Indeed, we chatted with a number of local regulars. They were keen to talk politics once they realized we were Americans. They knew a lot about American public affairs. Once though an old man had such a thick brogue and was so drunk he and I couldn't understand a word the other said and Marlene just laughed at us.

Eventually we made it Blarney where the immense castle impressed us. Queen Elizabeth wanted Blarney Castle to add to her military networks. But every time she wrote demanding it, she received effusive but vague notes from Lord Blarney. She became so frustrated that every time a message was sent from the castle she would proclaim, "It's just more Blarney."

Thus the Blarney Stone supposedly gives you the gift of gab. My friends think I already have an overflowing cornucopia of that gift. A bad flu was circulating that fall, and the climb was up a narrow, terrifying seven stories of a one-person circular stairway with no handholds. Marlene didn't even try, and I decided after the first three stories I had no interest in kissing the germy stone. Instead we found a pub with good crack and chatted up the locals.

"Ah, ye were smart to forego the stone. We have two tourists with flu in hospital right now," one local told me and then ordered me a hot whiskey with honey as I started coughing.

There was one road we traveled that was like a freeway after the narrow twisting roads we usually encountered. At a pull-off I saw that Tinkers, the Irish Gypsies, had claimed it. They had RVs parked, clotheslines hung full of billowing laundry, and had set up a kitchen and a children's play area. I marveled that the police had not run them off.

Jimmy Stewart with Bagpipes

"Turn right," I said to Marlene, then screamed "Left! Left!"

She abruptly jolted us into the left lane to avoid an oncoming bus. We had discovered it took two people to drive. One to actually drive and the other to keep screaming about hugging the left side of the road as we navigated the narrow roads lined with stone walls and hedges.

"Oh my God, what does that sign mean?" Marlene asked. The ominous sign read "Accident Black Spot".

"I have no idea but you had better slow down," I replied.

The traffic signs were interesting. We never figured out "Go Mall" or "Go Mall Tisteach", nor the ominous "SLAM!". "Traffic Calming Ahead" was always comforting but "Acute Bends Ahead" or even worse "Dangerous Bends Ahead" were alarming. Bends, we learned, are not a deep-diving ailment, it meant curves. It was nerve-wracking until right on the roadbed there was help; approaching a dangerous bend the word Slow would appear, a little farther on it would turn into Very Slow, and on the bend itself "Slower!" "Hedge Cutting in Progress" meant trouble because Irish roads are so painfully narrow and the hedge cutter would force us into the oncoming lane. The roads are so narrow sometimes there would be a sign "Danger Oncoming Traffic in Center of Road" and we lost a side mirror once to one of those stone walls while coping with that.

My favorite sign would be posted outside a village "This is a Tidy Town" those signs told us. Indeed, they were, hedges and gardens manicured and not a smidgen of litter about. Irish males must be very secure in their masculinity or only women run town councils. I can't imagine American men agreeing to calling their burgs "tidy towns". They'd go the tough guy route, "Death Penalty for Littering" or "We shoot litterers" or something close to it instead if they even cared.

We drove into a tidy village – Kinvarra on Galway Bay. Like so many Irish towns it was colorfully painted and decorated with a castle at the edge. We decided to stay and looked up a nearby bed and breakfast listed in the booklet we had been handed with our car rental. I spotted what looked like a grocery store where we could ask directions, but it turned out there was a pub in back. Three jolly middle-aged Scotsmen on vacation were quaffing their Guinness. They loudly welcomed us and insisted on buying us a round.

One of the men was carrying a bagpipe. He was tall and handsome and had big enough lungs to handle the bagpipe. We admired the instrument and he promptly played a couple tunes for us. He introduced himself in his thick brogue as Jimmy Stewart.

"Like the movie star but he didn't play bagpipes, and," he winked and laughed, "unlike him I am very much alive!"

We finished our drinks and left to claim our room. That done we went back to Kinvarra to find a cozy restaurant. We had finished our shepherd pies and were just tucking into dessert when the three jolly Scots walked in.

"And here's me lass without me," Jimmy Stewart told the others.

"Bon appetite," I called back.

"Let's find a pub," Marlene suggested so we set off and discovered Mary Green's. Mary herself presided over the taps. She told us she was the fifth generation of Mary Greens to rule over the pub.

"Mother to daughter to granddaughter and so on. Me own daughter Mary works here when she's not in school," she shared.

It was a venerable pub and the bent shelves groaned with the weight of the largest selection of potables we had ever seen. Marlene's favorite beverage was not Guinness, but Colorado's own Coors Light, a sacrilege on the auld sod I thought.

"I don't suppose you have Coors Light?" she asked Mary.

"And why would you be thinkin' that?" replied our publican as she fetched out a glass and cold one for Marlene.

Just then in walked our still jolly Scots.

"And here's me lass again, out on the town without me!" Jimmy Stewart clutched his heart and wailed, "Tramps, tramps ye are, to break a man's heart so."

We were still laughing as he launched into a bagpipe concert. Mary Green poured drinks for the trio.

"He'll be thirsty after all that playing," she confided in a low tone.

Jimmy Stewart accompanied Marlene and me to our car when we left.

"And haven't I at least earned a kiss?" he asked me with a mournful look on his face.

I leaned up and kissed his cheek. He smiled broadly.

As we drove off waving, he called, "And now me day is complete!"

The King of the Buskers and the Prehistoric Museum

Marlene and I were on the Dingle peninsula when we decided to get adventurous and drive out to wind-blasted, rocky, inhospitable Slei Head. It is the westernmost point on mainland Ireland - a peninsula off the Dingle peninsula famous for its prehistoric stone ruins and its miserable weather. The Blasket Islands are off that part of the coast and the government had relocated all the island residents because it couldn't afford to keep serving them. In the summer months some go back to run small businesses for daytrippers but they are otherwise abandoned now.

We explored the stone Fort Dunbeg that dated to 500 BCE. It was a wild lonely place with the ocean roaring, the wind roaring even louder, and mist soaking everything.

Tim Long was the modern keeper of the fort and sold us our admission tickets. I thought about the soldiers stationed there in the ancient days. I stopped to chat with Tim as we left.

"Do you ever feel like the ancient soldiers must have, that this is a rotten duty assignment?"

Tim grinned at me, "Nah. Me hut has heat. And I get to go to a rugby game in a few hours. They didn't."

We wound our way around the tortuously twisted one lane road dodging very large sheep including some colorfully painted rams. At one point we passed the wildest golf course I had ever seen. It was a boulder studded raw field but golfers under their huge umbrellas were making the most of the challenge.

We spotted the Celtic and Prehistoric Museum, and we couldn't resist a visit and a chance to get warm and dry. There we met Harris

Moore, who had once been an American but has since been misplaced or displaced in the midst of those rock-filled fields where once the poorest ancient Irishmen, chased there by more bellicose and better armed tribes, tried to plant crops.

Harris Moore began his odyssey as a very young man when he went to Europe. He vagabonded around for a few years earning his keep as a street musician – a busker. Eventually he became "King of the Buskers" for fifteen years. Apparently, one does not simply open one's guitar case for tips and start strumming. It's far more orderly than that and buskers recognize a self-imposed authority. Moore got to assign the prime corners to the best musicians and deal with local legalities and such on the musicians' behalf.

While he was busking, he began slowly collecting ancient things he found in flea markets and from dealers. He met "a crazy old man about to die" who had a fabulous collection. The fellow recognized a fellow fanatic and left Moore his collection.

Moore's passion had gradually turned him into an expert. He gave up busking, although not music. The buskers had to find a new king while he became a museum broker for antiquities.

"But I kept the best for myself," Moore grinned.

He made a few trips back to the States, but always returned to Europe in search of more ancient goodies. He finally decided he had enough goodies to open his own museum instead of collecting for others.

His museum is remarkable. In addition to a lot of early Celtic items, he has jewelry, pottery and metal items from ancient Baltic people and other regions. He has a wonderful collection of Cro-magnon items and animal antlers, but his "finest buy" was the "largest intact mammoth skull ever found", that he purchased from a local fisherman who fished it up in his nets.

"The fisherman is still in therapy," Moore joked as he showed off the massive skull.

His days as King of the Buskers may be over, but now Moore makes recordings of Celtic music that he sells world-wide. Warm and dry again, happy with the purchase of a duplicate of one of his prettiest Celtic rings, Marlene and I set off charmed by the man who had definitely become one of Slei Head locals. Dodging herds of sheep we made our way back to tamer, warmer, welcoming Dingle Town.

Limericks in Limerick

Marlene and I reached Limerick in the middle of a downpour – nothing unusual for Limerick, or indeed, all of Ireland. We found our B&B and met our charming hosts, a late middle-aged couple, Miriam and Ian, and settled into our cozy room. Any room would have felt cozy after a long rainy drive, but this one was superbly so and at first we were tempted to just sit pat and order in a pizza.

But this was Limerick of such fame and how could we not go out for a pub crawl? We mustered our spirits, bid our hosts a farewell as we set out on an adventure. Marlene was great to travel with because while she demanded her comforts, she was always game for an adventure, and she had insisted on taking over the left-handed driving. Even on local road trips she insisted on driving and because she made a lousy nervous passenger always back-seat driving, I always let her. Her driving was always better behind the wheel instead of the driver even if she did earn an occasional speeding ticket.

But we were on foot right now. Even in a blowing gale I made her stop on a bridge and regard the Shannon River that I had read about so often.

"Come on, Marlene, we can't just rush over the bridge. Soak it in for a few minutes and I'll stand you the first round at the first pub," I chided. We did.

After two minutes Marlene announced, "Yes, I have soaked it in and am now soaked. You owe me a whiskey."

We entered, enlarging a puddle at the entrance of a pub and found ourselves warmly welcomed by an equally drenched happy crowd of locals.

"And ye are being from where?" asked the publican.

"San Francisco," I quickly replied. We had learned if we said America we might get a lukewarm reply. California would draw a question about Hollywood, but San Francisco made everyone light up happily.

"Aye, then ye're bonny California gals and we had best make ye welcome," said a young man who was with a party of his peers from Kilarney. They demanded and got us extra chairs for their packed table.

We chatted, shared drinks, and then they announced they were moving on to another pub where there would be Trad that night and invited us to join them. Never ones to miss Trad we went with them.

The new pub was just a couple doors down and indeed the Trad was playing including a bodhran, a small drum that requires a lot of skill to play. I had already learned the words to a few songs so could join in the singing with everyone else. I love cultures that aren't afraid to sing publicly. When I lived in Greece any busload of passengers and even the commuter train from Piraeus would burst into song as soon as the engines started. Ireland was a perfect country for me. Marlene, a bit shy, generally hummed.

After a while Marlene said she was tired and after a nightcap in a quieter pub she would like to go back. We hit the third pub for her nightcap and made our way back to the bridge over the Shannon.

At the B&B our hosts greeted us cheerily asking if we'd had a good time. "Indeed. You have lovely pubs and lovely people in Limerick, but we are worn out and ready for bed," Marlene and I let them know.

We got back to our room and into nightwear when suddenly Marlene announced, "Oh my God, I don't have my purse. I must have left it at a pub. It has my passport, my ticket home, our B&B vouchers and all my money. Oh, my God!"

"Calm down. Let's think it through. Do you remember when you last paid for something?"

"I'm not sure. I think you paid for the nightcaps. We split at the trad pub. I am so tired, but I had better get dressed and go out looking. Will you come looking with me?" Marlene was distraught.

I was in my pajamas and groaned out, "Okay, but let's ask our hosts if they can call so we only have to go to one place."

Our hosts were totally sympathetic. They asked us about where we had been. We remembered the name of the first pub. "There's a string of them along there. Don't you do anything. We shall go out and inquire for you. You just settle down," Miriam assured us, and poured us a glass of sherry.

"I can't believe these people. They are so nice," said Marlene as we carried the sherry into our room.

"I can't believe you losing your purse," I retorted.

We sat down and Marlene said, "I think it has stopped raining."

She opened the curtains to look and there on the windowsill sat her purse. We both looked at each other in horror. "Oh my God. We've sent them on a useless errand," she cried while also relieved she had her documents and money. "How can I make it up to them?"

"I suggest you leave them a big tip," I replied and reached for my notebook. I was in Limerick. We had just had a misadventure, I was tipsy and feeling in the mood to write some limericks in Limerick. Our hosts were incredibly gracious when they learned they had been on a wild goose chase, Marlene left them a huge tip which I am sure made them happy, and I left Limerick with these verses.

When Marlene had herself whiskey,

The lass became very frisky.

With a wink and a nod

A quick prayer to God

She engaged in behavior quite risky.

Andrea Granahan

******

Marlene, a redhead Scot lass,

Was refined, not at all crass,

But lost her purse

Caused all Limerick to curse

And of herself, made quite an ass

I don't think Marlene appreciated my limericks and didn't ask for a copy of them.

Missions Accomplished

The news was suddenly full of predictions of "the storm of the century" coming to Ireland in the next day or so. It sounded alarming. We were headed to the east of Ireland then north to Dublin where we would catch our flight home. We would be on the road during the storm.

When I asked about it at a pub the waitress laughed, "It's naught compared to the storms ye get in California."

She was right. The rain was heavy but the winds were just moderate. We got lost in Cork, which was not a pleasant town compared to other places we had seen. We stopped in Waterford and toured the famous glassworks. I am too clumsy to prize breakables in my life, but elegant Marlene had to have a Waterford goblet.

We pulled into Portlaoise (pronounced Port Leesh) after hours of driving through rain and found a cozy pub. Soup and sandwiches and, at last, colcannon were on the menu. Colcannon is mashed potatoes and cabbage. It's a comforting dish on cold, rainy night. The server asked what we wanted to drink and I was about to request a hot whisky when Marlene said, "Could you make hot chocolate with Irish whiskey?"

That sounded good so we made it two. When it was delivered with a generous topping of whipped cream the server asked, "What is your name, Miss?"

"Marlene."

"Oh good. We thought it such a nice idea we will add it the menu and call it The Marlene," he smiled at us. We found our B&B. The minute we walked in the door I smelled an earthy toasty aroma. Our landlady had introduced herself as Lily Saunders. She was a cheerful, welcoming woman.

"Is that a peat fire that I smell?" I asked.

"Aye, it is. The mister has a bog. The mister lives for his bog," she laughed. All the peat I had seen up to now had been in the form of pressed briquettes like charcoal. I had begun to think I'd never see real cut peat in Ireland, but there it was burning cozily in the fireplace.

The next morning, I asked Lily if I could buy a piece or two of peat to bring home "so my children can smell what their Irish ancestors smelled."

"No ye couldn't, but I'll happily give ye some, after all, the mister has a bog." She gave Marlene and I each a peat block about a foot square and about six inches thick. Marlene and I vowed to get rid of some clothes to make room for it. It would later cause consternation at customs, then laughter as customs officers found out what it was. I saved it for our fire on Christmas day so the kids got an aroma for a Christmas present.

We bid Lily farewell and headed for Dublin. It turned out to be a nice, if somewhat sterile city. We weren't there long, just overnight after we turned in our micro-mini-car with relief. We found a pub with the Trad that had a neon signing banning drugs and nuclear weapons.

The pub had Irish stew which I ate with gusto and washed down with one last Guinness. Marlene and I toasted each other as I realized I had accomplished all my missions: Yeats, shamrocks, peat, Trad, colcannon and Irish stew.

Section 6:
London and Paris (and Quebec!)

The Diva and the Starlet

I love both Paris and London, each for very different reasons. Paris knows it is beautiful, takes it for granted, and can sometimes neglect herself dreadfully. London is less self-aware and despite its more ancient history, seems younger, less experienced, and much more fast-paced.

To use a metaphor, Paris is an aging diva. Everyone treasures her for what she was, and she still has traces of her former beauty although she sometimes forgets to bathe or comb her hair. London is a young starlet, eager for attention, wearing the most outré fashions, and although she's clean, is sometimes lacking in grace, tending to show off her gaudy jewels.

I don't think I saw anyone in London under twenty-five or so who wasn't tattooed and or heavily pierced. Short skirts and long scarves decorated the girls and sometimes the boys. The pubs were noisy, lively places at quitting time each evening. The atmosphere in the streets was electric. Paris was much more sedate to my great surprise. Things moved at a slower pace, and it seemed there was always time to have a cup of coffee or a glass of wine at a café and maybe engage in a leisurely discussion.

I saw few animals in London – maybe an occasional cat in a window. Paris loves its dogs. Dogs sit in the kiddie seats in shopping carts as their masters shop. They sit at the table in restaurants, sometimes eating from their own place setting, sometimes humping someone's leg. The dogs, even rather large ones, ride the metro even in rush hour. I have read the astonishing statistic that more than 600 people a year are treated in Parisian emergency rooms from having slipped in doggy doo. Parisians feel they pay enough taxes that the state is responsible for cleaning up after their animals, not them. I saw one doggy doo street sweeper. It was cute – very small, and in no way up to the job. So, while strolling the lovely tree-lined boulevards with the wonderful architecture, you have to either stop to admire things, ignore the sights and look down, or suffer the consequences of walking and gawking maybe in an emergency room.

I saw few examples of public displays of affection in London – just an occasional couple holding hands. In Paris, the lovers are shameless. No one ever tells them to get a room. No park is complete without a pair locked in a passionate embrace. They decorate every landscape, and no one minds a bit.

Foodwise, there is no comparison. They just don't get it in London. Thank goodness for the Indians – they have the only edible food in the city that's affordable. Parisians celebrate food. Even buying a fig is a special occasion. The customer does not touch the food, only the vendor, and he will comb through every piece of fruit he has to find you the best one and hold it high for you to admire before he sells it to you. A cup of coffee and a piece of bread at breakfast is a work of art. In London they flung Wonder Bread toast and watery bitter brew at us for breakfast in our hotel. Londoners, however, know their ales, and visitors, like the natives, come to rely on that for basic nourishment.

Street sports are big in Paris. One afternoon a street crossing a major bridge was shut down for roller blading competition during rush hour. A very serious timekeeper kept track of how long it took each skater to run an obstacle course. In London they only stop traffic for political demonstrations – a very popular and colorful activity.

Theater dominates London. Street performers earn tips. Art dominates Paris. One never knows when public demonstrations of either are likely to appear. One morning in Paris I awoke to the sight of yellow footprints decorating the alley in back of my hotel. For blocks in either direction the bright footprints made their way, detouring around a drunk who lay in the gutter, dancing their way across town. Why or how, no one knew.

I saw just one Parisian man wearing a beret, alas. In London I saw one man with an umbrella and homburg hat. He was very kind when I asked the way to Drury Lane (I was determined to buy a muffin there). He gave me a brief historical tour of the area, but when I asked if I could take his photograph, he refused saying he could not because of the Secrecy Act. I had found my very own English spy. John LeCarre was right, they abound.

Getting around in London is easy as they have a good underground "tube" and efficient bus service. I always preferred the bus because you could see so much more of the city. The Metro in Paris is filthy but very fast. The buses are much less organized and the drivers are not helpful. I learned to never sit down in a Metro station and in places discarded gum had actually been pounded into form of pavement. The drunks like to use Metro entrances as pissoirs at night, so you always hold your breath as you go down the stairs. But the trains whip you across the city in minutes. In London the "tube" was spotless. You just had to "Mind the Gap" as a loudspeaker warned every time the doors opened. The gap was a good foot wide. The gap has been known to eat small children.

You can see why I love each city for its own special qualities. There's no way to choose one over the other. They are both noisy, smelly, wonderful cities. It all depends on which one you want to date.

I have thrown Quebec City in this section because I was so startled to find such a European city in North America. I felt I had been taken back to Paris.

The Dark Side of London

It's in the kitchen.

There's an old joke about hell being a place where the Italians are the managers, the French the mechanics, the Germans the lovers and the British the cooks. I won't attest to the other things, but it's true about the Brits' cooking.

It amazed me what they could do to perfectly innocent ingredients.

Our hotel room came with a "complete English breakfast". The first day a plate was put in front of me. A fried egg that had been cooked until it was hard-boiled was floating in a puddle of water with a dollop of grease on top. It was cold. A spoon full of Campbell's pork and beans had been scooped directly from the can with all the juice and was mingling with the egg puddle. A burned, cold sausage, and a slice of fatty ham, burned at one end and raw at the other (British bacon) accompanied it. Fortunately, there was lots of Wonder Bread toast and the coffee was hot.

My table mate was not so lucky. He had asked for a soft-boiled egg. The bottom half was hard boiled while the top was raw. We puzzled over how that could be accomplished.

There is great entertainment value in British breakfasts. We always ordered the eggs even though we never could eat them, just to see what they had done to them that day. Scrambled eggs were watery or, as once happened, served so crusted they were in flakes.

In the pubs I figured traditional fish and chips would be edible, but the fish was soggy, the chips were greasy and they came with "traditional mushy peas". The latter are dried whole peas cooked in highly salted water then partially mashed with a potato masher. Those were not edible. I figured they invented roast beef and Yorkshire pudding so it should be good. They had apparently attacked the roast early in the morning, shriveled it to leather, then sliced it with a food slicer and dumped it into a bin of mix-made gluey gravy. I kept the hard lump of Yorkshire pudding from rolling off the table. It could have killed us.

Each meal we had led to new horrors until we discovered they knew how to make edible creamed soups.

Not only are they lousy cooks, but when they do have something that tastes good they give it a very unattractive name so as to keep more of it for themselves. Brown sauce (like our steak sauce) was the only thing that made the meat edible. Clotted Cream sounds like something you'd throw away but it was lovely on hot home-made scones, likewise lemon curd. But the one that really got us was the traditional English dessert of "Spotted Dick". It turned out to be bread pudding with currants served with warm vanilla custard, but with a name like that...

In fact, I have a theory that the British empire building and years of tenacious colonization can be blamed directly on their bad cooks rather than corporate greed as I had thought for so long. Those fellows were just looking for a good meal. No wonder they didn't want to let go of India – they finally had a cuisine worth eating.

Someone else has also made an interesting observation: the English are so nice and friendly and the food so bad, they stand in contrast to the French who are marvelous cooks but have a reputation for being snooty. Maybe one could plan to visit London but fly to Paris for dinner, not talk to anyone, just eat and fly back.

But there was one good side effect of the British cooking – it made the airline food taste just great!

A Love Story Found
in a London Pub

I found this tale of love and devotion in a pub called Gallagher's in London. Gallagher's was like so many London pubs, a very cozy place. It's as if the "publican", the bar-owner, has personally opened the doors of his home to you. In addition to the bar and tables it boasted comfy living room furniture, old-fashioned lamps, doilyed sofas with end tables and a tattooed barkeep named Patrick.

Patrick was covered from the top of his shaved head to his feet in beautifully wild Borneo tattoos which he had obtained while he was in the Royal Navy. I am not an ink fan but these were works of art. He also had many face piercings, actually piercings all over.

"The Royal Navy let you get those in Borneo?"

"Nah. They cashiered me," he told us, "for having anarchistic tendencies."

George Lucas apparently loved anarchistic tendencies. He had hired Patrick for one of his Star Wars movies, and Patrick was on a Hollywood list of special extras. I worried about Patrick. After he had pulled up the trouser leg to show us his tattooed ankles and feet and announced, "They are all over, and I mean all," he winked at us. "Some jewelry, too."

But then he revealed he was battling cancer. Tattoo inks hold known carcinogens and have never been tested for health consequences. That was a lot of ink Patrick had exposed himself to.

Patrick had befriended me and my travel companion, Marlene, and on a Saturday night he introduced us to Peter and Emily, a young couple.

Each Saturday her parents watched their little girl so they could have their outing to Gallagher's.

The two were from another city in England where they had gone to school together and been high school sweethearts. Then her father had lost his job and moved the family to London to take another. They lost contact with each other.

The move was the beginning of a downward spiral for Emily. She fell in with a rough crowd, got pregnant and then got hooked on heavy drugs. Peter had gone on to learn a trade and find work in London. He tried to locate Emily's parents without success. From a mutual friend he heard that Emily had a job working for an insurance company somewhere.

Emily, under threat of losing her daughter, was scared into trying to pull her life together. She had lost other jobs but gave it a go again, finally landing an office job at another insurance company.

"I was a lost soul," the pretty, dark haired woman remembered sadly. "My sister had organized the family to take Sally away from me if I lost this job."

Peter still determined to find his lost childhood love began the laborious task of calling every insurance office in London asking for her by name. One day he called the right one and Emily answered the phone.

"And who is this?" she asked suspiciously.

She didn't believe it was him, but he insisted on seeing her. She was terrified of what he might think of her but she found nothing but devotion.

"He rescued me and Sally," she said with love in her eyes as she gazed at her hero.

With his dedicated help she freed herself from the drugs and the pair moved in close by to her parents who adored Peter – and why wouldn't they? Peter was a sweet-faced man with very bad teeth and a splendid heart. The couple had been married for seven years and he still clearly adored his wife and bad teeth and all, she looked upon him as her shining knight.

And Patrick served them up another pint, gleefully grinning. "Right romantic," he concluded. "Knew you being a writer would appreciate that."

As for Marlene and me, we had our pictures taken with Patrick. When I returned home I told my kids I had met someone I cared about in London.

"I knew this would happen," declared my daughter-in-law.

I offered to show the kids a photo of their future stepfather and pulled out my photo of Patrick. They knew my attitude towards ink as I had threatened to disown them if they ever inked up. I got them good. They still laugh, but I do care about Patrick – a lot.

Changing the Guard

Marlene and I were at a pub near Buckingham Palace where we had discovered they made an edible tomato soup. Someone mentioned it was near time for the changing of the guard. We thought it would be fun to see and figured it wouldn't take very long.

We had severely underestimated the value the English put on pomp and circumstance. A huge crowd gathered.

I climbed up on a wall to try and get photographs, hanging on to a wrought iron fence that topped it. The lonely Queen's guard stood in a

one-person sentry box that was tall enough to accommodate his ridiculously tall hat. A troop of soldiers wearing the same type hats marched in formation and then took positions around the sentry box. Then a band marched in and began playing music.

From the opposite side of the great courtyard another band marched in and a battle of bands began. I laughed out loud when the bands joined together to play Abba's "The Dancing Queen."

Then the infantry marched in in full force. Once they were situated in front of the battling bands, the cavalry rode in both the horses and riders in splendid colorful costumes. Dragoons came next.

Then wildly ornate coaches rode in pulled by teams of magnificent horses delivering foreign ambassadors to visit the queen.Other musicians arrived with long flag-bedecked trumpets. They blared away. The coaches made their way through an  arched gate out of our sight. The dragoons, the cavalry, the trumpeters, and the infantry dispersed with great fanfare. The soldiers marched off and finally a small squad marched the guard off, leaving one lonely soldier in his tall hat behind to guard the Queen. It had taken quite a while. Marlene and I looked at each other in wonder at all the fuss and pageantry and its anti-climatic ending.

"So that's how they change the guard," said Marlene as we looked at the lonely guard who had been changed, guarding the palace.

How They Gonna Keep Me Down on the Farm After I've Seen Paree?

It was an impulse trip. There, big and bright in an e-mail, was a bargain good for eight hours only on April 15, tax day. It was about 5:30 in the morning, but I called my friend Linda who sleepily agreed to go with me. A week in Paris, airfare from San Francisco and back, hotel and breakfast for $700 plus airport taxes - the company was sold out in just two hours, so it was an impulse I was glad I had - sometimes leaping then looking is a fine thing.

I spent the next few weeks before we left trying to revive my high school French. Back in high school I had a friend who was French-Swiss who taught me the proper way to pronounce things. Our teacher at school had a raspy voice and a thick Brooklyn accent so pronunciation was not her strong point. My good French accent proved to be a liability once in Paris. Linda and I would try to ask directions. Because I had asked so properly the person would gesture and answer back with a whole lot of fast French I couldn't understand. But I'd thank him or her and walk in the direction that had been pointed out.

"What did he say?" Linda would inquire.

"I don't have the faintest idea, but he pointed this way and I'll ask someone else at the intersection."

"I thought you knew French," Linda fumed.

"Well I know how to ask, and that's more than you know," I testily pointed out.

But we did find our hotel, stopping at a café for *kir royale* en-route to celebrate our arrival in Paris. I had read about the champagne drink and couldn't wait to try it. It tasted great and left us both in a better mood.

At the hotel the elevator was so small that either two people or one person with a suitcase could fit into it, not two people with even just carry-ons could. So we ascended one at a time.

Our first room looked out over a lovely avenue with a wide median that the locals used as a park. The room was decorated in what Linda called "Early French Bordello" because of its red flocked wallpaper, but the avenue provided so much entertainment for us during the day, we thought we'd keep it. Then we discovered that neither the mini-fridge nor the telephone worked. But the worst problem came at 3:30 a.m. when a local market set up on the park-like avenue. The French never do anything without arguing, and they do it very loudly.

Our concierge was very understanding and said, "I can fix a telephone. I can fix a fridge. But I cannot fix the noise."

He moved us up under the roof to a room overlooking a quiet alley. It had a beamed ceiling and was much larger. Everything worked. We happily settled in and planned our attack on Paris.

I had competed in a contest online and won two tickets to the Eiffel Tower. We were lucky I had won because the line to buy tickets was hours long, whereas we just had to turn ours in to the elevator operator to sail up, and up, and up. We loved the view but the height made me dizzy, so we left to stroll the Champs Elysees. The Louis Vuitton store cracked me up because the entrance on the corner was shaped like a great suitcase. I've never been a fan of Louis Vuitton because the initials are plastered all over it. If I am a walking ad for someone, I feel I ought to be paid for my services, not charged for it. The famous boulevard lived up to its reputation, but it was very crowded and full of traffic.

I have read about *flaneurs,* the "strollers" along an avenue. I am afraid the age of the flaneur is over on the Champs Elysees. Everyone seemed in a hurry. I wanted to be a flaneur badly, but not here. There is a department store along the Seine that I had read had a rooftop restaurant that offered a superb view of the city. Linda liked that idea and on a treesy street I did get to be a flaneur after all. I discovered one had to flaneur carefully because of doggy do. If I wanted to admire a building or a view of the river, I had to stop to look or take a big risk.

I bought a tiny watercolor from a mustached street artist who flirted outrageously with us both, making Linda, who was sad about being newly divorced, very cheerful. We ate croque monsieurs happily as we enjoyed a view of Paris that included the Eiffel Tower, something the tower itself could not offer. I recalled that Balzac said he ate lunch every day at the tower restaurant because he hated the tower so much and that way he didn't have to look at it.

Over the next few days we did the usual touristy things. It was an anniversary of the liberation of Paris in World War Two and the Parisians were celebrating for months. They had blown up black and white photos to six feet high and hung them all over Paris. It was as if the French had opened their old family album for us. There were photos of old women and men tearing up the city's cobblestones to make barricades. There were pictures of young children carrying baskets of debris to help and bringing their elders food. There were pictures of the celebrations afterwards.

We got to explore Notre Dame before it burned and heard the children's choir. We met the man who had tamed the sparrows in the gardens outside. He, like so many of the French, was a chain smoker, and Linda was put out when he accidentally burned a hole in the sleeve of her favorite outfit as he handed her a bird.

The food was wonderful. The waiters were not rude like we had been told to expect, but they were knowledgeable and insisted on imparting their wisdom. We just let them tell us what to order and were never disappointed. We both became especially fond of the onion soup.

On our last day we decided to stay in our neighborhood. We bought some fruit and for dinner just ordered bread and a cheese board. As we ate the simple and tasty food we watched the dog walkers and lovers stroll by, almost all carrying baguettes under their arms. A colorful sunset gave way to a purple dusk and finally a dark night lit by the lights of Paris. What more could you ask of Paris?

Naked Yoga

Our room at the top floor overlooked an alleyway that had a soup kitchen run by the Mother Teresa order of nuns. Before it opened each afternoon, the clochards (drunkards) of the neighborhood gathered outside. The apartments across the alley were very nice, at least the top floors were, with broad terraces decorated with many plants.

Linda and I watched a young couple get ready to entertain, peeking from behind our curtains. They fussed a lot over their table setting and some flowers. They opened their wine to let it air. Their next door neighbor was a very handsome Black man with a magnificent physique. He spent a lot of time on his terrace.

One morning, a day when I wanted to go to the Louvre, Linda decided to stay behind because she wasn't feeling too well.

"But you go and enjoy the art. I know you've been eager for this," she told me.

I took the metro to the Louvre and was dismayed to see an immense line. I decided to try to use my press pass. In Italy the entrance guards had sneered at my pass and waved me to the back of the line. I expected the same treatment in Paris, but instead I was delighted when the guard personally conducted me inside with a bow. They respect the press in France.

I had three pieces I really wanted to see: Venus de Milo, the Mona Lisa, and the Etruscan tomb with the married couple above it. Venus was easy to find and I had her to myself, but when I went to see Mona Lisa there was a huge mob around her. I gave up and instead communed with another favorite Da Vinci, that I had nicknamed Madonna on the Rocks. I did have her to myself. On the way to the Etruscans I discovered some amazing frescoes and several other items that made my heart happy.

With my mind full of the beauty I had seen, I wandered over to the Jardin de Luxembourg to watch the children sail boats in the basin. Hemingway bragged that when he was broke he had strangled pigeons and hid them in his baby's stroller so his wife could cook them for dinner. I passed by lovers embracing on the grass, an old woman feeding the pigeons, not strangling them, and a man asleep on a bench with a newspaper over his face muffling his snores.

I stopped at the park café to have an iced chocolate drink and enjoyed the sight of a little girl with her father, sipping the same drink in clear ecstasy. Finally, I headed back to the hotel, stopping for some good bread at our favorite bakery and a bottle of wine.

I knocked on our hotel door.

"I'm not letting you in unless you've brought wine," Linda told me.

"Little pig, little pig let me in. I've got wine and treats."

Linda was grinning from ear to ear and it wasn't just because of the pastries and wine. I started to tell her about the wonderful art I had seen but she interrupted me.

"I saw a wonderful sight while you were gone, too" she said excited. "You know our handsome neighbor across the way?"

"Yes."

"Well, this afternoon he came out on his terrace to do a long yoga session."

"Nice," I replied.

"But that's not the best part," Linda went on as I poured us each a glass of the wine. She began to giggle.

"Okay, what?" I demanded.

"He was completely naked! Now, you tell if you saw something better."

The Drunkard and the Angels

I woke early Sunday in Paris. It was an hour before the hotel served its breakfast of good coffee and croissants, but I needed caffeine, I craved caffeine, I *had* to have caffeine. I went to find a coffee shop. Paris does many things well – art, nightlife, food – but coffee shops on Sunday, isn't one of them.

I wandered on in vain. I saw a bakery ahead; one that sold wonderful bread on weekdays. A clochard - a drunken bum – stood in the entrance, a bottle of wine in one hand, his penis in the other as he urinated on the doorstep. A bakery – a basic food place for God's sake – couldn't he find a more sanitary place to piss? That's what I was thinking as I sidestepped his spatter and averted my gaze.

"Bonjour, Madame," he blurted out in slurred speech. I just kept walking.

"Bonjour, Madame!" he shouted, though he could barely articulate.

I continued on my way. Then to my back, very clearly and loudly he angrily shouted, "Cunt!" And so I learned we and the French share more words than I had suspected.

Later I hopped a metro for mass at St. Eustache Cathedral. I am not at all religious, but I had heard it had the best organ music in the whole city. I went for the Bach.

The elevator from the metro to the church grounds was appalling. Too many brethren of my bakery friend had made use of it in the same way. The grounds outside the cathedral were thronged by dog-loving Parisians. Parisians do not believe in cleaning up after their animals.

Once inside, I gratefully learned cathedrals are the only places in Paris where dogs are barred. I was handed a program complete with a musical score I was expected to know how to read. I was humbled by the paucity of American public education as I looked at the complicated piece. Before the music began a jet plane flew overhead. The stones of the church captured the sound, turned it into a G major chord and reverberated with it. I was astounded. How did it do that?

Then the organ began. If the stones could capture a jet, imagine what they did with one of the finest organs in Europe, one used in the finals of all international competitions. But this was a musically spoiled congregation. The organ was not enough. A hundred-voice chorus stepped in. I was in music orgasmic ecstasy. Then they brought in the ultimate weapon. A woman looking like a 50-year-old Alice in Wonderland complete with long blonde locks and a blue headband stood up and raised her arms in command.

Everyone opened the music score and began singing, including her. Wrapped in sheepskin and drenched in a tub she might weigh 95 pounds, but it was all lung. The stones carrying the sound of that mighty organ, the chorus and the cathedral full of singers could not drown the soaring tones of that tiny, aging French woman.

For an hour I was surrounded by angels.

From the clochard at the bakery to the stones of St. Eustache ringing with all that music –"music heard so deeply it is not heard", a Frenchman said, I will carry to my grave the memory of that Sunday.

As I said, I am not religious, but if I lived in Paris you bet I'd be a regular churchgoer – clochards notwithstanding. The stones of St. Eustache can withstand whole cities of drunkards.

Quebec City –
Europe Without the Euro

On a snowy day, having worked up an appetite roaming a warren of cobble stoned streets and gazing at seventeenth century buildings clustered under the city walls, I suddenly got a whiff of aromas that made my mouth water.

I followed my nose into a small bistro, *Le Lapin Sauté*. A fireplace on one wall drew me like a magnet. Low wood beams held bundles of drying herbs. Some old copper pots hung on the wall, others were in use in the kitchen emitting the enticing smells. The place was full of people talking animatedly in French.

I stumbled over my own French but Pierre, my waiter, good-humoredly repeated the specials and translated for me as I pored over the menu. *Cassoulet*, a classic dish, jumped out at me. Before long I was contentedly washing down the succulent meal with some red wine.

"*C'est bonne?*" Pierre asked. I gave him a thumbs-up sign and he laughed.

Paris? No, I was in Quebec City, North America's answer to Paris.

Many Americans still tend to think of Quebec in terms of its French fur trapper history, envisioning wooden palisades in the wilderness. While Quebec is proud of that part of her history, and an edgy touch of the wilderness still permeates the sophistication, this is a city that has been civilizing itself since the early 1600s.

For proof of just how sophisticated this city has become you need look no farther than the magnificent *Chateau Frontenac*. This hotel, in the grand Canadian style of the hotels at Banff and Lake Louise, towers over the city walls and dominates the skyline.

The five star institution boasted Chef Jean Soulard who had won France's highest award, *"Maitre Cuisinier de France"* hosted a television cooking show and gave cooking lessons at the hotel. In homage to Quebec's wilderness tradition he includes wild game on his menu.

Also in keeping with the wild history, the hotel has a ghost who haunts the hotel. The lady had such a lovely time over a hundred years ago when she visited the chateau she has never left. An actress playing the part to the hilt frequently entertains the guests.

She was not the only lady to grace the city. In fact, in the 1660s, King Louis XIV of France , delighted with the furs coming from his new outpost, decided it should become a permanent settlement. To do that, the trappers needed wives.

So King Louis rounded up young women orphans from the convents of France. Rumor has it that a few ladies of the night were included for instructional purposes to prepare the girls for life with lusty furtrappers. Called *"Les Filles du Roi"* The King's Daughters, they all sailed over, 700 in one ship alone, and were greeted by hordes of happy trappers.

Their mission was to copulate and populate Quebec, one they accomplished with vigor. The average number of children per family until thirty years ago was between 13 and 16. Finally, at that time the daughters of those huge families realized they had a choice and it was a resounding "NO!"

Instead of dealing with so many children they don't know what to do, Quebec is now facing an aging population and not enough young workers, an altogether new problem.

The British, eventually disturbed the peace of France's colony by invading it. As the *Quebecois* defended the front at the confluence of the St. Lawrence and St. Charles rivers, the redcoats came in the back way marching across a field owned by a farmer named Abraham in 1759. Today Abraham's Plain is the site of the annual Winter *Carnaval*.

The Brits allowed the French to keep their language and religion (something they didn't do for their own Catholic countrymen at home). Luckily the French also kept their cooking skills.

While the rest of Canada may survive on marmite sandwiches, and under-seasoned sausage, in Quebec even the fussiest gourmet would have to work hard to find something to complain about, and one doesn't have to frequent the Chateau to find fine cooking. Small bistros pepper the city (no pun intended). They import their wine but do make their own ice wine, a real delicacy. The one possible exception to the excellent food might arguably be *poutine*. It was the French furtrapper's answer to fast food. It is French fries topped with fried cheese curds and glued all together with gravy. *Poutine* is a great source of amusement in Quebec cartoons. It sits in the stomach like a brick – you can eat it once to hold you over for a week of chopping wood in the snow.

Quebec makes the most of what it has and in the winter she plays with the cold. The commuter ferry crossing the St. Lawrence is swapped out for an icebreaker. I rode it one day and standing in the bow I felt like an Arctic explorer as we plowed through the ice. Before the icebreakers were purchased the *Quebecois* cleverly built temporary winter bridges of ice to cross the river. Many restaurants construct "ice bars" outside, illuminated at night with fiber optic lighting, and they even build their famous Ice Hotel. Now that's something even Paris doesn't have.

The European feel of the city is especially evident behind the high walls the British built to keep us Americans from invading. These days we invade with dollars instead of bayonets. Pierced by two gates that had to be widened in the 1950s to accommodate motorized traffic, they surround a wonderful maze of streets that make up the *Vieux Quebec*, old town, of the city.

Artists, craftsmen and artisans joined forces to preserve and protect the colorful heart of the old town called *Quartier Petit Champlain*. The shopping opportunities get visitors drooling and spending.

Entertainment is also big in Quebec and it has given the world such phenomena as the Cirque de Soliel and Celine Dion. During Carnaval, traditional Arcadian (translate that as Cajun) music from the backwoods days is popular and fur coated people wearing the traditional arrowhead patterned woven sash lead street dances in the old town.

Everyone speaks French, but anywhere near Quebec City they also speak English. The Separatist Movement had its heyday and got rules passed requiring all signs to have the English fifty percent smaller than the French. But when it came to a vote, the *Quebecois* voted to stay with Canada, so it just seems like another country. The money is definitely Canadian and our dollar goes a lot farther in Quebec than it does in Euro based France.

They are a fun loving people who welcome visitors and, hey, there's no doggie poo problem like in Paris. It's not only closer, it's a lot cleaner.

Surviving the Ice Hotel

I stood frozen. It wasn't just the bitter cold of Quebec in February. I was looking at an Eskimo's wet dream.

L'Hotel Glace, the Ice Hotel, is the biggest, most magnificent, most elegant igloo anyone has ever imagined. I knew it was insane – a spoiled Californian going to Quebec in mid-winter? Nuts. But now I am glad I went even if I was crazy – as crazy as les Quebecois, I learned.

It was a cold, snowy, wild week in the frozen North. I arrived in the midst of their Carnaval – a Mardi Gras in the snow. (Well, if they are going to celebrate it, it has to be in the snow up there.) I went to a snowy Nordic spa with an icy waterfall to splash in next to the hot tub. I saw truly mad Quebecois frolic in public in the snow wearing bathing suits.

"I may have to write about how you Quebecois torture yourselves," I said to my guide, Sylvan.

"No, Andrea, you must understand. We embrace winter, so we can enjoy it. Otherwise, it is just a long boring wait until spring," he laughed.

So here I was embracing winter in a big way in a dwelling made of ice. I took a daylight tour of the palace that exists only three months of the year, from January through the end of March. Artists and architects help design it and a crew of 74 works around the clock for three weeks to construct it each year. During daylight hours for $14 Canadian, the public can tour it, but at nightfall it belongs to the overnight guests.

As dusk falls, the hotel takes on an eerie beauty as the ice glows. I toured the lushly carved theme suites lit with fiber optic lights embedded in the ice. There's even a honeymoon suite with a specially built fireplace that sheds no heat so the room won't melt.

I went off to a fine gourmet restaurant on the resort grounds where I gorged on fondue, I met a bride and groom, newlywed, married in the fairy-tale lovely, ice wedding chapel. The bride wore a white silk dress and high white fur boots. They eloped – no worries about guests. "You can only have the chapel a half hour because the seats are ice and guests get cold," the bride laughed. Their love and a fur robe kept her warm through the ceremony.

Before being turned loose, we guests had to have our special "sleep training". Ambroise, in his French accent, showed us the sleeping bag, good to 40 degrees below zero that would be waiting for us in our rooms. He whipped one out of its bag. "To be warm you need to get much hair in 'ere," he stated. Easy for him to say. He had a thick, full ponytail. One of our numbers was bald, another, a girl, sported a crew cut. "So you must shock eet much." We were dumbfounded.

He looked at our blank expressions and then demonstrated, shaking the sleeping bag vigorously. We relaxed and laughed, "Oh, air – shake it to get air in it." He suddenly understood our confusion and grabbed his ponytail, "No, not zis." We were to put anything we didn't want to freeze in the bag, and go cool rather than sweat because that would freeze us to our bags

Ambroise then told us before bed to go to the courtyard where the only sources of heat were located – the bathroom building, hot tub and a sauna, to "heat ze core" of our bodies. If we used the hot tub, we were to don a hat so the rising steam wouldn't freeze our hair. We made our way to the N'Ice Club. The music system was protected in a fur-lined wood box, the iced speakers belted out loud music. Nooks of snow held ice tables and chairs. I got a drink in a glass made of ice. "Hey, my drink froze," complained one guest. "No problem," the bartender said. "We have a refrigerator in a tent outside. I'll get you a warm one."

If the hotel was cold, the music was hot, we danced in our heavy coats, scarves, boots, earmuffs, mittens and fur. In Quebec, fur does not inspire protests, but envy. Coveting warmth is a blatant sin up there. The most successful pickup line men use is, "Come with me. I'll keep you warm". As much as we danced, we knew we had to go bed eventually.

I was clever and came up with strategy. I dehydrated myself the last two hours (no plumbing in the ice and there were lots of snowy corridors between my room and the bathrooms). When one of us put Ambroise's warning to the test, and removed his hat in the hot tub, he timed it and found it took 20 seconds to freeze his hair. I opted for the dry sauna, wore my long johns under the fleece robe we'd been issued. I also took my outer clothes to warm them by the stove. I ran pell mell back to the room and stuffed the hot clothes down into the sleeping bag where they could warm my feet. I was toasty on my glowing bed of ice. I tied the neck muff of the sleeping bag around me, pulling up the hood with the built-in pillow, tied it so only my face was exposed to the night air. I was in a warm cocoon.

Between me and the ice there was a piece of plywood and a thin foam mattress, but the magic sleeping bag did its job. Wake up call was at 8:30 because at 9:00, the hotel opens to the public and some tourist is liable to photograph you at your morning worst if you want to sleep in. My clothes that had warmed my toes, had been kept warm by my body heat. I wriggled into them in the bag while my roommates cracked apart the frozen folds of their garments. I slipped out of the warm mummy bag into my boots and coat, ran for the bathroom and reception buildings where there was hot coffee waiting.

Over breakfast with other guests, I heard the stories. "My contacts froze. I forgot to put them in the bag. When I had to get up I couldn't see and got lost in the hallways looking for the bathroom."

"When I got to the bathrooms, I jumped into the hot shower and thought my family would have to move up here because I never wanted to leave it again. I used the hairdryer under my pajamas to get warm again."

We agreed it had been a unique experience we wouldn't have missed. I was smug as I ate my Eggs Benedict. I had stayed warm, dry and asleep until the wake-up call.

Yes, I know how to embrace winter now. Merci, Sylvan. Merci, Ambroise. Merci, beautiful Quebec.

Section 7:
Catalonia and Spain

I made two trips to official Spain. That was because I went to Barcelona first and discovered I was in Catalonia, not Spain. Even its language was different. I loved Catalonia. My husband and I had always admired the architecture of Antonio Gaudi and Barcelona was his city. Once I realized how distinctive Catalonia was, I realized I also wanted to experience Spain. I made a trip to Madrid and Sevilla, and surroundings. I loved Spain as much as I loved Catalonia. I will make another trip to official Spain to visit Basque country someday. I am sure it will be equally different and that I shall love it, too. Spain never disappoints.

Barcelona – Not Spain, Catalonia!

I wanted a mother-daughter trip to Barcelona with my daughter Heather. She had just spent two years as a caregiver for a boyfriend who died of cancer. I had plenty of frequent flier miles and I wanted to do something fun for her after all her hard work and sorrow. I also looked forward to some time alone with her. To my dismay, she invited her new boyfriend, Peter, to join us our last week in Barcelona.

I had rented an apartment in the L'Eixample district for a month. I got there a week before Heather was to arrive. The friendly taxi driver who met me at the airport understood my Spanish, but he spoke Catalan.

"I am happy to be here in Spain," I told him.

"No. Not Spain. Catalonia!" he said emphatically.

I realized Catalonians are fiercely proud and protective of their culture. Under Franco their language was outlawed and he posted signs that said "Speak Spanish, Quit Barking." Catalans pronounce Barcelona as we do, with no soft Spanish lisp. It is a much crisper sounding language than soft Castilian Spanish.

The owners of the apartment, two young men, met me to show me how the apartment worked. It was a two-bedroom place because Peter would join us. I spent my week alone exploring the wonderful city and learning the neighborhood so I could find things Heather would love. There was a lot.

L'Eixample was a wonderful neighborhood. The small balconies off each bedroom overlooked a wide boulevard. The center four lanes were dedicated to one-way traffic leading to the city center. On either side of those lanes was a broad park-like area with a bicycle and a pedestrian path, many trees and flowers, and some tables here and there set out by neighborhood restaurants. On either side of the planted areas were two lanes for local traffic. The buildings at each intersection were chamfered, the corners cut off, so every intersection created a small plaza. That made everything seem open, sunny and airy.

There were many small shops and cafes. I quickly discovered who had the freshest produce, and who sold the best cheese in the nearby side streets. Each morning I'd see white city-owned bicycles using the paths to commute. Only city residents could use them and were issued an annual card that would unlock them from the stalls set up for them throughout the city.

L'Eixample was the brain child of Ildefons Cerda, a brilliant urban planner before the world ever knew there was such a thing. In the late 1800s Barcelona had clearly outgrown its old walled medieval center and the city fathers knew the walls had to come down and the city expanded, so they gave Cerda the job. He went into the old dark medieval part of the city known as Gotic (Gothic) and talked to people who lived there in the midst of the Industrial Revolution. He discovered they were unhealthy, overcrowded and desperately needed sunshine and fresh air. Then he designed the city on a grid with lots of open space. I wish other cities had learned from him.

I took a hop-on, hop-off tour of Barcelona. Sometimes these are useful, sometimes just boring. But in Barcelona it was run by the city, not private enterprise, and was excellent. I learned the neighborhoods. I rode on the upper deck and a few times had to dodge the parrots. Barcelona has a huge population of Monk (or Quaker) parrots. They live in the palm trees that grow all over the city and can be a pest sometimes – especially on the top deck of tour buses.

I roamed the mile long Ramblas that leads to the sea. It is a pedestrian, leafy avenue lined with cafes and restaurants. All sorts of vendors set up stalls, and young men try to hawk junky toys that fall apart right away. The Ramblas leads to the dock where cruise ships like to drop off their passengers and where a statue of Christopher Columbus is pointing the wrong way to America.

I saw from posters that Catalonia Independence Day was coming up the next day and asked a young woman at a kiosk on the Ramblas if there was a parade or festival.

"No, but there is supposed to be strike," she told me.

"A strike? No fireworks?"

The next day I roamed the city some more and headed back to the apartment. I went out on the balcony and saw lots of people heading towards the city center. They were all carrying the yellow and red striped Catalonian flag. Some people were wearing them like capes. Little kids, young parents pushing strollers, older people using canes, everyone was filling all the lanes of the broad boulevard so there was no motor traffic able to use the road. Some people carried signs demanding independence.

Interested, I immediately went outside and joined them. I wondered where everyone was going. The street became so packed that halfway to the city center the crowd had to stop. I darted into a metro station. Hordes of flag carrying people filled the stairs and train cars. I got off at the plaza at the center of the city.

"Senora, for you." Someone handed me a flag. I accepted it gratefully.

Once up in the plaza, I saw it was mobbed. People spoke on loud-speakers, some people played music, probably the Catalonian anthem. It was all very festive and peaceful. Young people climbed the fountain in the center of the plaza to wave their flags. News helicopters spluttered overhead.

"Indepenencia!" was the cry.

Eventually, I got to the edge of the crowd and made my way home at dusk. I went out to a sidewalk café for dinner and people were jubilant everywhere, all still wearing or carrying their flags. Whole building facades were draped with the flags. Everyone joked, laughed and were celebratory. I was convinced and became a champion of Catalonian independence from that day on.

I Looked Good on the Radio

Heather came and I met the airport bus which I learned had a stop right outside our apartment. I was bubbling over with joy at seeing her. I met her at the stop with a handful of wildflowers and showed her a newspaper photo of the independence demonstration the day before. The paper said a million and half people had showed up making it the then largest demonstration ever in Europe. It had been taken by one of the helicopters that had been above us.

"See if you can find me. It's harder than finding Waldo," I told her. We laughed.

She was excited because it was fall and the city would celebrate its famous and infamous Merce Festival the last week we were there. Infamous because it involved a lot of fire and fireworks. She showed me a video on her computer and I was astonished at what I saw. People built seven story human pyramids, paraded with fireworks, projected light shows on public buildings. Some of it looked very dangerous.

"Mom, I want to buy a fireproof hat. Let's get you one, too."

"No thanks. I think I'll stay at a distance from the fireworks, so I won't need it."

The hats were on sale everywhere in the city along with fireproof capes, and even whole fireproof suits for children were available and selling fast.

Heather didn't want to take the bus tour but I talked her into it because the tourist office, wanting to accommodate a travel writer, had given us free tickets for the week and we could just use it for public transportation. To her surprise, she loved it and it was very convenient.

We used our passes to visit the Miro Museum on Mont Juic. It had a great view. Inside we discovered works by not just Miro, but some gifts given to him by other artists. We found a fountain made by Calder that flowed with not water, but mercury. The Catalans had safely put it behind glass to protect the public from the toxic metal fumes. Calder had made it for Miro because Franco had bombed Miro's hometown near a mercury mine out of existence. It was a condolence gift.

We explored the market where we ate Catalonian butter and squashed tomato sandwiches and very expensive ham. We went to the "Block of Discord" which got its name because so many architects competing with each other put up buildings on the same block. One was by Barcelona's most famous architect Antoni Gaudi. He has left his mark on his city. We went to see Sagrada Familia, his wildly decorative basilica. The exterior was an art deco dream. The interior was just as beautiful with columns like flower stems, blossoming high above. Heather and I explored it well and even found a restoration of one of his string models in a museum in the basement. Gaudi used to take string and hang small bags of sand from it until he got the exact arch he wanted. He then photographed it, turned the photo upside-down and told his contractor "Build this."

"It's supposed to be finished in 2023. We'll have to come back then," I told Heather after reading the explanation for all the cranes surrounding the basilica.

A cousin of ours we had never met was coming to Barcelona and we agreed to meet outside the cathedral on Sunday. Heather and I were outside watching some women beginning to get ready to dance the Sardana, a traditional Catalan circle dance, when a young woman came up to us and asked if we were from California. It was our cousin Alyson.

We instantly liked each other and moved closer to the dancing women. They had all tossed their purses in the middle of the circle so no one could steal them as they danced. Just then a radio reporter tapped me on the shoulder and held his microphone out to me.

"Are you a visitor to our city?"

"Yes."

"And you like Barcelona?"

"Very much."

"Did you know this is Catalonia."

"Yes. Not Spain, Catalonia."

"And do you know any Catalan words?"

Fortunately, I had taught myself good day, please and thank you so I could recite them for him. He seemed surprised. Then he asked me if I knew what was happening in front of me.

"The women are dancing a folk dance. I think it is called the Sardana. It is quite beautiful to see."

He moved off. I suspected he was looking for a more clueless tourist. Heather said, "Yesterday marching in a demonstration, Mom, and today wowing them on the radio. I think you are taking the city by storm." She and Alyson laughed.

"And she looked great on the radio," Alyson quipped.

We all laughed again.

We left and went to visit Parc Gruell, an incredible creation by Gaudi. Alyson was traveling with a friend who it turned out was a bird expert who worked for Florida zoos. We sat at a shady table next to a palm tree which turned out to be a convention center for the Quaker parrots. She did not approve of them.

"They've taken over so many cities now and drive away the native birds," she explained. Hooligan birds roaming in gangs, and I had thought they just added a bit of color to the birdscape.

We then explored the city's famous flea market which was rich with antiques. A gun dealer had everything from old Spanish muskets from the 1700s to brand new Uzis. He was sure as Americans we wanted his guns, but we told him we interested in old keys. He pointed us to friend's booth.

"Sure, no guns?" he asked.

"No guns."

"And you are Americans?" he laughed.

We found ancient huge keys fit for a Moorish castle and bargained for them.

We bid farewell to our cousin and her birdloving friend who were flying out the following day.

"I'll have to weigh my luggage now that I have bought something," Alyson said. "I am flying Ryan Air. I might have to throw out some clothes or wear two tops and pants."

The budget airline had minimal, strict luggage weight limits and made up for low fares by overcharging for every ounce overweight.

Heather and I decided to go up the coast and explore the Costa Brava and visit the village where Dali had lived, Cadaques, and visit his country home in Port Lligat just a short walk from Cadaques. We booked a room and took a bus up the winding roads. Pristine white villages decorated the coast and we left a mountain top to hairpin down to lovely Cadeques. We instantly fell in love with the place and enjoyed a seafood meal by the harbor. The next morning we set out for Port Lligat only to discover we should have made reservations months before.

"But if you are willing to wait, we always have cancellations. If you are right here, then I can give you those tickets," the kind woman at the ticket booth told us. We thanked her in Catalan.

The wait was pleasant. The courtyard was lovely and overlooking the peaceful bay. We could also see sections of his fence decorated with great eggs like they were waiting for a giant to come have breakfast. We kept chatting with the woman who was a little bored by just asking people for tickets and so enjoyed real conversation. After two hours, she grinned and beckoned us over to her.

"Here are tickets, just go in and enjoy."

We thanked her profusely because we had seen she had a waiting list, but had put us at the top either because she liked us or because we hadn't wandered off like the others who had been hoping for a cancellation.

There was an extra large egg on a patio over the sea that was cracked open so people could go inside it. We got silly and photographed each other as hatching chicks. The house was labyrinth.

On a terrace overlooking a pool, Heather started giggling.

"Look, Mom, the pool is penis shaped. It pierces the draped grotto at the end." We both went off into gales of laughter.

Dali's studio was surprisingly small but at one end of the room there was a slot in the floor and a pulley overhead so he could raise and lower paintings he was working on that were too large for the room.

We had Dalied a long time and it was time to return to Barcelona and our pleasant apartment. We had a lovely week together, then Peter arrived, and despite having another person in the apartment, I was alone again.

The Gates of Hell

Heather and I ate up Barcelona like it was dessert, before her boyfriend Peter came. Then it was no longer a mother-daughter trip. As long as it made Heather happy, I was fine with it. That had been the point after all she had been through. Unfortunately, Peter got some sort of stomach bug and Heather was constantly heading out to a pharmacy. They spent time in their room listening to Gypsy jazz, and went out on their own a few times.

I chose to just continue seeing Barcelona on my own. I made my way to Tibi Dabo, the highest hill in the city. I took a funicular to the top where there was a charming amusement park built in the early years of the twentieth century. When airplanes were invented the owner built a two-seater airplane on a crane that went in circles out over a cliff. The owner was a dentist who built the park so people would take their children to higher, cleaner air and keep them healthy. More modern rides have now been built below the beautiful carousel and scary airplane ride. It's still getting the kids to a higher altitude and cleaner air.

I also visited Montserrat which housed a medieval monastery. Even without the monastery, Montserrat was worth a visit.

Location, location, location. The monks must have thought like real estate salesmen. Even approaching on the train from Barcelona the mountain itself made my jaw drop. It so abruptly takes over the landscape around it. A smaller rail train like a glorified funicular took me from the commuter line hair-pinning up the mountain to the monastery and the village near it. Locals had set up stalls offering up products from the mountain. I tasted some of the remarkable honey and bought jars of it to have for breakfast and to take home.

Back at the apartment the three of us shared the honey. Peter was feeling better so we all went out to dinner together.

Then it was time for the Merce Festival. In the medieval Gotic part of town, in the largest plaza, wild light shows went on by night and human pyramids by day. Fire dancers and fire eaters were everywhere. I learned that Barcelona challenges another city each year to come up with a light show. This year they had chosen Quebec City. That's the land of Cirque de Soleil and other wild extravaganzas. Quebec City had chosen spectacular La Sagrada Familia as its canvas for the light show. I didn't want to miss this.

I went to take the metro to the basilica, but every car was so jammed, I gave up and splurged on a cab. The crowd was huge, and very respectful. The music began and the lights turned the building into waterfalls, oceans full of creatures, forests, singing crowds. It was magical and at the climax the Catalonians burst into loud applause and appreciative cheers. When I saw the metro stairs mobbed I decided on a cab again, but walked for blocks and blocks for an hour before I finally saw one to hail.

I was still full of the magic of the light show when Heather opened the door. I had tried to talk her and Peter into seeing it with me but they had declined. Now they were sorry.

The legend has it that the day before she was martyred St. Merce was tempted by the Devil, and when she refused him, he opened the Gates of Hell and loosed all his demons upon her. The night before the climax of the festival Catalans reenact that and hold a wild parade – the one Heather had bought fireproof gear for.

Peter had a relapse of his stomach ailment. I left the apartment and started wandering around town enjoying the festivities. I noticed at the ends of many closed off streets ambulances were parked and medical crews were setting up first aid stations. I felt a little nervous about that. I entered a plaza and noticed a weird construction and a stage. I went up to look at it and found myself pinned up against a temporary railing. I tried to move away but a crowd had formed behind me. So, I stayed. I figured something was about to happen. The sun set and suddenly people in grotesque costumes stepped on the stage and fire torches were lit.

A man with a deep, mean sounding voice began jeering and laughing in Catalan. He had big horns and I realized he was supposed to be the Devil. With no intention, I was standing right beside the Gates of Hell. I longed for Heather dressed in her fireproof clothes to be there instead of me. I had on a gauzy dress and had a fan. The Devil suddenly set off an explosion and the Gates of Hell opened. Floats kept pouring out, each one with its own monsters shooting off fireworks. I used my fan to bat the sparks away. Monster float after monster float came out and set off on a kilometer-long parade to the sea. When the last one came out the crowd followed the parade. Drums were beating everywhere putting out wonderful rhythms.

The crowd danced and walked, dodging more and more fireworks. Part way to the sea I was tired and hungry, but the crowd was packed around me. Then a drummer got a very good beat going. I began dancing with man in front of me. He was masked as a demon, as many were. I danced and went to turn around him. Then I turned around and began dancing with the next person, and one by one I danced my way to the edge of the crowd and into an alley. A few blocks down I found a restaurant that overlooked the parade route and bought myself a meal and welcome cold beer after breathing all that fireworks smoke.

Back at the apartment I found Heather had missed the parade and fretted that I had not bought a fireproof headscarf.

"I was fine. I used my fan to protect myself," I explained.

The next night, the last of the Merce, I was home early, and laying in bed reading when the building began to shake and I heard loud noises. The apartment was equipped with triple glass windows because of the traffic noise of the boulevard. They were very noise proof. When I went out on the balcony the noise was deafening. Heather and Peter were on their adjacent balcony and handed me over a glass of wine.

"There are three fireworks displays going on at the same time in different parts of the city," Peter said.

I sat and watched. I felt like a Syrian under artillery bombardment but knew at least no one was trying to kill me. Every Catalan was just celebrating Merce reaching heaven.

Shade and a Place to Sit

It was in Madrid a year later that spinal stenosis invaded my life. That and a knee that was giving out. Walking more than a hundred feet became painful unless I took a lot of Ibuprofen and gave it a chance to work. The Catch 22 was that I needed to eat something before I took the pain killer. That meant I had to walk a block and half in agony to the nearest coffeeshop each morning to buy something for breakfast before I could medicate myself, then it took about a half hour for the pain to ebb.

Fortunately, I was in Madrid. Because of their hot climate, or perhaps because the Moors owned Spain for so many centuries and loved gardens, the Spanish believe in shade and benches where you can enjoy the shade.

I would spot the next bench or ledge where I could sit for a moment and fight my way through the pain. It only took a few minutes for the spasms to subside, then I could walk again until it started once more. But I was determined not to let it ruin Spain for me.

Thus, I made my way a mile on a leafy boulevard from the metro to the Prado bench by bench, blessing the Spanish at each one.

The Prado is amazing. I was very pleased that unlike so many other museums in some other countries, the art had not been stolen. It had been commissioned and paid for.

The collection of Netherland paintings from the 1400s and 1500s is spectacular. Hieronymus Bosch's famous *Garden of Earthly Delights* was commissioned by a Spanish nobleman and finally made its way to the Prado. It was the star of that gallery but there were many other painters from the same period. It confirmed my belief that great artists do not come from barren soil. There has to be a lively community of artists experimenting for a true master to take root and flourish.

I have found when there is a huge museum like El Prado or the Louvre or the Met, and there is limited time, it pays to learn of their collection beforehand. Then I select a few pieces I have always longed to see up close in person, and make my way to them. Along the way I always discover special pieces that will linger with me the rest of my life, but I don't get overwhelmed or give short shrift to the art by trying to see it all.

So, I came for Bosch, but found Velaquez. There were pieces by him I had intended to see, but I discovered a whole treasury of his work. Among his contemporaries, his work shines off the walls. That's something else museums have taught me; look at an artist in context. I went back three times. I came for Goya's *Third of May* execution painting, and found his Black series and discovered Gisbert's painting of a massacre at Malaga.

The Black Goya gallery was truly terrifying. I had only seen one of them, Saturn devouring his child, in reproduction. There was a painting called *The Witches' Sabbath* that made my blood run cold. I noticed something interesting. There was a peculiar type of face with thick drooping lips and a chin that outweighed the rest of the features. I had seen it before in the carved faces at Salisbury Cathedral in England where the artist used local medieval villagers as his models. I looked more closely and wondered if there was an extinct genetic trait for that very ugly chin structure.

A few days later I was in a restaurant when a jolly group of middle-aged women came in and one of the women had that exact face. I tried not to stare. I could see that she was affluent and was well-liked by her companions. I wanted to gaze at her but stole glances instead. Then I began thinking that men could hide such an ugly face behind facial hair, but a woman could not. When I walked to the busiest plaza in Madrid, I realized one of men begging there had the same chin under his beard. Goya had alerted me to something fascinating. The gene was not extinct, just rare and mostly hidden.

When I finally found the gallery at the Prado that housed *The Third of May*, I was again astounded. I had only seen small productions of the painting so had not realized the man being executed in it was life-sized. The painting was huge and the colors much more vivid that I had ever expected. It was overwhelming. On the opposite wall another execution was taking place. It was also huge with life sized figures. This was the gallery of executions.

But while the Goya was filled with violent emotion, the other execution was methodical. It was by Antonio Gisbert and it depicted a scene from Malaga when a group of intellectuals attempted to restore Spain's republican government from Napoleon's occupation, so it was from the same time period as Goya's execution. But the men were lined up to be executed (some bodies on the beach already) and a priest was there as soldiers blindfolded those about to be shot.

I sat there a long time looking from one painting to the other. The Spanish had kindly provided a bench just for this kind of contemplation. Was it worse to be murdered in a hot frenzy, or in cold focused purpose? Even the colors in Gisbert's depiction were colder, grayer, more blue, while the Goya blazed away like the bullets being fired.

At long last I left the Prado to ponder some more over a late lunch and a dose of Ibuprofen. The café had a couple trees for shade and its own resident song sparrows. Every café seemed to have its own natural aviary. Once again I was able to sit in shade, this time with birdsong to entertain me. God bless the Spanish!

The Blabla Car

In Madrid I was staying at an Air B&B with a lovely blonde hostess named Marimar and her college-age son Pedro. I had been there a week and wanted to travel to Seville where I had rented another room for me and my granddaughter Eva, who was enrolled in a university for a semester in Spain.

My travel choices, I thought, were bus or train. Train was expensive but faster, about three and half hours as opposed to over seven by bus, so I tried to book us tickets online. There was not a single seat available. I was disappointed but went to book bus tickets which took seven hours, but were a little cheaper. They, too, were sold out.

Pedro heard me muttering and asked what I was doing. I explained, and said, "I guess I am going to have to rent a car."

"Let me try," he offered.

He was very computer savvy and of course his Spanish was better, so I turned my laptop over to him.

"Ah, I think I know what's happening," he said. "It is Feria time so everyone in Europe is heading to Sevilla. But don't rent a car. Just try Blabla Car."

"What on earth is that?"

He explained it was a way for people to pay for their expensive European fuel when someone wanted to get from one city to another.

"I just go online to Blablacar.com?"

He punched it in for me and there it was. I simply wrote in Madrid as my starting point, and Sevilla as my destination and the date I wanted to leave. Immediately over a dozen possibilities popped up.

"Check out the feedback section to be sure there are recommendations about the driving," Pedro suggested.

I looked at all the ratings and saw one car with room for two leaving the next morning when I wanted to go with high ratings for a safe driver. I emailed him and grabbed his two seats with room for some luggage. At dawn my granddaughter and I took a taxi to our rendezvous point, and sure enough about fifteen minutes later our driver pulled up. We loaded our luggage and were on our way.

We drove through the lovely province of Estremadura. It was full of castles. It seemed there was one on every hilltop. Then I spotted storks and woke my granddaughter out of her doze to look at them. The man sharing the back seat with us was pleased that I was so thrilled. He was from Estremadura. He explained it was their state bird.

"They like to nest in the parapets of the castles," he told me.

He was being dropped off in a town along the way and told me there was a Roman bridge in the town. The driver spoke up, "We are going to make a brief stop somewhere where there are bathrooms anyway, so why don't we make a brief detour to see the bridge?"

So we did. The trip took about three and half hours even with the pit stop and detour, and we were dropped off at the main square in Sevilla where we could take a cab to our room. The entire thing cost about a third what the bus trip would have cost.

So, after ten wonderful days in Sevilla (with a side trip to Granada and the Alhambra) when it was time to return to Madrid, I didn't even try trains, planes or buses. I went directly to Blabla Car. The trip back was even cheaper and among our passengers were three kittens being rescued from a kill-shelter and taken to one that always adopted out its rescues.

I made friends with a young Spanish and Lebanese couple and with the young woman who was rescuing the kittens. We made one pit stop to get the kittens water and the rest of us coffee.

On my return home I learned Blabla Car was a French innovation. There are cost limits. Drivers are not allowed to make a profit on their ride-sharing, just get their costs covered. They register online, pay an annual fee, and get their own travel costs covered. I wish we had it in the US. From now on when in Europe my intercity travel is going to be on Blabla Car. Merci, France.

How I Went to Spain and Learned to Love Polka Dots

I was in Sevilla and I was seeing spots before my eyes. No, it wasn't jet-lag.

Every woman in Sevilla was dressed in her finest polka dots. They were celebrating Feria, the uninhibited paean to spring the week that follows the somberly, even spooky, religious Holy Week.

Sevilla has a dress code for women for festive occasions that has lasted centuries because it works so well, and no occasion is more special than Feria. A low-cut dress hugs the form to mid-thigh then explodes into acres of ruffles – all the better to dance in. The sleeves, likewise, at the shoulder or below the elbow burst into yards of flounces – all the better to wield a fan or castanets. Add fringe to the bodice or don a fringed shawl, and don't forget a fan and big earrings. Then top the whole outfit off with a bright flower on top of the head, and you suddenly understand why men the world over have sung for centuries about the ladies of Spain with longing.

It was as if the city, like a spring garden, had suddenly burst into bloom. Every female in Sevilla from infant to crone had blossomed out in glorious polka dotted flounces. Miles of ruffles engulfed the city.

227

Not just the ladies, but the elegant horses of Spain dress up for Feria. During Feria everyone who has a horse, and, since it is a status symbol, there are a lot of them, brings out their horses and carriages. The buggies are polished and painted. The horses are brushed until they gleam, and their manes and tails braided or intertwined with ruffles, flowers, pom poms and fringe.

For several hours each day they parade a route in the fairgrounds with regulated stops for water and rest. The men sport elegant nineteenth or early twentieth century garb complete with high hats, and fill their buggies with the ladies and their overflowing ruffles. Solo horsemen make sure a pretty lady of Spain is perched side saddle behind them. Everyone in Spain fills trains, buses, and planes to come see the lovely spectacle.

The horse parade comes to a sudden halt at sunset so the dancing can begin.

The fairgrounds are lined with striped tents, all privately sponsored. At the back of each there is a small bar offering simple snacks. In the tents are some tables and room for the musicians and dancers. Some tents are small, some huge. They and the streets are lit with strings of round lanterns that look like more polka dots.

Everyone dances the Servillana, a folk flamenco as opposed to the intense classical form of the art. It's a complicated dance with four distinct movements and a long pause between each movement. It was originally a courtship dance, and the mamas and papas of the senoritas demanded that the men could look at, but not touch their daughters, so hands are always up in the air. At the very end, the couple could briefly put one arm around their partner while raising the other arm in triumph.

The drink of the night is usually white wine mixed with Sprite. No one wants to get so drunk they can't do the intricate steps of the dance, but they stay relaxed and hydrated. Sevilla is serious about keeping Feria available to all and regulates the prices of the refreshments each year. Nobody gets to gouge anyone.

While the tents are private, the guards are generous about letting visitors in for the festivities, and often the dancing spills out into the streets. The spring nights can get hot and the ladies' fans are put to good use, sometimes by the men who beg to borrow them. The celebration lasts late into the wee hours because it seems Spaniards, unlike other humans, don't need to sleep. Even if they managed to catch a few zzzs for an hour or two it was soon time to groom and decorate the horses for the parade again.

I wondered about the profusion of polka dots after I saw a VW bug painted with them and even a few motor scooters likewise adorned. I discovered it was in defiance of the horrible villains of Spain.

While the Moors held sway from Granada for centuries, Christians (Orthodox, Catholic or whatever), Jews and Gypsies were totally welcome and free to worship however they wanted. As long as no one messed with the Caliph's many wives and paid their taxes, everyone got along.

But Ferdinand and Isabella (yes, those of Columbus fame) married, joined the kingdoms of Spain and Catalonia and conquered the Moors. They were under the spell of Torquemada. He's the guy that invented the Spanish Inquisition and the Auto-da-Fe in which any non-Catholics were burned alive in large groups. He also sent the same rules to Latin America after Columbus found it. A lot of natives were broiled alive under the rule of the priests that accompanied the Conquistadors.

The Moors were kicked out along with the Spanish Jews. The choice was convert to Catholicism, leave, or get burned alive if someone suspected your conversion wasn't sincere enough. The Gypsies pretended to be Catholic but they danced out their anguish and rage, inventing flamenco. (Now you know why they stamp their feet so much during that dance!) Gypsy women, who had always honored the moon, sewed small round mirrors on their dance clothes to mimic the moon. Eventually as more sophisticated fabric printing developed, polka dots emerged as the new little moons to pay homage to an ancient faith and defy religious persecution.

After learning that, I appreciated the dancing and the joyful polka dots even more. I kept thinking "Take that, Torquemada!" as the partying continued until dawn during Feria week.

At Concha's

When I got to Concha's place, I instantly felt at home even though I was in the heart of Spain - Sevilla.

Her apartment on the second floor (the first floor according to Europeans) was spread out and had a balcony overlooking the narrow medieval street below. A small plaza opened up at the end of the building, providing enough morning sun to help a wild jungle of a garden thrive on Concha's balcony and yet enough afternoon shade to provide relief from the burning afternoon sun.

In back there was a private courtyard garden at ground level where a neighbor parked a red, white polka-dotted Vespa.

A massive piece of dark wood furniture, a sort of sideboard, cabinet, and wanna-be mantle took up an entire wall of her large main room. It had to be deconstructed then reassembled to have got it up the stairs and through the apartment door. Concha told me it was an old family piece. Old in Spain means OLD. It boasted a few hundred years at least. In the States some millionaire would have had a grandiose room designed around it. At Concha's it simply took up space and served to store a multitude of items. Clothes, books, and seldom used cookery items shared space with family heirlooms and photographs.

My bedroom was on the plaza side and my window overlooked it and part of the street. Another inner bedroom was occupied by an Israeli girl who had come to the city because her flamenco teacher at home had told her she was ready to learn from the masters in Sevilla. She spent seven or eight hours a day in classes, came back to shower quickly then spent her nights watching the best flamenco artists in the world.

Concha's kitchen was roomy with a table at one end. It had a washing machine which I could use, a real bonus in Europe. The jungle on the balcony had a handy clothesline.

I settled in for a cozy ten-day stay in sun-blasted Sevilla.

Concha instructed me about a farmer's market down the street and cheerfully made me café con leche each morning. I learned the small coffee bar a few doors away had freshly squeezed orange juice as long as the oranges lasted each morning. I made sure to get there early enough to get a big glass to sip as I ate a flaky pastry.

All would have been perfect except for an ambitious shop owner on the plaza, He decided to add to his family income by opening a bar after hours on the plaza. It was illegal and Concha had notified the authorities who ignored her protests. Each night beginning about 11 p.m. carousers would gather to drink, sing and argue outside the shop. I didn't mind the loud singing so much, but the arguments drove the noise level up by many decibels. The Spanish are passionate people and argue very well. I finally decided to do as the Spanish do and give up sleep.

Really, it is amazing how little sleep they need – a couple hours in the afternoon, a couple hours in the evening. Dinner begins at 10 p.m., partying begins after midnight following the leisurely meal, and lasts until 3 or 4 a.m., a short nap, then a small quick breakfast, a late leisurely lunch followed by another nap. That's it. Yet they have the energy to dance, work hard and court each other. No wonder they conquered the globe at one point.

I absorbed the illegal outdoor speakeasy into my routine, but another night brought a new sleepless surprise. Throughout the day as I wandered the beautiful city I had periodically heard loud booms as if someone was setting off daytime fireworks or the city was under artillery fire. It was the week of Feria when Sevilla parties even heartier than usual and I assumed the noise was coming from the fairgrounds that were the center of the celebrations.

The speakeasy celebrants had gone home and the shopkeeper locked up about 3 a.m. I had just fallen asleep when I heard a massive roar outside my windows. I jumped up and ran on to the balcony wondering if a revolution had broken out or WW III had just erupted. Concha was there and pointed down at a massive  procession of men. The men who had been shouting at each other suddenly broke into song and they carried a huge empty platform.

"They are practicing for next Easter when they have to carry the Virgin statue through the city. They must train to get strong enough to carry the weight," she explained.

"At three o'clock in the morning?" I asked.

"That way there is no traffic to get in the way," she said. "Did you hear the cannons today?"

"Yes. I thought it was from Feria."

"No, it warns the men to be ready to march. They put weights on the platform and take it all the way through the city. It happens maybe once a month, then more often shortly before Easter week."

We watched the noisy procession march down the winding street out of sight, then went back to bed.

The next day Concha surprised me by making her family recipe of gazpacho. She and I laughed about the rude awakening in the wee hours as we enjoyed the savory cold soup. It tasted divine in the hot afternoon. She helped me wash a load of clothes and she filled me in on the news about town. I asked her about the beautiful dresses every female from infant to crone wore during Feria.

"Every year some fashion person writes in the newspaper that this year there are supposed to be three layers of ruffles, or nine, or six, whatever. Only the rich ones listen. Mine I have passed on to my niece. My sister has my grandmother's, Concha said. "They are too expensive to always get new ones."

I saw what she meant. Polyester versions cost upwards of three hundred euros. My daughter studied flamenco and when she performed in public she was allowed to wear a troupe dress that everyone shared. I hoped to find one I could afford to bring home for her. Concha advised me to wait a couple days when there was a neighborhood flea market in the little plaza that I had begun to think of as "ours".

Sure enough, a flea market sprang up and spread itself down the winding lanes that fed into the plaza. Amongst all the goodies I spotted a bright red, white polka-dotted flamenco dress sporting four generous layers of ruffles. I checked it out. It was pure cotton. Then I noticed the hem – it was weighted. I knew this was the dress for a serious dancer. The rope weight in the hem helps the skirt flare out smoothly and gives the dancer control over the acres of fabric. My budget was fifty euros or less and the *dama* selling it and I bargained. I carried the many cubic yards of polka dots back to my room triumphantly. Concha looked at it, and then at my single suitcase and scratched her head.

"How?"

I puzzled it over and went to a Chinesi – those are general stores owned by the Chinese. They don't close for siesta like the other shops. They carry everything except food, selling just a few prepackaged snacks. The Spanish like the Italians will only buy fresh food from each other. Every few blocks there is another Chinesi –

they label themselves as such. I threw myself on the mercy of the family, explaining I wanted a bag that would shrink something. The young son instantly knew what I meant and to my great relief hauled out a half dozen in various sizes. I bought the largest one.

Concha watched curiously as I stuffed the voluminous garment into the bag, then opened a plug and squeezed out the air. The whole thing flattened to a couple inches. Later, at home, I greatly enjoyed handing the bag to my daughter who looked at the broad polka dotted pancake, puzzled, then burst into gleeful laughter when she unzipped it and the dress exploded out.

When I told Concha I wanted to see real flamenco, not a tourist show, she advised La Caja Negra. My seldom seen Israeli flatmate seconded the choice. "Real stuff," she said. "Serious."

I met with my nephew and granddaughter who were staying in Sevilla and we set out at 11 p.m. for Caja Negra. It wasn't easy to find because the only sign was tucked out of sight by a huge exterior swamp cooler.

"Boy, they are really trying to hide," commented my nephew.

"Means it's really good," replied my granddaughter. "Its name means The Black Box."

Inside its name proved to be truth in advertising. It was a rectangular room, floors, walls and ceiling all painted black. There was seating for about forty people but more piled in. I sat on an overturned trash can until a kind gentleman exchanged his chair for the can. My nephew and granddaughter stood at the back by a small bar. The stage at the front wasn't large.

A guitarist and singer stood at one side, and a young and older woman sat at the back in straight backed kitchen chairs. Then the star dancer came in. It was electric.

As the singer wailed in Spanish I could not follow, and the guitar passionately poured out music, the dancer proceeded to dance out a story of love and anguish, despair and triumph. She vanished offstage amidst applause and reappeared a short while later in a different dress. The spellbound audience watched again and sometimes called out encouragement to her and sometimes they clapped a rhythm. I realized flamenco is to dance what opera is to singing. It demands discipline, training, and reaches for another level that requires intensity from the dancer and the audience.

When the performance ended, the dancer suddenly became an ordinary person again not some goddess teaching us something important. The girl at the back was her daughter. The girl got up and danced a few moves to audience acclaim. The dancer acknowledged a former teacher of hers who also had to get up and dance while the audience cheered. She introduced her singer and guitarist then told us it was the guitarist's son's birthday.

The teenager was brought on stage, embarrassed as everyone sang Happy Birthday until his father handed him a guitar case as a present. The boy opened it and all embarrassment fled, replaced by look of astonished joy as he took out what was evidently a very special guitar. There was standing ovation and then everyone began to leave.

As we walked back to Concha's, we marveled at what we had seen. We bid each other good night.

The next morning as she made us coffee Concha grinned at me, "Caja Negra? You liked?"

"I liked," I replied and we both burst out laughing.

"I knew," Concha nodded wisely.

Section 8:
The World of Islam

When young I had been to Turkey and Lebanon. Turkey was my first visit to predominantly Islamic country. I was impressed with cosmopolitan Istanbul and even more by Beirut. It was before their civil war back when the city was called "the Paris of the Levant". The universities, including American University, provided excellent higher education to the entire Mediterranean population. Beirut's broad palm-lined esplanade and its skyscrapers delivered a sense of modern glamour that we had not seen in our beloved Greece, where we had been living for two years. Beirut also offered totally shrouded women beggars amid its mini-skirted throngs.

Decades later I wanted to understand that part of the world better. I had always wanted to see the ruins of ancient Egypt. Not long afterwards I took advantage of an invitation from Jordan's tourism department to visit that country. Like Egypt, Jordan is also a land that figures hugely in the holy books of three of the world's major religions: Judaism, Christianity and Islam, all three religions that came out of the desert. I would meet new deserts and learn from them.

Law and Order Istanbul Style

My first experience of a largely Islamic country was Turkey. It was in the late 1960s that we took a road trip from Greece to Istanbul with another couple, Brian and Nicole. They had fallen in love with each other while visiting the Greek island where we were living. Then they had fallen in love with our children. They had a camping van and invited us along, offering to let us camp in the van with our two kids while they stayed in lodgings.

"You speak Greek, and we don't," said Brian, a New Zealander. We had learned young Kiwis were expected to roam the world widely after they left school, then settle down and raise sheep and children. Nicole, a Quebec native had a more adventurous idea about life and Brian liked her point of view.

The trip proved more adventurous than we had planned. We had tried to cross Yugoslavia (remember that long lost country?) and into Bulgaria to get to Turkey. Yugoslavia had been a storybook experience for us with pretty villages made slightly exotic by the mosques alongside churches. But Bulgaria proved to be a horror back in those bad old days, where unlike Tito-led Yugoslavia, it was firmly behind the Iron Curtain of the USSR. We were harassed by the border guards and held up for three hours while they hoped for bribes.

Bleak impoverished villages with homes with cardboard instead of glass in the windows, were surrounded by tracts of mud while in the center of the village there was suddenly a new factory lit by otherwise non-existent electricity. We saw shops with lines outside while inside there were almost empty shelves, with only some gray-wrapped packages. We felt we had stepped into a political cartoon put out by the John Birch Society.

We cancelled our plans, opting for re-entering Greece instead and then going on to Turkey. When we asked a man the directions to the border town, he became belligerent, and when we tried to drive off he pulled out a gun. We stopped and it turned out our license plate was muddy. We cleaned it off and he waved us on.

"Let's get the hell out of here and back to Greece as fast as we can," my husband insisted.

The Greek border guard got into the van and demanded all our passports. He told us we had to spend the night there in the van until late morning before we got our passports back. We were eager to be off at dawn. Since I spoke the best Greek, except for our kids who were much more fluent, I protested.

"We want to leave early. This isn't hospitable," I said.

"You must wait," he was very authoritative.

I turned to my husband and said in Greek, "It's the same as Bulgaria."

All of a sudden the Greek border guard stiffened and said "No! It is NOT the same as Bulgaria."

He flung our passports back at us and said. "Leave when you wish."

I was happy and proud of Greek insistence on freedom at that moment. I thanked him and told the others in Greek, "We are truly in Greece now."

The guard smiled and wished us good night and good sleep.

We got to Istanbul the next day. The traffic was overwhelming. There seemed to be just one traffic light in the middle of a huge square and everyone ignored it. We saw a driver frustrated by delays drive up on the sidewalk in his VW bug scattering pedestrians everywhere.

It was getting late and Brian and Nicole needed a place to stay. The first few places had no rooms available. Finally, a place had a room and they went to book it. A short time later Brian came back out.

"The landlord says he has completed his Hadj, the pilgrimage to Mecca, so he can't let an unmarried couple stay in the room together. I let Nicole have the room and I'll sleep in the front seat of the van."

But in a short while a very distressed Nicole came pounding on the van windows to wake us. After we got her calmed down we learned what had upset her so.

The very virtuous landlord had given her a room with a hole in wall and was letting men pay him to peer in at Nicole. Brian stormed off in a fury. He returned with Nicole's things and their money in hand. We all slept in the van, very cramped.

The next day we found them a charming hotel frequented by international students. They happily settled in while we illegally camped on the street, using the hotel room facilities. After the bizarre first night we gratefully got the kids in bed early after washing them up in the hotel room. My husband and I poured ourselves a glass of wine and sat back toasting our success in finally relaxing in Istanbul. The curtains in the van were pulled closed and we had no lights on so we wouldn't be discovered and chased off. We peered through the gap in the curtains that separated the front of the van from the sleeping quarters and watched Istanbul street life.

We were impressed to see there were uniformed street patrols. The night watchman would walk a block and blow a whistle on the street corner. I wondered if it kept the neighborhood awake, but maybe it just assured them. There were others that greeted each other at intersections and were fairly regular on their patrols. We saw two women talking animatedly as they walked down the block together. Suddenly a man ran up behind them and grabbed a purse from one of them and ran off. The women began shouting and the night watchman ran up to them. They pointed out the direction the thief had taken and he ran off.

"He'll never catch him. The purse snatcher has too good a lead," I whispered.

But in a few moments two guards returned with the purse snatcher held between them. One of the cops triumphantly returned the purse and the women happily walked off. The cops dragged the culprit with them as they walked down the street. As they reached our van, to our horror the police rammed the man up against the van and began beating him. My husband and I held our breaths as the van rocked with each punch but it suddenly stopped. There was some chatting then all three men walked off together into the night laughing and joking.

We looked at each other nonplussed.

"He must have offered them money to not arrest him," I offered.

The following days were spent in a whirl of beauty as we visited the treasures of Aghia Sofia, Top Kapi and the spice bazaar. We went up and down the Bosporus on a delightful ferry going from Europe to Asia, back to Europe with each stop. We headed back to Greece with wonderful memories, but the most vivid one for me was witnessing crime and punishment Istanbul style.

Cairo

When Linda and I flew into Cairo, my first impression as our plane approached, was that it must be made of sand. A great Khamsin, a wind from the south-west Sahara, had blown in an impressive sandstorm. I was told the sand is so fine it seeps through weather stripping around windows into the homes and shops. It is like talcum powder, and poses a real health risk.

We were tired from a twenty-three hour journey. Linda had not been able to smoke at the Malpensa Airport where we had a lay-over in Italy and was having a nicotine fit. Then it was announced that we had to wait in the airport another two hours as the tour directors had to meet another flight bringing in more people on our tour.

"I want to smoke," Linda said. She kept insisting she didn't smoke that much, but I thought her addiction was well entrenched.

"Ask where their smoking area is," I suggested. She learned there wasn't one and sat down in a pout glowering angrily at the airport workers. "I am always thoughtful about smoking and not bothering others, so the least people can do is provide me with a place to do it."

Finally, we set off in a bus for our hotel. There was no smoking on the bus either. We drove through the sandy streets, admiring how rapidly the Cairenes were cleaning it up. Things that looked like snow plows were scraping it up and everyone was sweeping sidewalks. Trucks were collecting it from overflowing trash cans full of the powdery stuff.

The hotel on an island in the Nile, was very grand looking. It had been a palace built for Princess Eugenie of France for the opening of the Suez Canal in 1869. We were ushered up the elegant entrance and into a gilded lobby with a grand marble staircase.

People carrying trays of glasses filled with iced, bright red hibiscus tea decorated with flowers swept down the staircase smiling and welcoming us to Egypt. Linda instantly cheered up and sipped the delicious tea. We were introduced to Attia, who would be our guide and he told us our schedule. In an hour we were invited to a welcoming cocktail party in a silk-lined tent in the gardens.

Our room in a modern addition to the palace, had a balcony overlooking the gardens. I changed clothes to go to the party, but Linda declined so she could sit on the balcony and finally get her smoke.

Over the next few days we were to get to know the wonderful, dirty, polluted city of Cairo, the marvelous treasures it held, and its friendly, welcoming people. It is the most crowded city I have ever visited. That's because Nasser was a military man and he took over when the Army chased the fat old playboy, King Farouk, out of the country.

Nasser centralized everything in military fashion. If you need a driver's license, if you need a building permit, if you need a passport, if you need anything at all, you have to come to Cairo to get it. Getting anything in Egypt takes time and money. People travel from all over Egypt and finding somewhere to stay while you make your way through the bureaucratic maze is not easy.

The next day, as we passed a large cemetery Attia pointed out "grave sleepers". Families build small roofed tombs to honor their dead, and now they were renting them out to desperate people who needed a place to sleep. In parts of Cairo, apartment buildings were full of people before they were finished. Developers didn't have to pay for permits until their buildings were finished, so many simply never finished them. A five story building full of people had no electricity or elevators. Sometimes a building had no running water.

Our tour included a dinner with an Egyptian family. The family was affluent and lived on the fourth floor of a family home. There was an elevator and on every floor there was a family member with their own families.

"My in-laws live on the ground floor, my brother-in-law and his family live on the second floor, sister-in-law and her family live on the third floor. When I married my husband we added this floor," Sarah, the lady of the house told us. Her husband was out of town on business, so she and her teenaged daughter entertained us. She worked as a manager at an electronics company and wore a business suit with a short skirt.

We were served veal, two chicken dishes, soup, okra, cucumber salad and an elaborate dessert. The apartment was very elegant, with a huge salon that had several suites of furniture separated by decorated pillars, a fireplace, a grand piano and an immense television set. Sarah told us of the problems raising children in the electronic age and the changes in Egyptian life.

I admired her daughter Nina's English.

"We insist our children learn a second language. Our son Amin is learning French and Nina is learning English," Sarah said. "My son is at a French class right now."

I asked the teen what she did for fun. Her face lit up when she told us she and her brother went to an uncle's house out in the country every weekend and had a barbecue.

As we left, the lady who lived on the third floor joined us on the elevator. She wore slacks and a long-sleeved top and had a scarf around her neck. She chatted briefly with us but as we walked across the courtyard, Attia came in the gate. The woman instantly pulled the scarf over her head. She didn't mind her hair showing around Western men, but when a fellow Arab came, so did modesty.

The following day I met Tracy, an English woman who had been married to an Egyptian, had a daughter and had lived Cairo for ten years. She told us all about life in Cairo.

"Everybody drives and no one has insurance. If there is a fender bender the crowd gathers and they decide who is at fault and that driver has to give money to the other driver right then and there," she told us. "Parking is a problem, so if a lot is full, you leave your car in neutral if you are blocking someone. That way they can push your car out of the way when they want to leave."

I was to see nonchalant auto action in Alexandria a few days later where our bus was being escorted by police on motorcycles. A car drove around the bus to pass it on the right and hit one of the motorcycles. The cop got up from the ground, dusted himself off, picked up the cycle and examined it. It was undamaged and the cop just waved the car around him. I couldn't believe it. A cop at home would have had the driver locked up.

She told us Egyptian families are extremely close and visit each other all the time. "In England two months might go by before I visited my parents. That's unheard of in Egypt. You are expected to visit every weekend at least."

Attia turned us loose in the Khan El Khalili, the world's oldest and largest bazaar. Linda was in her element. She had lived in Taiwan for two years and sharpened her bargaining skills there. In the perfumers' market I wanted to buy amber oil. A man offered me a half pint bottle for twenty dollars. Linda went to work on him and by the time we left his kiosk we had two half pint bottles and two pretty vials of it for twenty dollars.

There was a gigantic area full of toy kiosks that was doing a lot of business because Bayyam was coming up. That was a four-day festival celebrating Abraham sacrificing a lamb instead of his son Isaac. Kids get toys and new clothes as part of the festival. Also, families are supposed to sacrifice lambs. In the meat part of Khan El Khalili sheep carcasses striped with bright pink dye hung everywhere. There were also live sheep for families who did it the old fashioned way, killing and dressing out the lamb themselves. Traffic jams happened because the streets of Cairo were often filled with shepherds bringing in their flocks to the sacrifice. The gold market impressed Linda.

"I've never seen so much gold in one place before," she said awed.

Linda came to our room one day after going to a café for coffee, and told me a would-be gigolo had tried to pick her up with a line about knowing her from a sporting club. She laughed. Later I went to the café to get an ice cream and enjoy the rococo elegance of the palace and the same guy tried to pick me up. Then I realized a creepy looking man was following me when I left and was walking through the gardens. I vowed not to leave my room alone at the hotel until we left for Aswan the next day.

I thought it odd that the fancy hotel made me uneasy while I walked the streets of the rest of the city feeling more secure than I did in a California city. I had bought a headscarf and discovered it was very useful for street vendors. When I pulled it over my head they quit trying to sell me stuff, and respected my privacy.

Saqqara and Egyptian Drivers
(worst in the world!)

A few of us on the tour decided we did not want to visit a carpet factory and see child labor exploited. Instead we wanted to rent a van and go visit the Step Pyramid at Saqqara. Our guide Attia was concerned and demanded to arrange for a van for us rather than allowing us to do it on our own.

A driver came with the van. Egyptian drivers are the worst in the world. They don't use headlights at night, they don't accept the concept of lanes, and use their horns instead of brakes. At the last moment another Egyptian man stepped on board our van. Under his jacket he had an Uzi. He was our security guard. We hadn't asked for one, but the government is big on protecting tourists.

As we left Cairo for the countryside I could see the dramatic difference between the Sahara and the oasis formed by the Nile. It was a definite line. You could literally put one foot in lush jungle and the other in desert.

I sat back and wondered at the fact that the world's longest river, the Nile, crosses the world's largest desert, the Sahara, and forms the world's largest oasis, Egypt.

The pyramid was interesting, but I what loved best was that about forty boys in Boy Scout uniforms were there with their scout master. I saw he had grouped them for a photograph and I offered to take a photo with him and the boys. He was delighted and so were the boys. Afterwards they crowded around me to chat and they wanted a picture of me with them so the scout master took one.

The sun was starting to set and the gates would soon be closing. Our driver seemed to be in a hurry, so we got back in the van. Just then a police car came alongside and our driver talked to him for a few moments. The policeman started up his blue flashing light and got in front of the van.

We were driving at top speed down what looked like a two-lane highway following our police escort when we saw a semi-truck coming straight at the police car. We realized suddenly we were going the wrong way on a one-way highway. We screamed as we thought we were about to see a fatal accident when the truck driver managed to pull over in front of a car in the other lane just before he was about to hit the police car.

We got to a six-lane freeway and the policeman waved to the van driver and took off. It was Cairo's rush hour and the freeway was filled with traffic. Suddenly the security guard noticed the van driver had driven past the off ramp we needed. Traffic and all, the driver did a u-turn across the median to an orchestra of beeping horns he ignored and while all of us almost had heart attacks.

When he stopped we realized why he had been in a big hurry. We were at the carpet factory and the rest of the tour was there in the bus. He probably got baksheesh if any of us bought carpets woven by the children. None of us did I am glad to say.

An Afternoon in Aswan

When I flew into Aswan, a sun-drenched Nubian city on the island-dotted Nile, I knew I had to get away from my tour group. I was used to being a woman alone, choosing my own itinerary, not part of an official group. Before I could plan an escape, we immediately changed planes to go to Abu Simbel.

At the impressive and intimidating temples, I slipped away to commune with ancient Nubia in solitude. These temples were built by Ramses II to notify anyone attempting to invade Egypt from the south, that they had better be prepared to take on a powerful, well-organized society. That and the fierce Nubian warriors at Aswan seemed to do the trick for a few thousand years.

Back at Aswan there was no escape as we were herded aboard buses complete with armed security escorts taking us to see the infamous Aswan Dam. Damn all dams to perdition. I am generally not fond of dams because they have done in so many salmon runs around the world. I was especially biased against Nasser's monument to his ego.

Nubia, which had never known rain, now has even summer rains due to man-made Lake Nasser, over two hundred miles long. The Egyptians, who love to eat, complained endlessly that their fruits and vegetables no longer had any flavor since artificial fertilizers have replaced the annual replenishing of soil by the inundations from the Blue Nile. The dam destroyed or forced the relocation of ancient temple sites, not to mention whole Nubian towns and villages.

"Lake Nasser can supply all of Egypt with electricity for eight years even if there is no rainfall," our guide told us. I pouted. He went on to say how many Egyptians had been killed building it. I said that was because the great workers' experiment, the USSR, that had built the dam, ironically didn't give a damn about worker safety, only deadlines.

Our buses finally disgorged us at our riverboat where we were to start a leisurely cruise down the Nile in a day or so. We had 45 minutes to settle into our cabins before we were taken to visit a papyrus factory. No way, I decided. I had no interest in papyrus, but I was out of money and needed a bank with an ATM. I really wanted to ride a Nubian taxi –a flimsy vehicle with men, gelibayas flowing in the wind, clinging to the outside when the seats were full. Nothing doing, my guide said. There was a law against tourists riding them, so he summoned a "tourist taxi" for me. I ungraciously yielded.

Once dropped off, free at last and with money in my pockets, I set off on a jaunt down Aswan's beautiful esplanade. It was Bayyam, a Muslim holiday celebrating Abraham's sacrifice of a lamb instead of his son. Muslims consider themselves descendants of Hagar and her son Ishmael by Abraham, who had to wander in the desert.

Muslims kill a lamb and give one third of the meat to the poor, and another third to extended family. There were grinning poor Nubian women everywhere carrying buckets of meat home. A lot of Nubians are poor since their enforced relocation and loss of farmland because of the dam. On Bayyam, kids get new clothes and toys. It was the equivalent of Christmas or Easter in Egypt. People were having picnics, crowding the restaurants and outdoor cafes, strolling around in their new finery.

I stopped at an internet café to drop a line home. I wasn't hungry because we had been relentlessly fed, but I bought street treats. I quickly attracted an entourage of little boys. My broken Arabic from a phrase book caused them great amusement as we chatted. The Nile flowed sweetly by. Egyptians smiled and greeted me until one of the boys asked for money. He had a video game in his pocket and was well dressed. Before I could say no, a man who overheard the boy, stepped up. He berated the boy and then checked with me to be sure the children weren't bothering me. He asked me to not give them any money. I assured him I would not. The boy, abashed, apologized but immediately cheered up and continued chatting as the children and I strolled on.

I am fond of most Nubians. They are high-spirited and proud. They like joking around. All Egyptians do, but none more than the Nubians. I concluded that the Egyptian mirth flowed north from Nubia, like the Nile itself. The boy had been chided to remember his pride and even when I bought some Bayyam sweets to hand out to the kids, he refused it with a big smile. Before long I realized my parole had run out. I had promised our guide I'd be back at a certain time. I wasn't sure how far I was from our boat. I wanted him to feel secure about future escapes I was planning.

There were numerous "calashes" – horse or mule drawn buggies – along the esplanade. I chose one with a healthy looking mule (Missouri mules are a popular import there) and struck a bargain with the driver. The boys and I waved good-bye; I trotted back to join the group exactly on time. I was in a much better humor. Besides, our guide had arranged a sunset sail on an Egyptian felucca below the Aswan Dam. Not everything on a tour is bad – some of it is dam good.

Some Reflections on Piety vs. Reverence

I was in Egypt at the beautiful Philae Temple to the Goddess Isis. This temple is a very special place. It sits on an island in the Nile by Aswan in Nubia. After the Aswan Dam was built, the island flooded. Boaters made a game out of running their vessels between the half submerged columns. Finally, an international massive moving operation similar to the moving of Abu Simbel was undertaken. Another rocky island was sculpted to the same formation as the original island, and the temple lovingly moved piece by piece to its new home.

Unlike Abu Simbel, the Pyramids, and Karnak, it is human in scale. It was a women's temple and seems wonderfully welcoming rather than intimidating as so many of the other temples are. It is a beautiful place.

And so I was horrified to learn that early Christians had mutilated much of the art. It wasn't easy for them to do. They had to chisel deep grooves into the high reliefs on the pylons at the entrance of the temple.

Egypt was one of the first places to turn Christian. St. Mark came there in about 50 A.D. and since the Egyptians had an all-powerful god (Ra) whose son was sacrificed (Osiris) and a loving female figure to worship (Isis), and since they had already experimented with monotheism, it was an easy conversion. Unfortunately, the Romans who had just got rid of Cleopatra and put an end to the line of pharaohs, didn't like it and pursued the new converts relentlessly. They took refuge in old temples and then proceeded to desecrate them.

Attia, our guide, seeing our distaste at the destruction, said, "We don't call them vandals. We call them pious."

I roamed the temple, and when I was tired sat at a little café by the water, feeling very much like I was on the Mediterranean rather than the Nile, and reflected on piety. I came to the conclusion it is a very suspect emotion.

I appreciate others' heart-felt faith. In Bali I met the most religious people I have ever known. But what I appreciate is their sense of reverence. Piety implies a sense of self-righteousness and the conviction that one is better than his other fellow humans because of his faith. When that happens real reverence is gone.

In temple after temple I was to see the ruinous work of the pious who lacked all reverence even for inspired beauty. It reminded me of the pious Taliban blowing up the lovely Buddha. It offended me to the depths of my soul.

And before I left Egypt I told Attia, "Pious or not, they were vandals, pure and simple."

On the Nile

In Aswan we boarded our ship to go up the Nile. On other rivers one goes "down", but the Nile is unique and stubbornly flows north, not south disorienting everyone except Egyptians.

Linda and I were impressed when we stepped on board the Anuket. There was a lobby with a marble floor and crystal chandelier where we were welcomed and shown to our cabins. Linda who had been on cruise ships before marveled at all the space we had. There were twin beds, a couch, table and chairs, desk, a small refrigerator and good sized bathroom. Our glass windows opened up to create a railed balcony.

We went up on the sun deck. I saw that as we were getting ready to leave, two guards carrying uzis boarded, one at the bow and one at the stern. Another guard on a zodiac got between us and the opposite shore. I looked for Linda but she had disappeared. A crew member asked us all to meet in the lounge on board to get the schedule. Linda wasn't there so I went to our room.

She frantically grabbed me when I walked in. "You're okay. What a relief. Men got on board with guns. Are we being hijacked?"

"Linda, those were our guards. They are here to prevent hijackings," I chuckled. She smiled in relief and we went to the lounge to learn about Kom Ombu, our first destination. The lovely temple still had some of its original colors and we found an intact ancient calendar Attia taught us to read.

There were three seasons: flood, seeding, and harvest. The year had twelve months of three weeks, and the leftover days were given over to a festival. Back on board a wild wind came up that began blowing over the chairs and tables on the sun deck. The wind blew my journal out of my hands and I had to save it from going overboard by pouncing on it with my feet. Nubian women who had come on board to paint some of the passengers with henna had to retreat to the lounge to ply their craft.

I stayed up top fascinated by Egypt unfolding before me. In some places the narrowness of oasis Egypt impressed me. All the temples were built on sand, not the fertile land, but in some places dwellings had to be built on sand as well to get any crop at all.

I longed to see an Ibis but was told I'd have to go to the Nile in Sudan to see them. Ditto for crocodiles. Egypt has too much boat traffic.

The wind subsided and others came on top including Linda. We moved on to an area where the hills were farther away and allowed the oasis to become much wider. We passed dense areas of bulrushes. Linda joked about finding baby Moses floating in them. I thought about all the problems the three major religions had caused since that baby was rescued, mostly by fighting with each other, and concluded he should have stayed in the bulrushes.

We saw fellahin villages. The women did their laundry and bathed children at the river side. I saw just one operating shaduf – the ancient donkey powered waterwheels that irrigated the fields for centuries. Nowadays, they use electric pumps instead. The fields were wildly fertile. It was cauliflower season apparently because snowy looking acres of them were ready to be harvested. I knew cucumbers must be somewhere in there, too, because I never ate an Egyptian meal that didn't offer wonderful piles of fresh cucumbers. The people always waved to us and got excited when we waved back and called salem aliakum to them. They'd call back alaikum salem. Once a little boy in rowboat tried to row out to us but he was stopped and turned back by the guard in the zodiac who constantly circled the boat as we sailed along.

Each night we anchored, each day we stopped at every temple along the way. At Edfu we were stopped by a police boat that checked out our guards. Edfu was jammed with several tour boats and the crowds inside were too claustrophobic for me so I sat in the courtyard communing with a large black granite statue of Horus the falcon god and sketching the temple. There were a lot of birds living in the temple, especially swallows. There were enough to satisfy even Horus' appetite.

We anchored at Esna where I saw a minaret under a crescent moon and heard an especially melodic muezzin call people to prayer. I felt I had somehow slipped into a tale by Scheherazade. While an entertainer in the lounge offered piano music, I much preferred listening to Nubian music which to me sounded like pure Africa. I saw our cabin boy listening to some on a cd and asked how I could get one. He appeared later at the cabin to bring us a bottle of wine Linda had ordered and gave me a copy of his cd he had made. He refused any pay for it. Minarets, the moon reflected on the Nile, Nubian music…it doesn't get any better Linda and I agreed as we sipped our wine.

Giza and Bedouins

While Cairo belonged to the Arabs, because the Pyramids and the Sphinx were in the sands, Giza belonged to the Bedouins.

Attia warned us about aggressive vendors at the Pyramids. "For years they'd ask me again and again 'When are the Americans coming back'. You are about to be very popular."

While problems in the Middle East scared Americans away from Egypt, the Europeans and Australians weren't frightened away. It turned out they seldom bought souvenirs, while Americans did in quantity. Sure enough, when the bus opened its doors we were besieged by people trying to sell us everything from toy Pyramids to postcards.

The Pyramids took my breath away. I had thought of them as they looked on a package of Camel cigarettes. From a distance they did resemble that. It was only when you were right next to the Great Pyramid that you comprehended the size. They are manmade mountains. Like mountains they exfoliate and my favorite souvenir is a piece of the Great Pyramid I picked up from the desert floor.

Bedouin policemen mounted on camels stood guard, mostly making sure no one climbed the Pyramids. On one side of the Great Pyramid was a tunnel. It had been dug by Welsh coal miners who thought they'd get to gold. They gave it up after a while. That tunnel had been taken over by a Bedouin sheik who wanted to charge me to go in it. I declined. The official entrance was closed.

I did do the tourist thing and succumbed to a Bedouin offering a camel ride on a sweet guy named Moses. One camel ride was enough for me to understand the origin of undulating Middle East dances and probable backaches.

I did pay to properly enter a smaller pyramid that was open to the public. Going in was somewhat claustrophobic and when I reached the bottom I decided to leave. Then it became *very* claustrophobic because a lot of people had come in behind me. We had to bend over, head over ass, to ascend the steep climb to the exit. We had been offered an Egyptian bean dish at every breakfast called foohl. I now knew which people in front of me had eaten foohl that morning.

At the Sphinx I saw that the mighty statue that had stared across the Sahara sands for 6000 years now gazed at a Kentucky Fried Chicken outlet. As I wandered its grounds I ran into a group of Egyptian schoolgirls on a field trip. They wanted to touch my undraped blonde hair and I let them. Then they asked me to write something for them and oohed and aahed over my writing from left to right, the reverse of Arabic. They got to practice their English and I tried out my Arabic phrases on them. We were all pleased with each other.

Linda and I left the group to buy lunch at a café. I saw stray horses wandering around the streets. As the sun began to set I saw young men whistling for their horses. They began racing up and down the streets hitting cobblestones with whips to excite the horses and get them to move faster. None of them struck their horses just the pavement. I realized it was a regular pastime.

At dark we gathered with our group again to see a French produced light show on the pyramid. It was extremely well done and ended with the fruits of the Rosetta Stone that suddenly made ancient

Egyptian literature available to the world. The narrator read passionate love poems and letters to loved ones.

I bid Giza good-bye with real fondness – happy teenagers on horseback, passionate love poems.

Love and Marriage Egyptian Style

One afternoon the ship was going to pass by the sugar factories along the Nile for a few hours. Since it would be uninteresting the guides invited us to the lounge for "*Guides' Day*". "No topic is off the table: politics, sex, schools, whatever." They meant it and for a few hours we got a lot of insight into Egyptian life.

Attia described how he courted and married his wife. He met his wife at a friend's wedding. Both of them were much more modern than most Egyptians. She worked as a professional and lived with her family. Egyptians live with their parents until they marry as a rule, but Attia's job had taken him away from his birthplace in Alexandria to Cairo, so he lived on his own.

The two saw each other frequently over the next year although he wasn't clear about if they dated. That is rare in Egypt. But they had exchanged phone numbers, and somehow they both "accidentally" showed up at the same places at the same time. Finally deciding she was too good to let slip away, he asked her to marry him.

Now, here in America, that would have ended it because the couple would have simply set a date, met each other's families and got married. In Egypt things are not so simple. Until this generation, parents arranged marriages for their children, and while the current generation chooses their own mates, parents still count a lot.

Attia had to go to his parents, traveling to Alexandria, she to hers. He explained all the particulars to his parents and told his father what he would agree to about providing for his future wife. His wife-to-be also went to her parents and explained why Attia would make a good husband and how he could provide for her and any children they might have. Then the two sets of parents met to make arrangements.

"We couldn't say a word out of respect for our parents," Attia said. "So I am sitting there infuriated, listening to my father agree to things I had told him I *didn't* want, but I now had to accept."

He was already forty years old and because of his work as a guide for a foreign company, had been able to purchase an apartment. That was in his favor, but the parents of Egyptian women can and usually do require that their daughters have some sort of independent money of their own. Attia had to buy some gold for his wife worth quite a bit of money. Some couples have to work and save several years to meet their parents' requirements. It took a total of two years for Attia and his wife.

When the time finally came, the two fathers went to a mosque. There they signed a contract. They shook hands, their hands were covered with a handkerchief while an imam said an oath over it and the couple was married without even being present. They were then free to have a party that Attia had agreed at the meeting to pay for.

And that's how you get married in Egypt. It ain't as easy as running to a wedding chapel in Reno. In fact, the difficulty of providing all that is necessary is so onerous that the average age of marriage for Egyptian males is now 35, and for women 29. "For Egypt that is late, very late compared to what it used to be," Attia explained.

Attia said the stress of modern life had taken its toll, and the divorce rate has climbed up to thirty percent now. Individual couples make their own arrangements but the man is expected to give his ex-wife fifty percent of what he makes unless she remarries, in which case he is off the hook. If children are involved the women seldom remarry since stepfathers are looked down on.

And, yes, under Islamic law a man can have four wives, but there are catches. Most men find it hard enough to support one family, and the first wife must agree to any new wives. And Egyptian wives are as likely to do that as non-Mormon American wives.

A Coffee Break in Egypt

The day before we were to leave Egypt, Linda and I stopped at an outdoor café to have a cup of coffee.

The only coffee they had was Turkish coffee, a fierce brew served in teeny tiny cups. Even then you get to drink only about half of what is in the cups and the other half is coffee grounds. Once, when I lived on a Greek island, a wise woman had taught me how to read the future in those grounds. I offered to do it for my friend.

Linda was enthusiastic so when she finished her potent sip, I had her turn the cup upside down in its saucer and turn it three times. Then we sat and waited for the grounds to dry and leave patterns on the cup. When it was ready, I took it and explained how some shapes meant men, some women, small round drops represented coins and therefore wealth and such. Out of those patterns you read a course of action you can take in your future.

Apparently, the Egyptians around me realized what I was doing and suddenly we were surrounded by several. They insisted on buying me cups of coffee along with their own and asked me to read their grounds. We spent a couple pleasant hours with them all – each in turn buying me more coffee.

I can handle alcohol fairly well, but caffeine is another thing. By the time we left the café I had had about five of those teeny tiny cups of dynamite.

When we left to go back to our riverside hotel in Cairo, I was full of energy. We had a late night dinner on a houseboat palace complete with marble floors and crystal chandeliers. I danced a lot. It was midnight when the ensuing party broke up and our guide abruptly announced that we had a 3 a.m. wake-up call in order to get to the airport and go through the stringent security measures there.

Everyone else groaned, but I was still well enough caffeinated that I was up for it.

Linda and I went to our room and I began packing while she just fell on the bed. I looked upon the Nile with the moon shining down.

"Linda," I shook my friend, "I have an idea. We are just alongside the river. Let's take a walk see if we can find someone who'll rent us a boat for an hour and let's go rowing on the Nile. It would be a great way to end our stay in Egypt."

"Are you out of your bleeping mind?" was her reply.

I still tried to talk her into it, but she reminded me we had to still pack. We had bought some ceramics to bring back to our children from Egypt. I always fill extra space in my suitcase with bubble wrap and I travel with duct tape ever since I went to Africa and realized I could have fixed so many broken things if I only had had a roll of the useful stuff. I brought it out and carefully wrapped all our treasures, at that point there was no room in my suitcase for anything but the treasures and I still had a lot of bubble wrap left.

"Let's pop it," Linda suggested. Everyone loves popping bubble wrap especially the kind with giant bubbles like I had.

We giggled and popped a few with our fingers then I said, "Look we have enough to dance on it."

We spread it out on the floor and began boogying. It made loud satisfying pops rapidly, when suddenly someone banged on our door. I unlocked it and there stood our security guard who had been at the end of the hall on sentry duty. He looked very worried as he bounded into the room. Then he saw the bubble wrap and burst out laughing. He had thought someone with a gun had broken into our room. We shame-facedly put the rest of the bubble wrap in the trash can and promised to be quiet.

He went off shaking his head and still laughing.

In no time we were being loaded into buses headed for the airport. I sat next to Linda and remarked, "We got in more trouble with the bubble wrap than if we had rented a boat for a moonlight spin on the Nile."

Linda yawned, and sighed, "Andrea, from now on you cannot have ANY caffeine after noon. That's a new travel rule for us."

I have obeyed that rule faithfully ever since.

Just A-Goin' Over Jordan

It was my first and only emergency landing so far. I was not afraid.
I was too busy trying to calm the hysterical young woman beside me.
I was teaching her a yoga breathing exercise and she was finally not
yelling or sobbing although she gripped my hand so hard it was badly
bruised afterwards.

"You're fine," I told her, playing the part of a wise grandmother. "If
it was my time, I would know it. It's not so you're okay, too."

The intercom came on. "Do not be alarmed by all the emergency
vehicle lights when we land," the captain said as we approached the
runway. "We are doing fine."

He had earlier announced our wing extenders had frozen and failed
to bleed off airspeed. We were landing at 400 miles per hour and
relying on brakes alone to stop us on time. The captain had also
announced all other flights at JFK were stopped until we landed
safely.

We thumped down and the world sped past us in a blur and with loud
squeals from our brakes. We were safe, and although our tires had
smoked and tried to burn we even got to a gate – so no slides.

I should have realized there would be trouble on board.

I had flown from San Francisco to New York City via Miami on
American Airlines to give myself plenty of layover time to change
flights and still catch my red-eye flight to the country of Jordan
where a group of travel journalists along with me had been invited
to a twelve day "Royal Tour". Instead the flight from Miami to JFK
was twelve hours late. A short-lived thunderstorm had caused a half
hour delay and the original crew of the plane had been reassigned. It
took the full twelve hours to find a new crew. I finished the

paperback I had brought for the flight as I waited and left it behind for the next stranded traveler.

In Miami as soon as I was finally buckled in, I noticed the seat in front of me was broken and tilted sideways. My seatmate and I shook our heads. We had never seen that before. Then I noticed the inner plastic window shield was hanging loose by one screw. I realized the reading light was burned out as well. I pointed it out to my seatmate.

"I just hope nothing out there is broken," I said pointing out toward the engines, thinking it was a joke.

The joke was on me. The plane made alarming kathunk noises as it taxied. The airline was going through financial turmoil then in 2006 and not long afterwards the employees bought it out. Somewhere along the way routine maintenance had failed.

I rushed through the airport still hoping to catch the Royal Jordanian Airline plane. The plane had not left yet, but TSA was closed, the workers just packing up. The Jordanian desk was also closed, so no go.

Several of us lined up at the American Airlines counter hoping for hotel vouchers. The woman behind me had also been bound for Jordan. Because of the emergency landing all flights had been delayed, so she too had missed her connection. The hotels in the area were all booked because of all the canceled flights. The closest hotel with rooms was a forty-five minute drive away. American Airlines didn't care about me although it had made me miss my flight, but my new acquaintance was scheduled to fly out on American so the airline would provide a ride and room for her. She offered to share her free ride. Fortunately, the distant hotel had a lot of rooms. The next morning, I bought her breakfast out of gratitude for her sharing her rides from and to the airport. She was going to Jordan on an expensive tour.

Lebanon and Israel were hurling missiles at each other. Jordan was not involved but was losing valuable tourism dollars over the conflict. Thus, the invitation to us American travel writers. My new acquaintance had an early flight, mine was late, so I spent a day at JFK reading a novel I bought at a kiosk and learning to play and develop an addiction to Sudoku.

I discovered the gate used by Jordanian Royal Airlines was only available to it a few hours a day. Other countries got other time slots at the same place. At long last the TSA line formed for the plane to Jordan. I was wearing my press pass and suddenly heard someone shouting my name. Gisele from the Jordanian Tourism Bureau who had originally invited me came running up. She, too, had missed the flight the night before because of the emergency landing.

"Get out of line and come with me," Gisele said. "I am going to try and get us on first class."

I saw her waving papers at an official and the next thing I knew, long line notwithstanding, I was being ushered into the royal class cabin that had been designed for their king. It was definitely good to be the king, and it was very welcome after wasting two days in airports and the harrowing landing. Each seat was well separated from the others and could be declined to be entirely flat. We had seven feet of legroom. We each had our own attendant who promptly served us all cocktails, offered appetizers, and took a dinner order. I ordered a steak which arrived perfectly cooked.

We were given a "comfort kit" which contained expensive Dead Sea toiletries and we were offered the chance to shower on board. I checked out the ladies' shower (there was also one for the gents). It too had lovely toiletries. Full sized pillows were handed out and we got tucked in.

In the morning our ever attentive flight attendants were ready with coffee and a full breakfast. As we neared the capital city of Amman, I looked out at a new desert. I had seen the Sahara, but now I would meet the Arabian Desert.

The Hashemite
Kingdom of Jordan

The city of Amman was not much more than a mud village until 1921when it was declared the capital. They broke a World War I treaty with the Arabs as the Europeans are wont to do (ask any Native American!) then divied up the Middle East among each other, creating Jordan.

Lawrence of Arabia was part of the history, and the famous movie made about the era starring Peter O'Toole was shot on location in Jordan. And Jordan does not let you forget it. You hear the theme song playing everywhere: hotels, restaurants, tourist shops.

As it is a new city, Amman is dazzling. Built of a lot of white limestone, the government should issue sunglasses before you get there because it can blind you in the desert sun. Its many broad avenues are lined with trees and everywhere people have planted flowers. No one loves gardens as much as desert people do. It's exceptionally clean. To my surprise the Arabs there do not use Arabic numerals. They use an Indian numeric form since much of their trade came from India. I had fun deciphering license plates.

Our tourism office guides whisked us through custom formalities. We were taken to our luxurious hotel where a beautifully costumed man with an elaborate silver contraption with spouts on his back offered us glasses of mint lemonade as we entered. Our guides Gisele and Ibrahim enjoyed our surprise at the exotic offering.

There were ten of us in the press crew. We learned it wasn't just the current conflict next door that had prompted the government to invest in a press trip. The year before, in 2005, Jordan had experienced its own form of the 9/11 attacks. On 11/9 (a date deliberately chosen I am sure) a group of terrorists had entered four of the best hotels carrying concealed bombs and blown up the lobbies, killing sixty people, most of them at a wedding at the Radisson, and also one famous American film director.

Jordan was taking no chances. The hotel lobby had metal detectors and screened areas to the side for searches. One was manned by policewomen who searched any female who wore modest robes. Pant-suited or mini-skirted females could just walk through the metal detectors. One of the terrorists had been a woman wearing long robes who pretended she was pregnant. She survived her suicide attempt and had recently stood trial.

"She was executed this week," Ibrahim told us. I asked how.

"They strangled her."

Maybe the Jerk is You This Time

Like any traveling group, a press trip inevitably has one person who behaves inappropriately and embarrasses the rest. In fact, there's a saying among travel writers "If you don't know who the jerk is on a trip, maybe this time it is you."

This press trip was made up of mostly seasoned journalists. Gisele, one our guides, was a princess. Tall beautiful, multi-lingual, she was originally from Brazil but after traveling to New York she landed the Jordanian job and was making a real success of it. Ibrahim, our other guide was a single, fun loving Jordanian. Anita, a fellow journalist, was a Sicilian New Yorker who had lived in Iran for twenty years until she and her diplomat husband were forced to leave in a hurry when the revolution occurred.

"We could easily have been among the hostages, but we escaped just in time," she told me. Her husband had been transferred to Portugal and they now had a retirement home in New Jersey. She had four children, eight grandchildren and one great grandchild. Two of her daughters had joined her for the trip on their own dime. They were so happy to be united their joy infected all the rest of us.

Alexandra, one of them, lived in Wales with her husband and five children. They owned a business and she did all the computer and graphics work. She was a sculptor and studied physics and astronomy. Her sister Sally worked as an Arabist in Iraq for an American company. She also knew ancient classical Arab as well as modern, and studied ancient poetry, translating it. Ibrahim quickly became smitten with beautiful Alexandra and showered her with attention, much to single Sally's chagrin. I was smitten by the whole fascinating family.

We also had Dan, a Brit transplanted in America, who daily recorded a radio broadcast for a Christian radio station. He was very laid back and easy to get along with. He and I hung out a lot together. Stu was a young man who always found something to complain about and was singularly lacking in humor.

Nancy was a thorough career woman from New York. She had a caustic sense of humor and was very witty.

The jerk this time was Emma. An older woman and not especially attractive, she somehow had decided in a Muslim country that she was a beautiful teenager and could flirt with every man, squirming and giggling like a middle schooler. Nancy and I became friends when we confessed our mutual feelings about Emma to each other.

As we traveled around Jordan together we began a joke group project. We made up an Agatha Christie type murder mystery set in Jordan adding chapters as we traveled from place to place. At Petra we decided the novel should open with a scream coming out of The Siq the canyon leading to the ancient site. Once, as we created chapters for each other, Nancy leaned over and whispered, "Please let's kill off Emma in it."

Once when Emma and I were in an elevator in the Amman Marriot, a man got on. Emma went into her routine squirming, giggling, making totally stupid remarks to the man.

She got off before I did. Before she left she said. "Oh, now that your competition is going, you have the only man all to yourself."

When the doors closed, I turned to him to apologize for her behavior gesturing that she was crazy.

He shrugged and said, "It's okay. She's old and ugly."

I told Nancy the next day and she burst into laughter.

Switzerland of the Middle East

Jordan has no oil and is officially a "water poor" nation. But it has one incredibly valuable resource in the troubled Middle East – peace. It is not an easy item to export, but people flock to Jordan when they need it. And the small kingdom offers a neutral table when it is time to sit down and negotiate for it. Thus it earned its nickname "The Switzerland of the Middle East."

When I was there the Iraqi War was raging, and many Iraqi business people had hopped over the border to set up shop. The government allowed them to do so as long as they employed out of work Jordanians. There was a vast building boom going on. More recently peaceful Jordan has taken in tens of thousands of Syrian refugees.

Jordan's former king, Hussein, was nicknamed The Little King That Could by western diplomats. He tried to bring his kingdom into the modern world and created Royal Jordanian Airlines. His fourth and last wife was Lisa Halaby, an American architect and urban planner. She was named Queen Noor. She pitched in finding ways to make the lives of the women of Jordan better without upsetting cultural norms. Bedouin women weren't supposed to work outside the home, so she created craft co-ops that were so successful many women ended up hiring their husbands. Hussein's oldest son from his second marriage to an English woman, King Abdullah, carries on his father's work.

We spent two days exploring the 'lost city" of Petra. An amazing natural gorge called The Siq stretches for a mile creating the world's most dramatic city gate. I rode a horse-drawn buggy between its echoing, eerie rock walls.

Petra is huge. It holds some hundreds of carved tombs. The most famous one stands directly across from the The Siq so it is the first thing you see as you enter Petra. Anyone who has seen the movie *Indiana Jones and the Last Crusade* has seen the Treasury. However, it isn't filled with booby trapped caverns. It was never a treasury; it is a tomb. There is just one simple room with niches for the dead carved into its walls. But it has a giant, gorgeous exterior.

An ancient people called Nabateans inhabited Petra and it was on a major trading route. Early Christians later moved in and built monasteries on the mountain slopes. Ibrahim told us donkey pack rides offered to take us up into the mountains to the monasteries that were hours off for an overnight stay. The closest monastery was a two hour hard uphill hike. It was blazingly hot and I decided to forgo it. Instead I sat at an outdoor café eating chicken schawarma and bargaining with Bedouin kids for trinkets. I looked forward to the evening because we were to stay and walk The Siq by candlelight.

Bedouins lived in Petra more recently. When it was made a UNESCO World Heritage site they had to move out but Queen Noor had a new village complete with a school and health clinic built for them nearby. They were also granted the concessions within Petra so all cafes and gift shops were run by Bedouins. I saw some Bedouins, despite the rules, had managed to move back into some of the tombs and cave-like homes carved into the stone mountains. I saw curtains on the rock windows, camels tied up outside, washing hung on clothes lines.

All us writers were anxious to see The Siq and Petra by candlelight. The walk down the gorge was lovely and when we reached the end the sight of the desert floor lit by candles and small fires was breathtaking. It was as if we had stepped back in time to when Petra housed its ancient people. But a Bedouin man who was supposed to tell us caravansary tales began to speak, he broke the spell. The old grouch instead whined and complained and begged for money.

When we told Ibrahim and Gisele about it they were outraged and said they were going to arrange to have him replaced at the Tourism Board. He was paid to entertain visitors, not to wheedle money out of them.

The following day we visited Little Petra, an ancient caravan pit stop, also Nabatean and fascinatingly beautiful with its natural rock formations.

The Petra Hotel was very luxurious and had a rooftop nightclub. We were at dinner when Nancy told me she had met a taxi-cab driver who for just ten dollars each would drive us out into the desert to meet a Bedouin family at their tent. I was happy to go. Ibrahim was apprehensive. He insisted on meeting the driver, getting his cell phone number, giving us his cell phone number and telling us to call him if there were problems.

Instead it proved to be my most memorable night in Jordan.

We left the road and drove across the desert to one of the large black tents we had seen from a distance. It seemed the family was asleep and I was concerned and didn't want to wake them, but the family instantly poured out and welcomed us inside. The woman of the family put a kettle of water on a fire to make us tea. Her name was Naman and she and I instantly realized this was a meeting of matriarchs. The taxi driver, a cousin of the husband, translated for us. Naman's husband and their daughters sat with us around the fire as our tea brewed. She was clearly the most intelligent one of the family and the rest all looked up to her.

She had four children. Her son had a severe eye problem and could not bear a lot of light. Naman let me know she had settled their nomadic family near Little Petra so her children could attend school in the village Queen Noor had built and their son could get the medical care he needed at the clinic.

She let me know proudly that she had woven the fabric that made their home. It was a spacious five-room goat hair tent. It even had a shower room. I told her my husband and I had built our home, but her efforts outstripped ours. She learned that I had three children and six grandchildren. Nancy, whose life style was totally foreign to Naman, just quietly sat and watched us smiling.

After a while Naman suggested we all follow a Bedouin custom. We put out a lantern and left the fire to sit out in the desert under the stars and talk some more. The stars were brilliant, the night, except for an occasional goat bleat, was quiet. Our talk was punctuated by long, comfortable silences. Finally, the taxi driver told us Ibrahim had insisted we get back by a certain time, so we had to leave.

Naman came up to me and embraced me, kissing my cheek and I kissed hers. I handed her husband some money. "For your son's eyes," I said. Nancy also gave him some money. As we drove back to the hotel and night club, and a relieved Ibrahim, Nancy said, "That was magical." I agreed.

Wadi Rum – Me and Lawrence of Arabia

I felt like Lawrence of Arabia, or at least like Peter O'Toole who played the famous soldier in the movie, when the sheik (Anthony Quinn) astride a black stallion, commands him in a great voice to "Come to my tents at Wadi Rum!"

Jordan's magic rock formations and valley in the Arabian Desert began weaving its spell as soon as we approached it. Giant mountains of red rock rose dramatically out of the golden sands, and loomed over our small group.

Sculpted by the winds and sand the mountain outcroppings called "jebels" were twisted into columns and sheer buttes. Their massive presence reminded me of Yosemite Valley. A striking formation behind the visitor's center has been renamed Seven Pillars of Wisdom after T.E. Lawrence's book. In reality, the book is named after a passage in the Bible, not a place, although Lawrence really loved Wadi Rum and spent a lot of time there, accurately describing it as "vast, echoing and godlike."

The new visitor's center at the entrance to Wadi Rum fit perfectly into the landscape. Made of a stone that is the same gold color as the desert, it looked as if the French Foreign Legion should be stationed there. Instead, we were greeted by some members of the local Bedouin tribe and invited into a small restaurant for lunch.

As always in Jordan, the food was excellent: fresh salads, chicken stewed with vegetables and rice, the ever-present flat bread, and hummus.

After the meal we climbed into the back of a pair of jeeps and our new Bedouin friends drove us off into the roadless sands. As we raced across the desert just small piles of stones once in a while marked the way. My heart skipped a beat whenever our drivers leaped a dune. It almost stopped altogether as the mountains unfolded their beauty.

We stopped by some graceful dunes and got to climb them. We rested in the shade while our guide, Ibrahim, talked to us about Wadi Rum. He clearly loved the place.

Because it has some springs, Wadi Rum has always been populated. Even the mysterious ancient people who built the remarkable city of Petra in the sixth century BC, the Nabataeans, occupied it and carved a temple in one of the jebels. We could see some of their carvings on a wall chiseled out of the rock.

During World War I the Arab tribes, with encouragement and arms from the British, united at Wadi Rum to form the Arab League in order to defeat the Ottoman Empire. The Brits promised the tribes independence if they did so, but reneged on the promise, and, with the French, carved up the Middle East to suit themselves. They created such artificial countries as Iraq and Lebanon, thereby helping to create the troubles the area faces today.

Lawrence, who fought with the League, was glorified in the press by an American journalist. Jordanians may or may not know of Lawrence (and many look on him as an opportunist who used the tribes) but they all know of the Arab League and take great pride in its achievements. The League flag still flies over the fort in Aqaba on the Red Sea coast where it won a decisive victory.

Wadi Rum led a quiet life until it was invaded for two years by the film crew making Lawrence of Arabia in the 1960s. The movie attracted a few adventurous visitors afterwards. Then it sank back into its desert silence until 1984 when a British mountaineering team got permission from the government to explore Wadi Rum to see if it offered good climbing opportunities. It did indeed and the team wrote a good book about it.

Suddenly tourism took on a new importance. The Zalabieh tribe created cooperatives to provide guides, camps` and services. They used their new-found income to build a school and some even left their tents to move into new houses.

Back in our jeeps we continued to explore the desert. We passed Bedouin camps. They all had camels and some had Land Rovers parked beside their livestock. We stopped to look at some prehistoric petroglyphs on one jebel. A boy on his camel rode over to look at us curiously and grin.

We waved good-bye to him as we left to explore some more canyons between the jebels. We stopped in the shade of one and were invited to all split up and walk away so we could experience the desert alone for a while.

I wandered off watching the wind create dust devils in the distance, baking in the sun, resting in shady spots. I found the desert was not barren like the jebels. Small valiant shrubs grew here and there – camel food, I guessed – and I even found a type of wild melon growing on a healthy vine that crept over the dunes. It was a far cry from the really barren sands of the Sahara.

Eventually we all wandered back and found our drivers had taken out a small spirit stove and were brewing us all tea. The hot, sweet, strong beverage tasted good.

In the distance we saw a small camel caravan. Bedouins were leading some tourists to a camp. In the quiet desert we suddenly heard an engine and another jeep came roaring over the dunes from an entirely different direction. The Bedouin driving it screeched to a stop and hopped out to meet us. He had a big bristly moustache just like one man in our group. The two men grinned at each other and admired each other's ornamental face hair, good naturedly posing for photos. He was given tea, too.

The sun was westering and the color of the stone was changing in the light, getting more rosy and glowing. We drove madly, the drivers in a race with each other, and the desert dunes gave way to an enormous flat dry lake bed.

At the far side of the lake bed we found Captain's Desert Camp, our home for the night.

More Bedouins greeted us and led us to our individual tents. They were genuine handspun and handwoven goat hair tents. The Bedouin women take pride in their workmanship, sewing the heavy cloth strips into roomy shelters. In the rain the hair shrinks becoming water-tight and in the sun it stretches and lets air through.

This was a luxury camp. Sofas, tables and cushions surrounded a fire pit and one tent held flush toilets and showers. We were offered more sweet tea or spiced coffee.

Locals had showed up at the camp entrance with lots of noisy camels, offering us rides if we wished, but we elected to walk and climb the low jebel that sheltered the camp to watch the sun set.

The lakebed was surrounded by camps, some playing loud music, celebrating the next to the last night before Ramadan began.

When we returned to our camp our hosts were preparing a treat for our dinner – a type of desert barbecue, with the lamb and chicken being buried in the sand with hot coals. They unearthed our meal and unwrapped it with a dramatic flourish.

We sat on our cushions and ate under the stars. Afterwards we persuaded them to douse the lights. The night sky blazed with the

Milky Way. The celestial show was so spectacular some of us decided to sleep outside rather than in our tents.

In the morning, coffee and breakfast were prepared and we packed up to leave lovely Wadi Rum.

Ibrahim told us our next stop was Aqaba. Once again a scene from Lawrence of Arabia came to mind – when hundreds of Bedouins on Arabian horses and camels stormed out of Wadi Rum at full speed shouting "To Aqaba!" Remembering the wild, heart-throbbing scene, I stood in our van and shouted "To Aqaba!" My companions stood and shouted with me as Ibrahim and the driver laughed. No camels, no beautiful Arabian steeds, just a mini-bus but to Aquaba we went.

The Unexpected Roman Army and the Earring Guy

We spent a day and a night in Aqaba. The port is on the Red Sea. Jordan has gone to great lengths to protect the coral reefs that are in its waters. A bridge connects Jordan with Israel. There is a lot of traffic back and forth. The day after the peace treaty between the countries was signed, thousands of Israelis poured into Jordan to visit Petra. There was such an excess of tourism that the government appealed to the United Nations and got UNESCO World Heritage status to protect the precious ruins.

We rode in a glass bottom boat to view the fish and corals. It was so warm I was tempted to dive overboard but our guides gave a thumbs down on that.

That evening, as much as I enjoyed most of my travel companions, I needed a break and took a walk alone along the esplanade. I noticed a necklace my daughter would like in the window of a shop and went in to inquire about it. A man my age sat at a table where he had his jewelry making equipment laid out as he fashioned more pieces. He worked quietly as I browsed. I found another piece and approached him to pay for the two necklaces I wanted.

He was friendly and introduced himself to me, so I responded with my name.

"And you are from America?" he asked.

"Yes, San Francisco in California." He grinned.

He said I should have earrings to match the necklaces I was buying and he began making them for me.

"Gratis, free," he said. He then asked if my husband was traveling with me. I told him I was a widow and he then told me he was divorced. By then he had finished the earrings.

"But I can make you some to go with the necklace you are wearing. A beautiful woman like you should not remain a widow," he said.

It took a while before I could leave politely to return to the hotel. By that time I had seven pairs of earrings.

At one point our journey also took us to Jerash. It is an extraordinary Roman city remarkably well preserved. It's in better shape than the ruins in Rome. The Jordanians host an international music festival there every few years that draws thousands from Europe and Middle East.

As we were walking the "Street of Columns", an impressive sight, I saw a guide leading a group of tourists begin banging on a column with a pipe. It rang out with a musical tone.

I asked Ibrahim, "Are guides allowed to do that?"

Ibrahim laughed. "It doesn't hurt them, and he is demonstrating the ancient earthquake alarm system."

"What?"

He then explained that the stone used to create the columns was very resonant, and as soon a minor tremor started, gave off a sound. That gave the people of Jerash a few seconds to flee outside before stones began to fall. I wondered if San Francisco could import some of those columns.

Jerash also had an intact hippodrome where chariot races used to be held. There we were surprised by a show Ibrahim and Gisele had planned for us. There are a group of Jordanian men who have made it their passion to study ancient Roman warfare practices.

First, they had a chariot race for us. It was very exciting and looked more than a little dangerous when the horses rounded the sharp bends at top speed pulling those light chariots. That in itself would have made our day, but then an army of men dressed in ancient battle uniform took the field. Each man wore a sword and carried a shield and spear.

The "General" described what they were doing and shouted orders. As the men marched toward us sitting on the ancient stone grandstand he shouted "Turtle!"

Instantly the army disappeared behind an iron wall resembling a turtle shell. Soldiers knelt and on the edges raised their shields while those in the center held them high overhead. Every man was protected. They demonstrated several maneuvers including a typical battle stance.

"Each man stood in front for just six minutes," explained the General. "He had to fight his best but only that long, then the man behind him came forward to take his place. It was one of secrets of the Romans' success. Unless the enemy began to figure it out, the enemy always faced a fresh fighter."

The finale of the show was a gladiator battle. Fortunately, no one lost limbs, received real wounds or was killed, but we got to decide the fate of the loser, not with thumbs up or down, according to the General. The army had done its historical research and the genuine gesture involved the whole arm. We "killed" him.

The Jordanian Romans were so good at what they did, they had been invited to go on tour internationally. One of the venues, of course, was Rome.

Ramadan at the Dead Sea

It was the first night of Ramadan and we were in a very romantic resort and health spa, the Movenpick, on the Dead Sea. The place was built like an Arabian Nights fairytale village. An artificial stream led down the hillside to the infinity pools overlooking the sea. Gardens grew all along the meandering stream and songbirds had moved into the blossoming bushes.

The pools linked together except for the salt water one and I had swum from one to another, sometimes between fountains. Finally, I had gone down to the beach. There two Lebanese bathing beauties whose parents had fled to Jordan until the skirmish in their homeland ended, were totally covered in Dead Sea mud. It was very black mud and the young women looked tar babies.

We chatted and they persuaded me to rub some of the goop on myself. I did but in a few minutes it began to sting and irritate me so I ran to the shower conveniently placed nearby just for ridding oneself of the sticky mud.

I tried to wade into the water but it knocked my feet out from under me. I had to sit and hunch myself in to get in water deep enough to float. You can't swim in the buoyant water and you can't sink either. You also can't get sunburned. The sea is almost 1400 feet below regular sea level and there is all that additional atmosphere shielding bodies from the sun. A German man floating in an inner tube had very pale skin and the ladies told me he had been out there for a few hours and had not turned the slightest shade of pink.

I knew the sea was 1000 feet deep which made it the lowest place on earth. I made my way back up to the pool that overlooked it. I wanted to get the salt off of me.

That evening our Swiss host held an elegant sit-down dinner for us. Usually meals were served buffet style. The food was very good so I didn't mind the buffets, but it was a luxury to actually have someone serve us. Hans explained that this was an iftar, the meal after the sun goes down during Ramadan. The first iftar and last one of Ramadan are the most important.

Ibrahim told us about Ramadan fasting. People get up before the sun to eat a good breakfast so they can make it through the day. Those who are ill, pregnant women and travelers who go more than fifty miles are exempted from the fast as are small children. But children like to try. Ibrahim told us his five year old nephew bragged, "I fasted for two hours!" The family applauded him.

As soon as it gets dark everyone feasts at the iftars. After dinner we were invited to a silk tent lined with beautiful rugs and cushions and water pipes were brought out. All sorts of special desserts only made during Ramadan were brought out. Musicians came to play for us. It was all quite lovely.

I had thought of Ramadan as being stern and sacrificial like Lent, but I discovered it was anything but. Of course, I had had lunch and the devout had not.

Where Bible Stories were Born

Dan, our traveling Christian broadcaster, went into ecstasies whenever we got to see a place mentioned in the Bible, and there were many.

In the amphitheater in Jerash he learned Christians and lions had met many times. He stood where the slaughter had happened to record his impressions as he wept.

We visited Crusader castles where religious battles had raged in the Middle Ages. They were gloomy places. The best part of a castle for me was the sally port. The wide tunnels where armies rode out to battle were dramatic spaces full of echoes.

We were taken to Mount Nebo where a third century monastery sits and where beautiful mosaics were being carefully excavated by archaeologists. Dan and I stood on the peak where Moses and Joshua had stood so many centuries before as they plotted to invade the land of milk and honey then known as Canaan. Dan and I were duly impressed with such ancient history.

"Look off there," Ibrahim pointed in the distance. "That's Jericho. The oldest city continuously inhabited in the world."

I began singing the old spiritual *Joshua Fought the Battle of Jericho*, and Dan joined me. "And the walls came tumbling down," we concluded while Ibrahim looked amused. He didn't know the song but he liked it.

Ibrahim had explained that Muslims feel that like Jews, they are descendants of Abraham, but they feel they are not descended through Isiah, but through Abraham's other older son Ishmael, whose mother Hagar was turned out into the desert when Sarah gave birth. They also believe Jesus was a prophet, but because he was murdered, he didn't finish his task so must return. So, Muslims believe in the Second Coming. Mohammed, on the other hand, finished his job is the general belief. He doesn't have to come back.

Another place we visited was the River Jordan. It was less than impressive, alas. The Israelis have made the desert bloom by draining much of its water leaving only a small murky stream for much of the year. Jordan is in negotiations because its government says Israel has violated water agreements. Murky and sad, nonetheless, it was THE River Jordan. This is where John the Baptist baptized Christ.

A small hut of a chapel dating to the first century has been found and it is believed it is on the very spot on the river where the famous baptism happened. To get to it meant a hard, muddy crawl on a steep bank. Dan was game, but I was not, so I handed the local ranger who guarded the area, an empty water bottle to bring me back some of the water from the spot. I knew my mother, who was a devout Christian, would prize such a souvenir from the Holy Land.

The government is spending seven million dollars to build a visitor center nearby the spot. A traditional market place and a memorial to John the Baptist were on the drawing board, we were told. Maybe there will be new water agreements and there will be more water in the Jordan by then.

We left, driving to Zoar where Lot and his daughters fled when Sodom and Gamorrah were destroyed and mom turned into a pillar of salt.

On the way back to our hotel we crossed a bridge and Ibrahim casually mentioned that it was under that bridge that the Prophet Isiah had slept and had his vision of angels climbing a ladder to God. I was jolted. Another ancient place was just casually acknowledged. If you visit Jordan, don't bother with a guide book, just bring a Bible.

Are Arranged Marriages Doomed?

I was in Amman. We were due to leave in the morning. My fellow travel companions had left the bus with our guides to climb a high rock famous in an Old Testament story. I stayed in the bus with our driver Jamal. He and I liked each other and had often chatted during meal breaks and while driving.

Somehow the question of marriage in Jordan came up. I knew in many places marriages were arranged by parents, not by the young people themselves. I asked if he would arrange his seven children's marriages.

"My son is the oldest. He is almost old enough to be married but I will never choose his wife for him. When I was his age I loved a girl very much. But my father picked out a different bride for me and I obeyed him.

"It was a great mistake. I was never in love with my wife and she knew it. I later saw the woman I loved and realized I still loved her. We saw each other whenever we could. My poor wife – the only thing that made her happy was to have children.

"That is why I have seven children and she wants another until my son marries and gives her grandchildren. I can't deny her that happiness when I know I have never loved her.

"Because I obeyed my father there are three unhappy adults and too many children. So, no, I will arrange no marriages for my children and my wife agrees."

Section 9:
South of the Border

Off to Mexico in a Marshmallow

There was a memorable three-month trip to Mexico before I was widowed. Our daughter Heather was fifteen and in love. Her brothers were thirteen and four. The reason for the trip was my husband and I were homesick for Greece where we had lived for two years [see *It's Greek to Me,* my book about those years]. We thought perhaps Mexico could help us find that simplicity again so we made a three month trip to see if we wanted to emigrate.

We did not find Greece. Instead we found wild, vivid, colorful Mexico and eventually chose to stay in California. During our sojourn we had so many adventures, I have to share them.

We owned a Volkswagen bug and I thought it would suffice for a camping trip. A friend of ours laughed. "You may as well go on a pair of roller skates." David agreed with him and we went in search of a more comfortable vehicle. We saw an ad for a station wagon for $300 and made an appointment.

The small bungalow was at the end of a dead-end road. The wooly bearded young man who asked us in was very friendly and frank about the station wagon's shortcomings. We were having a conversation when a raccoon rolled out from behind his sofa.

"You have a pet raccoon?" I thought owning a wild animal was illegal in California.

"Yeah, I got a special permit because he was injured," he said calling Rocky Raccoon to his side. Just then a wolf walked into the room. My jaw dropped.

"Isn't that a wolf, not a dog-wolf mix?" David asked.

"Yeah, he was injured, too," our amiable host replied. "I've got a panther in the backyard. Want to see her?"

Indeed we did, especially my sons who were with us. I kept a wary eye on the wolf and kept my sons close by. The panther was in a cage fortunately, but what I also saw made my jaw drop again. There was a wooden kitchen chair with a motor underneath, a gas tank behind it, attached to a helicopter rotor blade above it. A safety harness was screwed to the chair.

"Oh my God," I exclaimed. "Do you fly that thing?"

"Yeah. Me and my girlfriend. She sits in my lap. We've got it up to 1500 feet. But she complains she gets too cold up there."

We closed the deal and drove off to deliver the VW bug to the friend who was buying it from us. We said we liked our new vehicle because it was so huge and comfy after the bug, but really I think we bought it partly out of awe of the eccentric seller. But it was really roomy. Our friend who had laughed at our plans to camp with the bug looked at it in admiration.

"Now that looks as soft and cushy as a marshmallow," he said.

So we promptly named our blue, slightly battered wagon Marshmallow.

We packed it with two old canvas pup tents, a camp stove, a pressure cooker, which I always found handy on camping trips because it cooked beans, stews and even pot roast in less than a half hour on the camp stove, and everything else it would take to live on the road with two boys. Heather refused to come with us (she was in puppy love and we would be gone for high school reopening) so we agreed she could stay with her grandparents. She promised to write at various American Express offices and waved good-bye as we dropped her off and pointed Marshmallow south.

Noisy Camping

We set up camp on a lagoon a couple miles from a village we could see on the horizon. We wanted to rest, and four-year-old Devin looked like he was coming down with a cold so we decided to make it our home for a few days. We set up two tents and I took advantage of our stay and the shore to wash some clothes. I used my pressure cooker to make some beans. We had picked up tortillas and vegetables at the village so enjoyed a leisurely meal.

The first night we camped a cow came walking through our camp. She leaned against one of our tents collapsing it, mooing as if she was annoyed. Startled awake, we shooed her away and reconstructed the tent in the dark and calmed the alarmed boys. I sang Devin to sleep.

The second night we were awakened by church bells ringing, whistles blowing, boats sounding their horns and general wild hullaballoo in the village which had all lights blazing at 2 a.m. We were to learn the later that the shrimp fleet had returned from a trip with a good catch. We had shrimp for dinner that night.

The third night it was dolphins that woke us. A loud splashing right outside our tents sent us investigating. I saw dorsal fins and for a moment feared sharks were right there near my children – then I heard the breathing and realized a whole school of dolphins had decided to visit the lagoon. They were jumping, splashing and obviously having a great party in the moonlight.

The next morning we all watched entranced as the dolphins leapt and played in the lagoon. The lagoon was filled with many small islets. There was one near the shore by our tents. Someone had gone to great trouble to connect it to the mainland with a concrete footing and cyclone fencing under the water. I couldn't imagine what purpose it served and just assumed it had something to do with a fishing technique.

I was standing on the shore when the dolphins all at once decided to leave the lagoon and head back to sea. Suddenly, a young dolphin, smaller than the others came streaking down the waterway between the shore and the islet. My heart panicked and I thought it was going to run into the underwater fence and injure itself because it was swimming so fast.

To my astonishment it stopped abruptly with its snout six inches away from the fence. I was amazed it was physically possible. The dolphin must have sent some kind of distress signal because the whole school of dolphins stopped and suddenly two adult dolphins came swimming at top speed to lead the young one out to sea.

"Honey, the dolphins are gone, and I don't think we're ever going to get a full night's sleep here," I told my husband. "Let's go to the nearest city and get a room for tonight."

He yawned and agreed.

Tequila and the Stray Horses

We drove to the town of San Blas on Mexico's Pacific. The beach was lovely – a nice sweep of sand shaded at the edges by palm trees. We set up our tent and took out our camp stove. We had stopped at a store en-route and were disappointed to find they sold no wine, just some tequila in bulk. David bought some of the unfamiliar liquor, filling a water jug we had. We were remarking that the coming sunset would be lovely and noticed everyone else leaving the beach in a hurry.

"Wonder why they want to miss the sunset," I said, when we suddenly learned the answer. We were engulfed by stinging *jejenes* – the no-see-ems of infamy. The boys came screaming back from the beach. We hurriedly just bundled up the tent and sleeping bags and jammed them in the back of Marshmallow.

We hadn't been fast enough. We all had nasty bites, but poor Devin got the worst of it probably because he was the shortest. I fetched out hydrocortisone cream and tried to doctor everyone.

"Let's just camp here," David said. The area where we stopped had once been under development but nothing had been built and it had been abandoned leaving just curbs and drains. There were no bugs and that settled it. I was worried about my boys and very grouchy as I set up camp again, and started assembling our dinner. At last the tents were disentangled from the mess we had created with our hasty departure. I was chopping vegetables when David asked, "Do you want some tequila?"

"Sure," I replied and was handed a water tumbler of it. The cheap stuff we had bought tasted very mild and I drank it like it was wine. It only hit me after dinner when our worn-out sons were asleep. I was in my sleeping bag when I crawled out of our tent to the curb and was sick. I was dizzy and cursing tequila when I saw what I was convinced was a hallucination.

There was gang of stray horses trotting down the street. They stopped to examine our camp then trotted on. I crawled back into the tent hoping the tequila hadn't done permanent brain damage.

The next day we packed up and moved into the San Blas campground in the center of town. The customs house from conquistador days had been turned into a small campground near the harbor. It was drowning in flowers and was along a pretty street lined with small hotels and homes. A block away there was a plaza where at night the townspeople gathered for the paseo, when young people walk in circles, the boys eyeing the girls and vice versa, all while under the watchful eyes of parents. Children played, street entertainers appeared, young husbands hired some to serenade their wives. We knew we had found a small paradise.

I learned to head for the shore just at daybreak when the *jejenes* had disappeared and wade out to the incoming boats to bargain for fish before the restaurant owners in town had got them all. The early rising Gringa willing to get wet amused the fishermen so they always saved some fish for me. We found a shop that sold wine and dumped the rest of the tequila.

Three nights later we stayed up a little later than usual sitting with fellow campers talking when I realized I had not been hallucinating. Down that pretty street just outside the campground, came the stray horses. It was the night before trash collection in San Blas and the horses knew it. They were like a gang of juvenile delinquents, kicking over trash cans and rummaging through the garbage. No one chased them, no one even seemed to notice them. They could just as well have been alley cats.

In the couple weeks we camped there we came to know them and expect them. I never quite got over the concept of stray horses, though. I still was wary of tequila. It was at least a decade before I would even agree to a margarita after that first encounter with the deceptive liquor.

Las Niñas

Patzcuaro was beautiful city. It was a great place for Marshmallow to break down. We rented two rooms in a posada along with kitchen privileges so I could make our meals. The señora who ran the place was a tough bargainer, but so was I and we respected each other.

The town was alongside Lake Patzcuaro. The lake was so large that a whole civilization existed on an island called Janitzio that didn't discover the mainland world until the 1930s when a teenager in his dugout canoe got caught in a storm and landed at Patzcuaro. Conquistadors came and went without the Janitzio folks even knowing. But on the mainland there was no ignoring the European conquerors. Even though the native Tarascans fought the Aztecs alongside the Spanish, the Spaniards treated them as a conquered people, not allies, afterwards.

Things got so bad word reached Spain who sent out Bishop Vasco de Quiroga who showed up had the head Conquistador hanged for his crimes against the Tarascans. He tried to bring the Tarascans into the then modern world of the 1500s. He set up each village around Patzcuaro with a different trade: one wove, one worked copper, one made ceramics, one made musical instruments, etc. They were like spokes on a wagon wheel with Patzcuaro as the hub. All would bring their work to Patzcuaro on market day. That legacy has lasted and we loved visiting the various villages and watching the craftsmen at work.

We especially delighted in Santa Clara de Cobre where copper was worked. Everything in the village was made of copper – street lights, railings, fountains. Every house had a forge and the sound of clanging hammers on metal was a symphony.

We spent a day visiting the Isla de Janitzio. The government guarded the native culture there carefully and limited visiting times. One improvement it had built was a communal laundry sink so the women didn't have to wash clothes in the lake. The pool sized place was a scene of neighborly chatting and playing children. Janitzio was only place where I saw women still making tortillas by patting them out on their thighs.

Patzcuaro had two plazas, one a very busy market plaza, the other a larger park-like place with a church and a lovely municipal building opposite. In between a great lawn, flowers and trees decorated the landscape.

We often went to the quieter square to eat a picnic lunch after we had bought supplies at the market plaza. One day we were sitting there when people started streaming into the plaza. The entire plaza filled, most of them native Tarascans. At the municipal building there was a balcony below a huge clock. A group of business suited men gathered on the balcony. One was clearly more important than the others and kept looking at his watch then the clock.

Suddenly a murmur began running through the crowd. "Las Niñas are coming! Las Niñas are coming!"

The self-important politician began to give a speech, pompously declaiming. In the distance I could hear drums. Suddenly the crowd parted and into the plaza marched about one hundred little girls, all dressed in pink dress uniforms and wearing white socks. Every one of them had a drum and they were beating their drums with all the energy they had.

The crowd cheered and shouted encouragement to them They marched in formation right up under the balcony. There was no way anyone could hear the politician over their glorious racket.

I could see the shawled Tarascan women looking at the lovely girls with fierce pride. I don't think the politician ever had a chance to finish his speech. Maybe that's what we could all use in Washington, whole corps of little girls with drums drowning out our politicos.

A Bribe and a Pickpocket

We were staying in Patzcuaro, Mexico. It was a market day and we stopped at a bank to cash some traveler checks (Remember them from pre-ATM days?) in anticipation of doing some shopping.

The bank clerk was friendly and when he asked for my husband's identification he burst out laughing at a photo my husband had in his wallet of our son at age two with his two buddies in his playgroup. All three toddlers were wearing hardhats, carried hammers, and were naked. He cheerfully handed us a wad of cash which I put in my bra.

We set off to the market. We turned down a narrow lane where a grinning policeman leaned against a vine covered wall. We turned right towards the market. The policeman instantly stopped us and as he stepped from the wall, pulled down a vine that showed we had turned the wrong way down a one-way alley.

He had a big grin on his face. Since I knew more Spanish than my husband I had to translate. He explained he would have to take our license plate off our car, haul us into the station and we would spend the entire afternoon filling out forms and pay a large fine. It was useless pointing out that he had deliberately obscured the sign indicating it was one way. He just wanted a bribe. He mentioned an amount.

My husband took out his wallet. He did not have the amount. In fact, he only had five pesos in his wallet. I was glad I had hidden our money in my bra. The cop's face fell, but he held out his hand and then he caught a glimpse of the photo that had made the teller laugh, and he chuckled. He saluted and sent us on our way as I called "*Buen appitito*" to him as it was lunchtime and he could buy a taco with our money.

At the market, it was crowded. I grabbed a bill from my bra, another five peso note, to give my husband as he cautioned me to hang on to the rest of the money until we concluded a bargain. My husband carried our youngest son on his shoulders as we made our way through the throng. We were looking at a pottery display when suddenly he was jostled. He had to fight to keep his balance with our son on his back so he wouldn't smash any pottery.

Immediately afterwards he discovered his wallet was missing. A pickpocket had shoved him to create the distraction. The pickpocket had got only five pesos, like the cop, but he had also made off with all of David's identification.

"Let's go back to the bank and the same teller we had so we can cash the rest of the cashier's checks that are in my name," my husband decided. That way we'd have enough money to continue the trip.

Sure enough, the teller remembered us and did not ask for identification again, and tousled our son's hair laughing as he recalled the photo. The photo, alas, was gone with the wallet. We ran into no more thieves on our journey, but to keep our cash safe, I had to increase my bra by two cup sizes.

The Coconut Beach

David and I and the boys found a coconut grove on the west coast of Mexico that had not yet been claimed for a resort by the nearby town. It was clear it was doomed because there were signs posted boasting of the coming development.

The camping was perfect if primitive. We had a long stretch of pristine beach to ourselves. There was no running water but there was shade from the trees, coconuts and a rudimentary outhouse. We could wash dishes and ourselves in the sea and use coconut water for making coffee in the morning.

There was a jungle covered peninsula that jutted into the sea just south of us and we discovered that a flock of parrots rose out of it every morning to congregate in a tree near the edge of our grove. They made quite a racket so there was no missing them. There was a small house near the tree and a man came out the first morning and set up some kind of net. In a short while he had caught a couple parrots that he put in a pair of cages he had made from palm ribs. We saw him hiking into the town to sell them. Later he came back with the empty cages. The process was to repeat itself every day of our two-week stay. The parrot population diminished until one day there were no more parrots left to rise out of the jungle.

We ran into other wildlife at the grove. A pack of stray dogs gathered one afternoon, barking and clearly excited by something. I went to investigate and discovered the biggest iguana I had ever seen surrounded by the snarling dogs. I picked up some coconuts and threw them at the dogs until they scattered. The iguana looked exhausted and was very still for while until it realized it was truly safe and I was no threat. Then it took off and vanished up a coconut palm.

Magnificent Frigate Birds that looked like pterodactyls flew overhead entertaining us.

Every couple days we went to town to buy some supplies, fetch water, and to get kerosene for our lantern and camp stove. One evening as we sat around a coconut husk fire, two little girls came with a jar to ask us politely if we had some kerosene to spare. We happily filled their jar and they went off to the little house. They were the parrot trapper's daughters.

The next morning a trio of fishermen came in a boat and met another two men on the beach who were carrying a net all bundled up. They unwrapped the bundle and it was a very long net. The men on the beach held on to one end while the men in the boat went out and made a large circle with the net. They returned to the beach and brought the other end of the net to shore. Then the hard work began. The men began pulling both ends of the net in. We saw they needed help and so we went to help with the pull.

I was astonished at the catch. There were fish of all descriptions, some of which the men tossed back. I was horrified to see a half dozen barracuda in the net. I had been letting my boys swim in barracuda infested water! Finally, the fishing was over. They handed us a couple fish as a thank you for our help and left happily with their catch.

That night the little girls returned with a bunch of plantains as a gift. We were delighted and since we still had one of the fish left, we gave it to them.

The following day a big, untidy policeman needing a shave showed up at our camp. He said he wanted to buy our gun. Gun? We had no gun and told him so. He kept asking, not able to believe we'd be camping without one.

"Colt 44?" he asked. Those were the only English words he knew.

"Sorry. No."

Finally, he left.

That night the little girls returned and they had brought us a bag of shrimp. I gave them some barrettes for their hair.

The next morning the policeman returned, obviously very hung over. He again asked to buy our Colt 44. We insisted again that we didn't have any guns much less a Colt. He hung around a while and finally left still unable to believe that Americans didn't have guns.

"It's time to get out of here. We'll leave in the morning before he decides to throw his weight around and search our camp for our imaginary guns," my husband decided.

That night the little girls came back and brought us a couple dozen oranges. I was overwhelmed by their generosity. Since we were breaking camp in the morning, I gave them a water jug we had been using. Their eyes got very big. They couldn't believe we were giving it to them. They gleefully ran home with it.

At dawn we began packing up and got ready to leave our perfect beach and coconut grove.

"I'll miss this place," I told my husband as we drove off. "But it's just as well we get out of here before we impoverish that generous family. I'm just happy they didn't give us a parrot."

The Sticks and the Carrot

I was in an airport wheelchair on my way to Puerto Vallarta for a writers' conference and a series of press trips. I had just had surgery on my back and was due for knee replacement in a few weeks. My doctors had given me eight weeks between the surgeries. With so many sticks in my life I needed a carrot, and the trip to Mexico was it. I could not stand for longer than ten minutes, nor could I walk any longer than that, thus the wheelchair.

But I made the most of my ten minutes of pain-free mobility whenever I could. I was eager to see Puerto Vallarta because thirty years before I had fallen in love with the lovely tropical town.

The town awoke from its sleepy existence in the 1960s when Liz Taylor and Richard Burton were steaming it up with their torrid affair. He was filming "Night of the Iguana". She was not in the movie, but came along for the sex.

Emotions ran so high on the film set that John Huston, who was directing it, gave each cast member a gold revolver with a gold bullet engraved with another cast member's name. Fortunately, none was ever used. The tabloid press flocked to the area to cover the juicy, scandalous stories and stayed in Puerto Vallarta.

Movie filming over, PV became the hippie destination of the 1970s, and many retirees have happy memories of the busy village. It is no longer the little town on Banderas Bay. These days Vallarta, with a population of 300,000, has been well discovered.

Thirty years before when my husband, sons and I had driven into town I had first been charmed by the women of the town washing their laundry at the river mouth. I thought I'd join them instead of trying to find a laundromat. This time women were no longer at the riverside. Washing clothes below the town's water treatment plant was forbidden. Instead a bronze statue of a washerwoman sat beside

302

the river. The picturesque town I had loved so much still existed but it was surrounded by resorts and large modern stores.

I was driven to one of the resorts where lush gardens were filled with noisy peacocks for a writers' conference. Their constant screams sounded like a person in distress. "Help! Help!" they'd shriek. Those stuck on the ground floor made plans to hold a peacock barbecue.

We writers were offered a food tour. I am not a fussy foodie. Instead of seven course dinners with a different wine with each course, although I do appreciate the work and nuances of such things, I much preferred a simple bowl of good soup and a glass of red. I had been on a couple such tours before and found them overly precious but this tour was totally different. In three hours, it made me a local. Local families were all part of it.

A taco stand that had a long line of people down the street turned out to have been in the same family for generations. The family made just one kind of taco, and they had perfected it. The newest generation proudly handed over the masterpiece. It was the best taco I had ever eaten.

Another family had a tiny place with just three tables and made nothing but ceviche. They had a boat and caught much of the fish they used. Another family ran a small back patio restaurant. The grandmother was chopping vegetables on the porch when we entered. She was known to make the best tortilla soup in town. It was. There was a small front porch with some tables when on certain nights the family projected old black and white movies onto their neighbor's white garage wall for their customers.

Yes, my kind of food tour.

One night the writers were invited to a dinner show. We took a boat out to what seemed to be an island but was probably just a jungle settlement that had no roads to it. As we disembarked, we saw a waterfall with a mermaid bathing in it. The path was lit with torches. As we walked, me hobbling on a cane, to the theater we passed rock outcroppings. There were costumed acrobats on them. On one there were people dressed and made up as owls flitting over the rock. People lizards occupied another.

Finally, we arrived at the stage which had a real rock Mayan-looking pyramid behind it. The whole area was lined with palms and jungle vines. The performance was stunning and reminded me of a Cirque de Soliel performance. The dancers and acrobats depicted a Mayan deer hunt.

At one point someone dressed as a quetzal bird came soaring out of a tree behind us on some kind of line hidden above us and landed in a palm tree next to the stage and as she did, men dressed as snakes writhed down the palm fleeing her. By the time we left and were on the boat back to PV I felt like I had visited another world.

We took a trip up the side of a mountain where enterprising villagers decided to capitalize on the busy tourist scene below them and open an adventure camp with zip lines, donkeys and horse rides. On the way up there we passed the water treatment plant and much to my glee I saw women washing clothes in the river like they had always done. I applauded the remote village that had pulled itself out of poverty by using its imagination.

I realized all the naughty movie stars that had put Puerto Vallarta on the map had led to the Mexicans developing a high degree of acceptance of all sorts of lifestyles. That, in turn, had made the town an international LGBTQ destination. The resorts were careful to designate whether they were "family resorts" or "adult resorts". The owner of a hotel catering to gays invited us to cocktails.

"For years, we gays had to go to seedy, run down places when we wanted to go on vacation openly. That has changed. Now we vacation like anyone else," he told us. His was a quiet, simple hotel with garden views, not an elaborate resort.

One excursion took me south of PV to Barre de Navidad. I knew this place had been essentially blown away by an especially fierce hurricane in 2012 and had to be totally rebuilt. I was very pleased to see it was a much better town. The high-rise hotels that had taken over the sandbar for which the town is named, had blown away, and now it was a public promenade with small restaurants and parks. The town mayor was a Gringo from Canada who had retired in Barre. The townspeople had elected him to help them preserve their environment as Barre was rebuilt. Barre was known for its sailfish and a busy charter boat industry added to the town's prosperity. A lazy lunch on a bamboo balcony over the sandy beach let me feel all was right in Barre de Navidad.

At the end of the press trip I extended my stay a few days, staying a posada in the "old downtown" area of PV, the part that used to be the whole town. I took a ferry to Palapa for a day on its beach. I hung out with some expats and locals.

I got myself to the airport and into a wheelchair again and headed back to the sticks of surgery and rehab leaving my lovely carrot behind.

Oaxaca

I ran to the window when I heard the chimes playing a cheerful tune on the street outside. "Beth it's the propane man. Let's let Alvaro know he's here because we are running low."

Another important delivery man used a loudspeaker to sing out a chant that sounded like a muezzin calling the faithful to pray. He delivered five gallon jugs of water just as the propane man brought five gallon cannisters of fuel.

I was back in marvelous Mexico with my buddy Beth, an artist, a bicycler and a very adventurous traveler. Except for the ugly border towns, every time I went to Mexico I seemed to find more to admire. Beth was an experienced European traveler, but it was her first trip to Mexico. I tried to explain that while Spain and Italy might vary by region, Mexico seemed to vary by town, so Oaxaca was as new to me as Mexico was to her.

Our apartment was on a quiet back street atop a hill next to a school that taught music. We could hear the children practicing in the distance. One of the young musicians was a tuba player and he practiced marching back and forth in the schoolyard as he played the oversized instrument.

"He's getting a workout as well as music practice," laughed Beth.

Our two bedroom flat also had a roof garden that housed the washing machine. The lush mini-jungle had a roofed section that offered a sofa, table and chairs in addition to a spectacular view. We could see the Sierra Madre mountains on one side and look down over the city on the other side to the foothills beyond.

Our hosts Laurie and Alvaro clued us in on the neighborhood, mentioning a newly opened organic farmers' market just two blocks away. The Zocalo, the park area in the central plaza, was a long walk downhill. We first went there early Sunday morning and had an elegant breakfast. The place was empty at that hour. We enjoyed the trees and flowers while we sipped our café con leche and fresh squeezed orange juice. The breakfast was half the price of just a cup of coffee at home.

We strolled to the Jaurez Market which was colorful and bustling. A group of ladies sold roasted grasshoppers as snacks, and as ingredients for cooking some of Qaxaca's famous dishes.

"Eww," said Beth. "Are you actually buying some?"

"Just to taste them. The Olmecs used them for protein for hundreds of years," I replied. I bit into one and gagged.

It was so spicy as to be fiery and the texture was awful.

At lunch time we returned to the Zocalo which was now so thronged with people, the flowers were hidden in the crowds. We sat outside to order and were interrupted at least six times by people trying to sell us handicrafts. Eventually a guitarist came and sang to us. He was good so we tipped him and he went off to sing at another table.

Up in our rooftop garden we settled in for a peaceful sunset when there were a series of explosions. Beth panicked at first but I ran to the edge of the roof to investigate and discovered our neighbor two doors down dressed in a black fire-proof ninja-like suit was setting off fireworks. Young Mexican men love fireworks and need no excuse to set them off, and apparently it is perfectly legal.

We were to get used to erratic explosions during our weeks in Oaxaca. They, like the church bells that were often ringing, did not signify anything or mark anything special. Fireworks and church bells just went off whenever anybody felt like exploding or ringing them. We just enjoyed them whenever they did.

Bulls and Wedding Dresses

My daughter was getting married soon and I decided to buy her a Oaxacan wedding dress – they are beautiful embroidered things. My guidebook said of St. Antonino was famous for them so we set out to check it out. To get there we first took a bus to Ocotlan where the same guidebook said there was a large market.

The market was not a handicraft market – it sold plastic kitchenware, cheap clothes and such for the locals although I did find a booth that sold local black fired pottery that was beautifully made. Beth and I had lunch then went to the edge of the plaza and asked a policeman how to get to St. Antonino. He frantically pointed to a flatbed truck full of people and shoved us toward it telling us to hurry as he signaled the driver to stop.

We climbed on board obediently and off we went sitting on the floor of the truck bed. The truck finally stopped in a dusty field filled with many people and a lot of noisy animals. Bewildered we sat there as the truck emptied until it was clear the driver wasn't going anywhere else. Cows and bulls were everywhere. One large truck trundled by us with the largest bull I had ever seen tied up in the back, looking very placid. He was so calm I was reminded of Ferdinand, the peace-loving, flower-smelling bull in my children's storybook.

There were no facilities, just dust, trees, and fields filled with very busy people and very unhappy cows, and more placid bulls. We had somehow landed in a cattle auction instead of a wedding dress village.

I joked with some of the women about finding cows not wedding dresses, and how I couldn't take a bull home with me on an airplane.

"Vestidos, no vacas," I told them. Dresses, not cows.

The ladies thought was funny and gestured that we should climb into a recreational vehicle shell on top of flatbed truck that was leaving. It had benches inside that were filled and people clung to the outside, standing on the bumper, hanging on to rails. A man pulled me inside and made room for me on a bench, but Beth was determined to hang on to a rail outside, laughing and handing me her camera to photograph her.

But the men did not let her stay there long, they pulled her in and made room for her on the bench, too.

The strange bus dropped us off at a turnoff which unlike the cattle market road was paved. A moto-taxi was there – a three wheeled motorcycle with seats for two in front and behind. The two men in it drove us to a village and dropped us off outside a fancy dress shop that was closed. In fact, the entire village was closed. If anyone embroidered wedding dresses they were hiding. We found one small store that was open that sold us cold drinks and the owner told us we could take a collectivo back to Oaxaca, there were no taxis. A collectivo was a sort of private bus service that used cars instead of buses.

There was stop where one was waiting to get a full passenger load before leaving. Collectivos don't adhere to schedules, they just wait until full. Eventually, there were six of us and driver was satisfied he'd make a profit. It dropped us off at a central location where we caught a taxi home, exhausted but exuberant. No wedding dress, but a fine adventure to tell our kids about.

The Unwanted Wonderful Tour

"I don't like organized tours. They're boring," Beth balked. "I prefer to go on my own."

"Well, we didn't do very well on our own trying to find the wedding dress village. Laurie [our landlady] says there's no public transportation, and the only way we are going to see the mountain villages is using one of the tours," I countered.

"Well, it is cheap," she said. The day's tour would take us to the rug making village, a mezcal hacienda, to the petrified waterfall, and to a town with gigantic tree. All that for about ten dollars, and it included lunch. Beth was sold.

It proved to a great day. We started at the town of Santa Maria de Tule that boasts the magnificent tree supposedly 2000 years old.

One of the highlights of the day was the weavers' village of Teotitlan. Many father and son businesses sold their handmade and hand-dyed wares. Marigolds provided yellows, indigo the blues, cochineal bugs the red, with lime mixed in for orange, and alum mixed to create purple. They used traditional and new, local designs. I heard the words "credit cards" mixed in the rapid machine-gun fire Mexican Spanish.

"I'm buying one," I told Beth. "This same quality rug in the Southwest made by Navajos that would cost my life savings. These are the same craft but by Mexican natives and I can finally afford one."

Our tour then took us to a mezcal ranch where the heady drink was made in the ancient way. A pit dug in the ground served as an oven to roast the agave plants, covered with dirt to bake for a week. It was then dug up and the roasted agave put into a mill run by a very bored donkey who walked in circles slowly to grind it to a pulp which then

311

went into a pool to ferment. The whole mess was then distilled in a charcoal fueled still, and results put away in barrels to age. We commiserated with the donkey who was taking a lunch break and went to the tasting room.

The final result was exquisite and we were showed the peppery tasting worm that eats the agave that is put in each bottle to flavor it. We were also offered dried worm ground to powder to serve on lime with the mezcal.

The rest of the day was taken up by a buffet lunch which we shared with a Canadian couple and a visit to marketplace and the ancient ruins of Mitla. The man of the couple had been, as I had, an investigative journalist and was now a professional political strategist. We had a lively conversation.

Driving through the mountains was impressive because the roads were so good compared to our potholed roads at home in California until the road turned to gravel.

Our guide had taken us to spectacular natural pool at the edge of an abyss. A petrified waterfall made its stony way down the mountainside. The pool was full of people, tourists and local families cavorted in its blue water. We had brought our bathing suits, luckily. Finally, it was time return home.

In our roof garden I teased Beth. "Organized tours, so boring."

The next day we packed to go home. The propane man played his jingle bells, two buglers were having a contest over who played the loudest in the school yard, church bells rang, and our neighbor set off some more fireworks.

Beth and I agreed that we would miss Qaxaca.

Section 10:
Peru, Land of Coca and Condors

When I got a form my doctor had to sign before I could go on a three-week adventure trip to Peru it did cross my mind that I might be too old for the journey. I was in my sixties but, while not ready to bench press 200 pounds, I kept active and worked out.

"Well, I'm not going to get any younger. I had better go now rather than later," I reasoned.

So it was I found myself with one young Irish woman and ten Brits and Aussies in their twenties, ready to run up mountains in a single bound. But I found I had made the right decision. We were told to bring soft-sided, luggage without wheels as streets were often cobble-stoned. I packed lightly but still dreaded having to wear the heavy backpack for long periods. As it turned out I never did. Someone, usually a Peruvian but sometimes one of my fellow travelers, was always at hand for the heavy lifting.

I usually shared rooms with the Irish girl, Catherine. Even though I was not only the oldest, but the only American, the gang never treated me as if I were an outsider or as an "aunty".

El Estomago del Burro
(The Donkey's Belly)

I nicknamed my taxi driver Mr. Toad because of the wild ride he gave me. We tore away from the airport in his aging car that had no seatbelts at top speed. It was late at night and I saw no traffic lights. Instead just before we got to an intersection he would blow his horn. I discovered that was how things were done. He who blows his horn first gets to go through, and cross traffic has to stop.

"What if you don't hear the horn blowing because you are blowing yours?" I asked.

"Accident," he said and I was not reassured. My stomach lurched as he screeched to stop outside my hotel. I had come a day earlier than we were to meet with our guide and begin our journey through Peru. The room was plain but had a private bathroom.

I walked all over town the next day but learned the archaeological museum was too far to walk. It took a lot of courage to take another taxi. Once again there was a lot of horn blowing. It was a warm, stuffy day, but the taxi driver kept the windows up to avoid breathing the traffic fumes.

I didn't care much for Lima because of its sky. There's a marine layer that lays a heavy gray blanket over Peru's coast most of the time and unlike California, it does not usually burn off in the sunlight. In Lima the blanket traps all the city's air pollution making it an unhealthy place to live.

The Limans call their sky El Estomago del Burro – the donkey's belly. Despite the donkey's belly sky there has been little if any attempt to control pollution.

The museum was a beautiful Spanish style building with many arches surrounding a courtyard. It was in a quiet residential neighborhood so there was breathable air.

The displays were beautifully done, and there was guard posted at the doorway to the "adult" section. The ancient ceramics depicted various forms of copulation between all sorts of partners and creatures, but I was offended that modern Peruvians included nursing mothers as "porn".

Then I found something wonderful no other museum I have been to had ever done. They had opened their stacks to the public. All museums have a lot of stuff that is not on display. Can you imagine what you might find in basement vaults of the Louvre or British Museum? In Peru most of what they have from the past is ceramics, a wealth of ceramics from many regions, many periods of history. They had decided to put them behind glass on many, many shelves in their storerooms and classify them by year and culture.

An afternoon studying the stacks would make anyone an expert in recognizing ceramics. I did just that, enchanted that someone had made it possible even if the museum people did think nursing mothers were pornographic.

At the other end of my journey I looked up my friend's relatives in the elegant Miraflores district of Lima overlooking the sea. They had a penthouse with a private elevator leading to the living room. I could see merrymaking crowds below at an amusement park. As we sipped coffee I was startled to see man hang-gliding right past their window. They laughed when I jumped. They were happy to have retired in Peru where the cost of living was so low and they were by the water.

Elevator and all, I was not impressed. Hang-gliders invaded their privacy, and they'd never be able to sunbathe by the sea with the donkey's belly hanging over them.

When Poop Was Gold

The sound of the birds drowned out the sounds of the sea crashing on the rocks of the islands. There were a couple million birds, shouted Ryan, our guide, over the racket. We were out at the Ballesta Islands formerly known as the Guano Islands.

The early name was apt as the rocky islands looked snowy with the many meters of bird droppings adorning them. They made Peru the richest country in the world in the 1800s. Everyone wanted the rich fertilizer and the Peruvians happily carried it around the Horn to Europe. The bird poop was pure gold.

We had been handed hooded ponchos to protect us from the birds. Catherine, my Irish roommate, had a long thin nose and with military precision a Peruvian Booby got her right on the tip of her nose, poncho notwithstanding. Our boat load laughed at the rueful face she made.

The sea wasn't high but still some on our boat were turning green as the swells rocked us. We were at the mouth of a large cave filled with sea lions, all making a great racket of their own. There were a few hundred of them, many with pups. The smell was gagging and we urged the boatman to leave the cove after a few minutes.

On one of the islands up a steep cliff we could make out the ruins of cranes and a building left over from Victorian days, also being buried by bird poop.

We learned the Ballestas, now that the world has started making chemical fertilizers turning poop into just poop again, have been turned into a wildlife preserve. Different varieties of birds come at different times in the year. Sea lions and seals take turns using the shores to breed. It was now an ecotourism draw. It had taken us about an hour and half to reach the islands. As we left the noisy wildlife behind and could hear each other speak again we all shared our wonder.

"Jesus, I didn't know there were so many birds in the world," said Stephen, an Aussie.

"I feel like I was in a National Geographic special," I replied.

"Dirty birds," mumbled Catherine and we all laughed.

Our hotel was charming. Like most of Pisco, home of Peru's national drink the Pisco Sour, the roof of the hotel was not finished. Rebar stuck up out of the concrete as though the owner planned to add another story. The government required a building tax when the work was finished, so the buildings never got finished.

There was a small restaurant and bar on the ground floor. Before dinner I went down to have a Pisco Sour and chatted with a young woman who was carefully cutting cheap paper napkins into four then folding each fourth into a triangle for the table settings. I asked for scissors and helped her. You know that imports are taxed and wages low when it is cheaper to pay someone to do such a laborious task instead of giving your guests a whole napkin.

One by one the others came down to get their own Pisco Sours. Ryan showed up to eat with us and tell us of the next day's itinerary to a sacred oasis. We all went up to the unfinished roof where there was a palapa and seats to watch a colorful sunset.

Ryan was a Brit in his late twenties. He had worked in the USA for a few years but when his American sweetheart broke up with him, he went to South America where he found his real home. He liked Peru and Bolivia, he told us, because of the native people, but he loved Brazil.

"Someday I hope to marry a Brazilian woman and have lots of little brown babies," he told us.

Sand Sledding and Grave Robbing

Ryan arranged for us to ride a public bus to Huacachina Oasis. I sat next to a Swedish woman traveling on her own. As we chatted, we drove by a sad sight. There was a high desert area full of thorny shrubs and on every shrub for a few miles there were snagged plastic bags.

"It always makes me want to cry," said the Swede. "In Africa I also saw this in the poorer countries."

The Atacama Desert got little if any rain, just occasional fog drip in some places. These poor shrubs shrouded in plastic would not get the benefit of even that bit of water.

Eventually we reached the Huacachina Oasis about lunch time. The oasis had been a favorite with Incan royalty who had come there for religious reasons and to play in the lake at its center. We ate lunch and enjoyed a magic show. Ryan then told us we were going for dune buggy rides and sand sledding.

The oasis was surrounded by a sandy desert shaped into steep dunes by the wind. My dune buggy driver, Pedro, was my age and began flirting with me ignoring the young people. He deliberately hit the crest of the dunes at high speed so we'd be airborne each time. It was a thrill.

Sand sledding was less fun for me, but the young men enjoyed it. I donned the goggles and went down one dune and that was enough for me. The sand got in my mouth and hair, so I contented myself watching the others and hanging out with Pedro.

Ryan finally rounded up everyone and got us into a van to travel to Nazca. Everyone was rubbing cream into their sandblasted faces.

In Nazca and we enjoyed a meal with an ethnic floor show at a local restaurant. Our hotel was simple but lovely. In the morning we took flights in small planes over the mysterious Nazca "lines" carved into the landscape but that can only be seen from the air even though they date to prehistoric times. The Nazca Lines are so mysterious that they gave rise to Von Daniken's far-fetched idea that they were made by ancient aliens from outer space.

Once I realized that the Nazca ancients used to have their shamans take psychedelic cactus to get guidance from the gods, I came up with a better theory. I have read Carlos Casteneda's books about Don Juan. I figure the shamans would come back from their "spiritual flights" and demand the people make a straight line for them. It became a shamanic fad.

In addition to glyphs of animals and people, there are hundreds of straight lines carved out of the soil crossing the undulating high desert. The darker soil on top was scraped away to reveal the lighter soil beneath. I found them arrogant, slashing the gentle wavelike landscape.

A German woman lived in Nazca for decades to study the lines. She thought them astronomic in intention, to keep track of stars and planets. She used a tall ladder to study them since they can't be seen at ground level and mapped them all. I visited her home that has been turned into a museum.. A model of the area maps all the lines and it's staggering how many there are crisscrossing the gentle desert landscape. There are literally hundreds.

Our last night, a local guide took us out to a pre-historic graveyard. It was the spookiest place I had ever seen. That's because of grave robbers. The ancients used to maintain family graves. A body wrapped in hides would be sat at the bottom of a square, rock lined pit and then mummify in the dry desert air. The next time someone died they'd be wrapped up and put next to their mummy relatives so they could keep each other company.

"We have a perfectly preserved grave to show you," our enthusiastic guide told us as we hiked across the desert at twilight. "Let's hurry before it gets dark."

When we got to the site her shocked expression told us something was wrong. The grave had just been looted, the mummies, unwrapped, had been stripped; fragile mummy parts scattered in the pit. I was not surprised to learn some scary scenes in an Indiana Jones movie were shot in that graveyard.

"I was just here this morning. I can't believe it. I have to report this to the police," she wailed.

As we made our way back to the road through the vast graveyard, I saw wispy things were getting caught in my sandals and the ground was crunchy. I used a flashlight to clean my sandals and to my horror discovered I had been walking on bones and the wispy stuff was human hair.

Saroche Creeps In – How High Can You Get?

We left Nazca in a luxury overnight bus. It was like traveling business or first class in a plane. We had stewardesses serving us meals, handing out pillows and blankets. After dinner we got to watch a movie before the lights went out.

Arequippa was a beautiful place surrounded by volcanos. Spanish colonial architecture graced its wide avenues. Bright pink and red bougainvillea decorated its many arches. Our hotel was luxurious. Arequippa is at over 7000 feet and Ryan thought it would begin to acclimate everyone for the higher altitudes to come.

I struck out on my own for a while. I knew some Spanish, the youngsters in the crew didn't, so I strolled about meeting locals and visiting sights. I watched a labor union parade.

That night there was also a religious procession. I got caught in it trying to get back to my hotel. The flood of people blocked my way and no one would let me escape the crowd. A young couple was pushing a stroller with a sleeping baby. They pushed it up against me. I feigned being dizzy and about to faint, so the couple shoved back into the crowd to move the stroller out of my way and allowed me to escape the procession to a side street to my great relief. I am always wary of people possessed by religious fervor.

My younger companions partied at the local bars and clubs and set themselves up for saroche – altitude sickness. They discovered hangovers and saroche don't mix well. A few of them spent the next two days in bed with oxygen tanks beside them, including my roommate Catherine. A couple of the women said a bar had run videos of a hideous form of bullfight. I had read about it and knew the government had outlawed it. It was an ancient sport which pitted a condor, a symbol for Peru, against a bull, a symbol for Spain, by tying the giant bird to the bull's neck. The condor eventually slashed through the raging bull's neck so it bled to death, but the stressed bird usually died shortly afterwards as well. I was glad I hadn't run into the video.

After two days adjusting to the altitude in lovely Arequipa and watching one more parade, we left to get really high. Ryan warned us we'd be going over a pass 17,500 feet high – that's a thousand feet higher than Mt. Everest base camp.

Lost Valley of the Incas

The Lost Valley of the Incas. That was where I was told we had to go if we wanted to see the great Andean condors, the biggest flying animal in the world. Biggest, highest - I ran into a lot of superlatives on this pilgrimage.

We left the lovely Peruvian city of Arequipa in a small bus. We were warned we were going to climb but before we reached the top of the pass leading to the Canyon de Colca we would stop for coca tea to prepare ourselves for the heights.

We drove for a couple hours on a paved road and just before the pavement ended we went to the Coca Café, a plain cinderblock building. A group of the local Indians were gathered outside to sell their wares and they had brought some of their charming baby alpacas. As I left the bus I felt a wave of dizziness and reeled for a moment. We were at 15,000 feet and still had 2,500 to go. I moved slowly and since I had no energy felt totally relaxed. I could see my fellow travelers responding to the altitude as well.

"Do you realize how much it would cost to feel like this in California?" I quipped. Then I was hit with a series of flash headaches.

In the café a cup of coca tea mixed with other herbs dispelled the headaches and brought the dizziness under control.

"Eat something sweet with the tea," Ryan told us. So I nibbled on a chocolate bar as I sipped the coca tea.

Suddenly a young alpaca that had wandered into the café stuck his head in my cup and began to eat my sodden coca leaves. We were all charmed. But the café owner's son soon came to shoo him outside.

Afterwards we left the comfort of tarmac behind and found ourselves winding our way on a gravel road up into wild vicuña country. We had to make emergency stops a few times for those who found the combination of bumps, curves and altitude too much for their stomachs. We all were thrilled when we ran into a few small herds of the lovely untamable vicuña.

The local guide, Jose, who had joined us explained that there are four animals in the camel family in South America, two in Asia and Africa. Scientists think that camelopards originated in the Americas and crossed over into Asia. Peru has all four of the Western varieties: llama, alpaca, vicuña and guanaco. We kept a lookout but never spotted the smaller shy, wild guanaco.

We finally crossed the 17,500 foot pass (the highest I have ever been outside a pressurized aircraft) and plunged down into the Canyon de Colca. It is the deepest canyon on the planet. (See, I told you there would be superlatives). The view as well as the altitude left us all breathless.

Back in about 1300, the pre-Incan people who lived there were invaded. The Incas were empire builders, the first Conquistadores of South America. But the Incan prince who came to Colca Canyon fell in love with the chief's daughter. She agreed to marry him only if he moved to her valley. He did and the pair were very happy. He built her a copper palace and they had many children.

In the 1500s the Spanish Conquistadores invaded. They tore down the copper palace, used some of the metal to cast a bell for the church they built, took the rest and left. After that no one even knew about the Canyon de Colca.

In 1969 some American aviators were making an aerial survey of the Andes for the Geographical Society when they thought the bottom fell out of their altimeter. They flew back and checked again. Yep, there was a canyon 10,000 feet deep below them. Then they saw the villages. They sent their aerial photos to National Geographic and called their article The Lost Valley of the Incas. In actuality, it is much older than the Incas. In 1970 the Geographic Society sent a Polish-led expedition to explore the canyon. They are still the only people to travel the length of the river that cut the canyon. At its deepest, the walls of the canyon are only three meters wide and sun reaches it for just minutes a day.

There was an internationally funded engineering project that carved a road to connect the villages to each other and the canyon to the outside world. The engineers also built a reservoir and irrigation system for the people.

We crossed a bridge at the high end of the canyon and went to the end of the road, arriving at the only hotel, a tiny six room one (another was under construction farther down the canyon). Two of our party had saroche (altitude sickness) so bad they took advantage not just of coca tea, but some oxygen the hotel offered and went to bed.

The rest of us went for a hike. The young and the restless opted for the high road. I took the lower and was glad I did. It climbed enough I needed to rest a lot. I finally reached a perch where I decided to sit and wait for the others.

There are some sacred places on earth. I have found myself swept away by a sensation I call "time out of mind" when I have found them. One place was in the mountains of Peloponnesian Greece, another in the Anasazi country of the Southwest, and here I found another. The Andes were cut by ancient stone terraces, built who knows how long ago. The scudding clouds made shadows on the landscape, and I was utterly alone. Past, present and future all folded into one. I had a little over a half hour of magic before I heard the voices of the others approaching and the moment was lost. The guide explained the history of the canyon as we descended back to the hotel. He stopped once and picked up a pottery shard and gave it to me.

"From the ancients to you," he smiled.

The next morning we wound our way up the other side of the canyon on the terrifying road the engineers had constructed as we made our way to the condors' end of Colca. Here the canyon became incredibly steep. We had to hike the last bit. Tourists come from Arequipa on day trips and some stay with families in lower levels of the canyon where there are fruit orchards.

We were early enough it wasn't crowded and we were in time for the early morning thermals, which the condors love. We were watching the world's biggest hummingbirds (they were the size of robins) feed off flowers when we saw our first condor rise up out of the canyon.

"It looks like a large crow," one of the Aussie lads said. Then it flew right over us and he yelped and dropped his expensive camera. It was like being buzzed by a small airplane. Their wingspan can reach sixteen feet. This time the altitude had nothing to do with our breathlessness, it was the simple magnificence of the birds.

In the time we were there we saw several condors. It was their nesting time, we were told. At some times there are as many as a hundred in that spot.

We left reluctantly after a couple hours as the condors began vanishing back into their canyon. We wound our way back up the pass to rejoin the outer world, saying good-bye to the Lost Valley of the Incas.

Condors, I kept telling myself, I have seen condors. I pinched myself. It was not a dream.

Cusco and Machu Picchu - Where Incas Still Rule

We left Arequipa, our plane slaloming between volcanos. I held my breath while we squeezed between impossibly high Andean peaks down to 11,000 feet to the city of Cusco.

As soon as we banked to land and I could see the city, I rejoiced. No flat topped, rebar prickly roofs here. Every building was roofed with red tiles. I gleefully emailed my daughter telling her "They have roofs here." She promptly replied, "What do the rest of the Peruvians do, use umbrellas?"

The minute we entered it I saw not only rooftops distinguished Cusco. A lot of architecture in South America is Spanish colonial, not Cusco. It is thoroughly Incan. Giant blocks of stone fitted so well together a piece of paper could not fit between them made great walls and large foundations for whatever else more modern had been built on them. The stonework had withstood centuries of earthquakes that had claimed everything else. I touched them with my palms in wonder, sensing the strength flowing from them.

Saroche claimed some of the youngsters so badly Ryan and the hotel owner sent for a doctor. They all, except for Catherine and I, had reserved space to hike the Inca Trail to Machu Picchu, a grueling steep four day trek. If I wanted an endurance hike I can always go to the Desolate Wilderness in the Sierra in California. I had come to meet Peruvians, not test myself.

The doctor met with all of us in the dining room of our hotel. "I cannot recommend doing the trail. At least five of those signed up are very ill. I can prescribe some medicine to help, but they should stay here where oxygen is available."

He left and to the others gathered to discuss it. They argued with Ryan about it. Even the most ill were determined and signed waivers that stated they were going against medical advice. Only Catherine decided to stay in Cusco.

The next day the group took off. Catherine managed to make it to the "world's highest Irish pub", that proudly sat on the main plaza, for lunch. It really was an Irish pub and run by an Irishman, not a Peruvian. Other "Irish" pubs had offered Guinness, had pasted paper shamrocks up but were actually Peruvian. She delighted in finding a piece of her home in such an improbable location. But then she opted for bed and oxygen.

I took off wandering the streets, totally enchanted with a city that was so uniquely different from any other I had seen. The streets were thronged by Peruvians in traditional dress. On one street an ambitious young family had dressed papa as an Incan. He had their strong noble features and in his gold headdress so looked the part I paid a few sols to take his photo. He posed alone, but then I insisted he pose with his family. They spoke Spanish so we conversed a while and we introduced ourselves. They told me the costume was his wife's idea.

"You have a handsome husband, Delores. You are smart to use him this way," I said.

"I am handsome, but she is the smart one," Incan Hector told me.

I went to visit the cathedral the Conquistadors had erected. The main point of pride was a painting of the Last Supper a newly converted Incan had painted in the 1500s. It depicted Christ eating guinea pig. Guinea pig was Incan livestock. The little critters took up little room and could be harvested for a single meal with no leftovers to worry about. The Incans considered them a delicacy for special occasions. Naturally the Incan wanted Christ to eat only the best in his painting.

Back on the main plaza, a dog came up to me and nuzzled my knees. I patted it and went to walk away, but it came after me nudging me in a different direction. Amused I moved toward it. It kept nudging me and I began to laugh.

"What is it girl? Is Timmy down a well?"

The dog made sure I followed it and turned down an alley off the plaza. It led me to jewelry shop where an elderly man was making beautiful elaborate earrings. He offered the dog a treat when I appeared in the shop.

"Smart dog," I laughed and patted it and admired its ability to find customers for his master. I picked out a few pair to bring back as gifts.

Back in the square, I saw men on bamboo scaffolding erecting odd towers and windmills out of bamboo. I went to see if I could rouse Catherine to go out for dinner. She was willing to leave the hotel on a quiet side street for a while. We found an upstairs place overlooking the plaza and ate on the balcony.

"What are those children doing?" Catherine asked pointing. Families were taking kids to all the businesses, door to door and the kids were carrying little hollow pumpkins.

"Oh, it's Halloween. I almost forgot," I exclaimed. "They must be trick or treating. I didn't know they did that here."

Catherine was so tired she took a taxi back to her room to rest and gulp down more oxygen. I could see excitement on the plaza was building and went to explore the town some more. The altitude was getting to me, but I did not have saroche, I was just moving very slowly and sitting down to rest whenever I could. I didn't mind. I was soaking in the growing festivity around me. I walked up a few blocks off the plaza to find a place to buy a glass of wine and sit down a while. Suddenly I heard a band coming.

Another Peruvian parade was on its way. Sure enough a bunch of lovely ladies in colorful skirts came dancing while the brass band followed. A few gorillas proceeded a very drunk old man dressed all in gold like Incan royalty. More dancers followed and one spotted me and swept me into the parade.

We all got to plaza where bands were coming down other streets to meet in the plaza. I was breathless and found a wall to sit on. A little girl about six came shyly up to me and sat beside me. Suddenly an older woman appeared and spoke to me in English.

"Her name is Carolina. Mine is Rosa. Can we sit with you?"

"Of course."

Carolina sat beside me and took my hand. Rosa explained Carolina was an orphan. Rosa was her aunt. The child's parents had been killed in an auto accident and Rosa now had to raise the little girl. It had been recent. Carolina attached herself to me holding my hand tightly. All the bands converged and began playing lively dance music. People danced, some solo, some couples, and many circle dances. Carolina, Rosa and I joined a circle and had a grand time.

I was surprised by all the children still out near midnight on a school night. But maybe the Peruvians let them sleep in I thought. I finally was ready for bed. I bid Rosa good-night and Carolina didn't want me to go. I hugged the poor motherless child and she finally agreed to go home with her aunt.

I spent four days in Cusco, loving every minute of it. I explored its amazing market where I discovered over a hundred varieties of potatoes in every color imaginable. Finally, it was time to leave and catch a train to the village below the mountain on which Machu Picchu sits. Catherine and I took the train to a hotel overlooking the wildly rushing Urubamba River in the town of Aquas Caliente. We had tickets for the bus up the mountain at five in the morning.

That evening we went to the hot springs that gave the town its name. As we soaked we watched a glorious sunset.

The bus was very narrow, just a row of single seats on each side. It was made for the narrow winding road that led to the mountain top.

It was very foggy at Machu Picchu because dense mists rise out of the river. Catherine and I wandered off in different directions. At first the ancient citadel made itself known to me as great stone terraces, and narrow stone paths just emerging out of mist. But as the sun rose higher and the mist lifted and evaporated, it was a great unveiling.

What was unveiled was a spectacular landscape. The steep jungle covered mountains surrounded Machu Picchu. The Urubamba roared below. The city itself was finally revealed in all its glory. I realized some of paths I had wandered were right alongside frightening abysses.

After an hour of roaming the ruins and taking photographs I heard someone calling my name. Ryan and a local guide, Daniel, had just arrived with the group who were all exhausted but triumphant after their four day hike and steep climb. Coca leaves had kept them going they told me.

They were disappointed that Huayna Picchu, a steep narrow peak right over one end of the citadel was closed because a land slide had destroyed the path and it hadn't been repaired yet. They would have added it to their endurance experience. Instead, Jose entertained us with a tour of the advanced drainage system the Incas had built to keep Machu Picchu and its crops healthy. We left the magic place at sunset reluctantly and caught the train back to Cusco and its small airport.

The whole way back I heard all about the hike, and I told them about Halloween on the plaza. We were all happy.

A Night on Lake Titicaca

Several times while in Peru, I felt as though I had passed beyond the end of the world. The high altitudes, the vast distances, new music, and native dress, made the world seem much larger than I had thought before reaching the Andes. Here on Lake Titicaca I felt that way again. Not only had we traveled far into the Andes to get to the lake, but we had been riding for hours in a boat across the immense body of water.

At about 12,000 feet my head was spinning and my breath short. I was traveling with a bunch of kids in their twenties, but they looked even more stricken with saroche, altitude sickness, than I was. They had nick-named me Iron Woman.

Our first day on the lake coincided with the first rainy day in three weeks. I huddled in my alpaca sweater and windbreaker.

We finally reached our destination, the island of Amantani. Here our tour leader had made arrangements for us to stay with a local family. A local guide, Daniel, handed out a page of Quechua words since the islanders did not speak Spanish. It was hard to pronounce. Each word sounded like a sneeze, and they seemed to take a lot of syllables to say very little. Hello was ayichanchu. Thanks was yuspargasunki. We practiced on each other.

The path from the dock up the hill was tricky since the rain had turned it into slick mud. We arrived muddy and bedraggled. Catherine and I were introduced to a short, barrel-chested man named Nicholas. He grinned at us and we ayichanchued him in our new Quechuan, then he led us up the mountainside on a sometimes stony, sometimes muddy path. We did our best to keep up with him in vain. At one point he stopped, took off the blanket he was wearing and piled both our packs into it and bundling it over his shoulder bounded up the hill ahead of us. We looked at each other in wonder. Was Nicholas part mountain goat?

332

The altitude had us breathless, and needing to stop often, but he'd wait for us and urge us on. The lake lay far below us. I discovered Nicholas knew some Spanish. He had once gone to Lima to work, he told me. That made communication much easier for me.

At long last we reached his house and he led us into a tiny courtyard. The house was made of red adobe. Many of the rural buildings in Peru are unreinforced adobe. It makes earthquakes, which they have often, a real peril, but it also allows abandoned homes to melt back into the earth – biodegradable architecture – a new concept for me. When a family can't afford the expense of a tin roof (a major wedding present for most young couples), they must keep their thatched roofs in good shape – a labor intensive, but cheaper alternative.

We climbed a stairway so steep it was really a ladder, and he led us into a spotless, charming room. It had been plastered, painted white and had a blue tarp ceiling under its tin roof. There were three beds and a table and chair. We gratefully collapsed.

A few moments later he knocked on our door and introduced us to his wife Justina. She was wearing the brightly embroidered blouse of the islands and a brightly colored skirt that billowed out. Their little boy, Jimmy, had been sleeping which is why she hadn't met us at the boat, too. They had brought us a thermos of hot water, cups, coca leaves and herbs, and some sugar so we could make tea that would help us with the altitude.

All over in the mountains people had coca tea for us. The hotels had great urns of it always available. All cafes carried it. It really did help ease the breathing and drove the high altitude flash headaches away. I had expressed concern over the narcotic possibilities but had been reassured that it takes over fifty pounds of the leaves to produce one gram of refined cocaine (which is illegal in Peru), and our tea usually had only three to five leaves in a cup. We would not get high from the tea, fortunately or unfortunately depending on one's desires, no matter how high we got via altitude. Coca leaves are sacred in Peru and part of all religious ceremonies. We had learned to treasure them as well.

The warm tea made us feel a lot better and we tried to rest from our strenuous climb but in a very short time, Justina came to get us. She gave us hats she had knitted and made us follow her higher up the mountain. The hats were so she could easily pick us out of a group of foreigners. We might all look similar to her at first but she knew her knitting anywhere.

It turned out the locals wanted to challenge us visitors to a soccer game. To warm up they played a couple spirited games among themselves.

"I'll be a cheerleader," I told Catherine. I was older by at least twenty-five years than my fellow travelers. Eventually enough of the group (there were ten of us) showed up and a team was formed. I thought for sure we'd be toast but the young Brits and Aussies of our group had played 'futbol' all their lives and played a darn good game. The islanders won but not easily. They were greatly pleased at being offered a real challenge.

The game had drawn out the entire island population. Lovely young women gathered in colorful clusters to knit, giggle, flirt with the young men, and comment on the lack of fashion sense of us touristas.

Daniel, who hadn't been able to resist from joining the game, told us something about the island. The island did not have power or health facilities – the islanders preferred their own traditional healers and only went to the mainland for help when the healer told them they had to.

The healer used guinea pigs to diagnose illnesses and determine cures, we were told. The all-important guinea pigs were also used in ceremonies such as weddings, when the shaman would kill and bury one under the foundation of the new couple's home to be. The family could then safely build a new adobe structure over it.

There were no vehicles. In the rocky, steep, and roadless terrain they'd be useless. They did have a school, and the children were learning Spanish as a second language. One person on the island had a solar panel that powered a small television and had named his kids after famous soccer players as a result. Sometimes a young male of courting age (16 to 18 years old there) might invest in a battery-operated radio to attract the girls' attention, but when the batteries ran out they were seldom replaced because they were expensive. Otherwise the islanders' only connection to the outer world was by boat. Once in a while an adventurous soul, like Nicholas, would leave the island to seek his fortune on the mainland, but they usually came back after a year or two, disappointed with urban life.

A Peruvian university had established the home-stay program, Daniel told us. At first, adventurous visitors had to sleep on the floors of the kitchen with the family guinea pigs – a form of livestock that provides meat as well as magic for the indigenous people. But grants had provided funding so the families could create guest rooms. The university was determined to minimize the impact of visitors on the Amantani culture while at the same time provide some cash income for the locals and education for the modern world.

Daniel's lecture over, back down the mountain we went, thoroughly frozen by this time as the rain had begun again.

Back at the house I discovered Justina in her tiny, raw adobe kitchen with a dirt floor. She was starting a fire in her small, ingenious clay fireplace. It had three holes in the top into which she set three earthernware pots. Just a few twigs were enough to get everything cooked. I asked in Spanish if Catherine and I could join her. She seemed to understand. I also gave her the staples we had bought on the mainland just before we had boarded the boat: sugar, rice, oil, and a can of Nescafe, a ubiquitous item in Peru.

"Catherine," I called from the bottom of the steps. "Fire, warmth. Come on down." She had taken refuge under the covers upstairs but came down to join us in the little room. She looked miserably cold.

Then Nicholas came in with five-year-old Jimmy. We sat at a tiny table lit by a single candle and began a game of table soccer since Jimmy had a small ball. It would roll off the table, and I'd hand him my small flashlight so he could find it in the dark little room. He brought out his school books and proudly showed us all the numbers he had written. He proudly recited his newest lesson for us. I helped him practice his Spanish numbers.

Another little boy a year or two older, Solferi, joined us. I had sheets of gold star stickers and fetched them out for the boys, pasting one on each child's forehead.

That did it. The boys began plastering each other with stars. Before long they were so covered with gold they looked like young Inca gods. Nicholas and Justina laughed. We were all happy with the result.

Nicholas turned to me and asked if I had ever taught school. I was surprised he had guessed I had once run a nursery school. He was pleased with his own acuity.

"I can tell. You know children," he told me in Spanish.

Daniel had told us before we docked that our hosts were to be our temporary parents. I told Nicholas and Justina that they were the ages of my children so if someone had to be a parent it was me. They teased me about my new grandchildren.

Solferi went home and Justina and Nicholas served us bowls of wonderful soup made of quinoa, the local grain, and vegetables. We were grateful for its heat and warmed our hands holding the bowl before we ate it. Then we were given great plates of rice and vegetable stew. The islanders only eat meat a few times a year, usually the ubiquitous guinea pig.

After dinner the couple came to our room bearing armloads of clothes. The women on the island wore lots of short skirts, "to look like flowers" Nicholas explained.

The couple proceeded to dress us over our slacks and sweaters. The blouses were so encrusted with embroidery they felt like armor. We only had to wear two skirts each – some of the locals wore as many as ten. A tight sash tied it all together and compressed our already beleaguered lungs. Nicholas explained that he had made the clothes. He had invested in a treadle sewing machine while working in Lima. Sewing for his neighbors provided the family with extra income.

Finally, they deemed us ready. Justina looked lovely. We looked ridiculous. We marched back up the mountain in the rain, worrying about getting the beautiful clothes muddy on the terraced adobe walls that lined the path.

At a town hall lit by candle lanterns, there were two bands playing. If soccer at these heights was hard, dancing was even harder. The dances lasted about twenty minutes, and got faster and faster towards the end.

There was no break between dances since there were two bands and one picked up the instant the other stopped playing. The whole town had again turned out and for a couple hours they exhausted us in wild dances. Jimmy and Justina and I danced non-stop. There was some warm beer from the island's only shop but Catherine and I had used the drafty outhouse back at the house earlier and didn't want to have to get up during the night in the rain to use it again, so we abstained.

Finally, I made excuses because Jimmy had to get some sleep. Justina and Nicholas pretended to agree he had to get up early, but I could see they were just taking pity on Catherine and me. They were ready to keep partying until dawn. We stumbled down the mountain through the cold rain. Back at the house, with a little help from Justina, we got out of our fancy duds. The family bid us good night. Then Catherine and I put on all the clothes we had with us, took the blankets off the extra bed in an effort to get warm and fell asleep.

The morning dawned with the sun and warmth. The rain had stopped at last. The lake, far below us, glittered blindingly in the sun. We were brought a basin of hot water to wash in, and some more tea.

Down in the kitchen the family had made pancakes for breakfast. This was a dish the university people had taught them to cook and they made them only when they had visitors. Jimmy was clearly enjoying the treat.

Nicholas liked having someone who spoke a little Spanish, and he liked having a visitor older than most of the young people who usually find their way to Amantani. His parents had passed on and he missed them. He seemed to have no trouble adopting me as a temporary Mom.

He talked to me about America and asked if we had more luxuries. I told him his life in Amantani was simpler and less stressful. He offered to build me a house next door so I could move in since he was my new son. "You can help us with Jimmy and we will make pancakes for you every morning."

After breakfast my new "daughter", Justina, and Jimmy, walked Catherine and I down to the docks. Nicholas bid us farewell and went out to his fields to work – there was a quinoa crop to tend. It had only been overnight, but it somehow seemed I had known the family a long time, and we all found it hard to say good bye. Jimmy hugged me a long time. We waved at each other as long as we could see one another as the boat pulled away from lovely Amantani

The People of the Floating Islands

When we stepped off the boat, the "land" trembled beneath our feet. Some people actually stumbled they were so startled. "I'm from California. I'm used to earthquakes" I joked. I just pretended to myself that I was still on a boat because, in a sense, I was.

The floating islands of the Uros people on Lake Titicaca in Peru are famous throughout South America. The Uros create their "land" from the long Totora reeds that crowd the lake for miles in certain areas. They tie the harvested reeds in bundles to make great rafts, sometimes anchoring them with stone anchors, but usually nestling them within the living reeds, then chop up more reeds to create an even surface to walk on.

Quechan Daniel translated for us and the locals told us about their way of life. Everything is made of the reeds. The Uros skillfully weave them into boats that are wonderfully buoyant. They weave their homes out of them. They eat the pith of the reeds, which make an asparagus like vegetable that is nourishing. They dry some of the pith and turn it into flour, which they make into bread.

They came by their skills about two centuries before the Spanish conquest when the Incas were busy empire building and marched to the lake. The Uros had lived on the shores until then, but the advancing Inca armies terrified them and they took refuge, hiding in the reeds.

It worked for a long time. The Incas marched right on by to go to war with the Aymaras who lived on the far side of the huge lake. The two armies battled back and forth for years. Eventually, the Incas gave up and marched off leaving the Aymaras triumphant.

"Aymaras are still very tough people," Daniel our local Quechan guide told us. "An outsider went to an Aymaran town to run for mayor. He made many promises so the Aymaras elected him, But he didn't keep his promises and the people hung him. The government sent police there and demanded to know who had killed the mayor. The entire town stepped forward to say they had because he was a liar. You don't want to lie to an Aymaran."

After a while the Incas did discover the Uros but considered them too poor to bother with and simply asked them to pay a token tribute of a hollow reed filled with rice once a year. The Uros began a small trade with the Aymaras and Quechans, providing fish and reeds for land-raised things. They eventually adopted a lot of the Aymara tongue although their dialect is still distinctly different.

But one thing didn't change, the Uros didn't leave the reeds. The Uros just stayed where they felt safe and figured out how to survive. To this day even finding the floating islands takes a canny guide and skillful boatman to find the water paths through the reeds. The labyrinth goes on for miles.

In the middle of the island where we had been welcomed, was a small hole where the Uros kids learned to swim. When you live literally on a lake, drown-proofing your children becomes a priority.

There was also a small lookout tower. Each island had one as we discovered when we climbed it. It was their way to stay in touch and signal each other as well as watch for trouble – or these days, visitors.

While the other Peruvian tribes revere Pachamama, Mother Earth, the Uros revere Mother Lake. The bountiful lake provides them with fish and reeds. And the reeds provided them with everything. I noticed some strange looking contraptions on the roofs of the straw huts.

It seems the Uros used to use fish oil lamps or candles for light but that created a serious fire danger. Some bright soul came up with the idea of a small solar panel that could light a single light bulb. Now each primitive straw hut had its own panel all throughout the Uros villages. They cook on fires carefully made on top of stones so as to not burn the ground beneath them. A kind Uros woman showed us how she made her flour, grinding it between stones taken from the mainland, and let us taste the flatbread she baked. I noticed a big pot of water at hand to douse any sparks that might fly.

Living on a floating island has its advantages. When the family got too large or if there were disagreements in a village, they'd simply saw off a section of island and float it away. That had happened recently on the island we visited. Our guide told us it used to be much larger. The islands vary in number because of that but there are generally between forty and fifty at any given time.

There were problems, too. The reeds had to constantly be replenished. We saw straw boats hauling in large loads of reeds for that purpose. If the reed mat got so thick as to touch bottom, it would begin to rot, so a boat would be hired to tow the island off into deeper water. If not kept up, the surface of the island can get spongy underfoot. The islands usually last a full generation – about 30 years, so island making is a constant project.

The surface of the island was strewn with chopped dry reeds. It was like walking where a bunch of hay bales had been broken open. The golden color contrasted vividly with the green of the surrounding reeds and the blue of the lake waters.

The Peruvians at the city on shore recognize the Uros' water rights, and in the market in the nearby town of Puno, they hold the monopoly on fish sales. These days, however, as the fame of their strange islands spread, tourism is becoming an important source of income. Most of the tourists are fellow Peruvians.

The women are very skilled needlewomen and their work is in demand by visitors, and the men, so good at weaving their own boats, also weave miniature toy ones to sell. Most of the people incorporate the visits from small groups like ours (there were 10 of us who had booked our trip through an agent in Puno) into their regular routines, and natural hospitality, but some only see dollar signs. One obnoxious fellow followed us when we went for a ride on a straw boat playing the flute very badly then demanding a tip. I told him to keep his day job. I think he got the message. I was happy to spend my money with the rest of the Uros but saw him as barely a step up from a beggar and I wondered if that attitude would spread among these innocent people whose unique culture had survived for so long.

Unlike the long-lived people who inhabit the islands of Titicaca where the average life span is 76 or more, the Uros suffer from arthritis and respiratory problems that result from their damp way of life. Their average life span is about twenty years less than their neighbors.

Since they did not speak Spanish, only their own dialect of Aymara, we could only communicate through our interpreter, but some things were clear. Many of the young people had paddled off in their boats to settle on shore and get jobs in town. From thousands, the Uros' numbers of those still on the islands is down into the hundreds now. While there was still a lively village life with people paddling between islands and hauling their catch to shore, I fear the Uros way of life will soon disappear.

The old folks do, too. They lamented the steady drain of their young. But I could understand the lure of a life with the bright lights and solid ground beneath one's feet.

In the Amazon Rainforest

Our plane left the dramatic city of Cusco behind. The Andes dominate the country of Peru in such spectacular fashion, it had come as a surprise to me to learn that well over fifty percent of the country is Amazon rainforest.

Soaring over the mountain peaks I could see rivers formed by the melting snow. We were going down to 7,000 feet. I had to chuckle, down to the altitude I drive up to in California to ski. In Peru I had learned altitude is a relative matter.

The mountains gave way to vast jungles laced with myriad rivers. There were no roads visible. When the plane descended I could see a settlement on the banks of a large river. It was the frontier outpost of Puerto Maldonado, and an important place despite its small size. We were met at the tiny airport by what could euphemistically be called a bus. The open wood-sided contraption had a tin roof and was gaily painted with jungle animals.

It took us "downtown" to the market area where we were free to roam until our canoes arrived. Puerto Maldonado was rife with wonderful tropical decadence. Corrugated tin roofs were rusty and the banana trees threatened to swallow whole buildings. It was early enough the heat was not yet oppressive but I still stuck to the shade.

People were sipping soft drinks at improvised cafes while an occasional vehicle stirred the dust of the streets. I strolled and chatted with shop and stall owners, buying some wonderful tropical nuts that had been roasted and sugared, until it was time for us to gather at the riverside.

The long motorized canoes were not docked as there was no real pier, but just beached where the road ended at the waterside. I was glad to see we had a canvas roof to shade us. With a mighty shove from the crew we were off, and the motor started putt-putting us down the beautiful Madre de Dios River.

We quickly left the homes and businesses behind and passed a few jungle lodges. We were going to a lodge next to the Tambopata wilderness preserve.

Thick jungle came right to the water and overhung the banks. The only signs of civilization were an occasional farm chopped into the greenery and barely piercing the wilderness. Sometimes there was a canoe beached or someone working to indicate there were inhabitants, but often the farms were abandoned and being rapidly claimed by the jungle again.

After two hours of nothing we were getting apprehensive. Where were they taking us? Finally, we rounded a bend and saw a boat landing and thatch-roofed walkways leading to some lovely buildings. A sign proudly told us we had arrived at Eco-Amazonia Lodge.

Our cheerful bearded host greeted us as we tied up and led us to a screened dining room where our welcome lunch awaited us. Chicken and rice wrapped in banana leaves and steamed were among the goodies the cheerful help served up.

Then they showed us to our bungalows. Raised thatch-work shaded catwalks above the verdant lawns linked all the buildings. When I left the walkway to step on the high grass, clouds of brilliant butterflies rose into the air. The bungalows had private baths and a screened porch complete with a hammock.

Another thatched building held a large swimming pool. We had been warned not to swim in the river – not just piranhas but very vicious parasites favored the river.

The main building housed a huge lounge. For three hours each night generators supplied electricity to run the blenders and ice makers so the bartender could make Pisco Sours or other exotic drinks, and everyone could watch soccer matches on television. There were spacious verandas and balconies with rocking chairs and hammocks where we could laze around and watch the river. Canoes from farms eking out a living delivered produce to the lodge.

The first morning after breakfast I met the garbage disposal system. Our leftover banana pancakes were put out on a tree stump and a flock of brightly colored macaws came out of the trees to eat them. At night a tapir who had settled in nearby came out from under the walkways to handle the dinner leftovers.

In the middle of the river was a small island, Monkey Island, where the lodge owners protected five species of wild monkeys. A young guide took us there for a hike and lured monkeys out of the trees with a bunch of bananas. He stood and gave a call and sure enough through the trees various monkeys came, and jumped on him for their treats. Monkeys are fine although I had one as kid who made life miserable for my family for a few months – Gina, a bad-tempered squirrel monkey. These were nicer than Gina, but still I enjoyed the wild orchids growing in the trees as much as the monkeys. Suddenly, my stomach began making very loud noises. Ever since I had made the mistake of eating a salad two nights before I had been feeling uneasy. I lagged behind the others and crouched on the ground until a wave of dizziness had passed and the stomach quieted.

Inland there was a lake an hour's hike away. The following day everyone was going to hike out to see it and a waterfall nearby. I chose to dose myself with immodium and make full use of the veranda filled with hammocks overlooking the river. It was a wise decision. The lovely Madre de Dios reflected the sky as it sluggishly made its way through the jungle to the Atlantic. Birds were everywhere although the macaws had taken off somewhere out of sight now that breakfast was long over. A noisy toucan seemed to take over one tree, and weaverbirds had filled a few others with their ornamental nests.

The next afternoon we traveled downriver to visit one of the farms that supplied the lodge. If a family can survive for a few years on the

Amazon the government will give them the land. The law is similar to our old Homestead Act that lured settlers to the West. And like life in the old West, it isn't easy on the Amazon. Because the lodge provided a relatively easy source of income, and because this family had relatives in Puerto Maldonado, they were able to send their children to school. Many farmers can't.

They raised some chickens, grew bananas and other fruit, and some sweet potatoes. They also fished. Their home was made of sticks and thatch. They cooked over a fire outside. It was a very lonely existence. I happily paid too much for some strings of seeds they offered for sale and hoped the money would go for some small luxuries to lighten their lives.

Back at our luxurious lodge the generators were fired up and the bartender began making cocktails. I got a cold beer and went upstairs to the veranda to watch another beautiful sunset on the Madre de Dios. We were leaving in the morning after three days in this paradise.

Screens, mosquito coils and Deet had kept us all from being eaten alive by the insects. We had the luxury of doing nothing when it got too hot. We could swim in the pool. We could just watch the wild life, not compete with it.

I thought about life on the farm we had seen and began to understand why ninety percent of the homesteading Peruvians here had opted for life back in the mountains leaving deserted farms behind.

I had read about rapacious explorers looking for gold and oil that had decimated the tribes in this area. I was glad they too had left, and that the government had begun protecting its jungles, learning that eco-tourism paid off. Some places deserve to left alone, to be touched only lightly. And this piece of the Amazonian rainforest was definitely one of them.

Section 11:
Chile, Uruguay, Argentina, Belize

Deep into the Great Recession I began being besieged by ads from cruise companies. With each ad the prices dropped. I had never been especially lured to cruises but I knew there was one place on my bucket list I could only reach by ship – Cape Horn. When I saw a two week cruise from Chile to Argentina that would take me around the Horn for $50 a day, I booked it. A friend, Nancy, wanted to join me which was fine, but at the last moment her boyfriend Roger also decided to come along, which meant, except for specific outings, I was basically on my own. That gave me the chance to also pursue another passion – Pablo Neruda. So, I left a week early for Chile. I stayed another week in Argentina after the cruise ended.

Neruda and the German Pirate

I flew into Santiago as the sun was rising over the Andes. The snow-covered, jagged cordillera against the sunrise was a beautiful welcome to Chile.

A taxi dropped me off at Marilena's small Bed and Breakfast. Santiago was a lovely town with a bad air pollution problem because it is nestled in a valley surrounded by the Andes with just one pass leading to the coast. All the exhaust from its busy traffic gets trapped in the city and no one has figured out how to deal with it yet. I was only there for a few days before I left for Valparaiso. There, I would meet with Michael, the German Pirate, who was to be my guide.

I needed a guide because I was on the trail of Chile's revered pack-rat poet, Pablo Neruda.

He was a poet beloved by the world. He was an ardent politician – a communist. He was a hero who once rescued 2000 people. Above all, he was a passionate collector, a true pack-rat, who collected everything, including, it seems, women.

I had read his work; loved most of it, excited by some of it, driven to righteous anger by much of it. But because of his legendary collections, I realized to really get to know Neruda, I had to visit the pack rat's houses. Houses, plural. He built three. Yes, he collected those, too.

La Chascona

His house in Santiago is called La Chascona which means a woman with wild hair. Neruda was married to his second wife Delia de Carril, an Argentine twenty years his senior, when he was having an affair with Matilde Urrutia. He and Delia had a home in Santiago, but he and Mathilde bought property and built La Chascona as a trysting place. She was the one with the wild hair.

I had arranged with my hostess Marilena to get reservations for me to tour it. A foundation guards everything of Neruda's closely and is very uncooperative about visitors, refusing to allow cameras and requiring reservations well in advance. Michael the German Pirate had promised to get me in Neruda's other homes.

It is nowhere near the sea, but Neruda and Mathilde's house still feels like a ship. Although Neruda was a tall and burly man, he favored small doors and narrow steep stairs like a ship. He designed an artificial stream to water his gardens and so he could always hear running water – it no longer exists, alas. His dining room is long and narrow, like a captain's dining saloon. Narrow walkways link living spaces, and secret back spiral staircases pop up everywhere.

The house overlooks Bellavista, a poor working-class neighborhood until Neruda moved in. Artists followed him, mingled with or grew out of the workers' numbers until now Bellavista is the lively, colorful, Bohemian district Neruda envisioned when he built his home there. Blue collar workers can still afford to live there.

The artist Diego Rivera painted a portrait of Mathilde with Neruda's distinctive profile emerging from her unruly curls. It hangs in La Chascona.

Neruda, wildly popular with Chileans after winning the Nobel Prize, ran for president, then turned around, giving his votes to Salvador Allende who was elected in 1970. In 1973 Pinochet led a US funded coup and took over the government after bombing the capitol and "suiciding" Allende. Pinochet sent soldiers to invade Neruda's homes. The soldiers tore apart La Chascona, destroying the stream while Neruda lay dying in a hospital nearby. They also painted over a mural locals had painted on a fence across the road to honor Neruda. When Neruda died a week or so later, Mathilde decided to hold his funeral in the ruins of La Chascona. It was pouring rain.

The city rose in sorrow and protest, to march by the thousands behind Neruda's casket to the cemetery. They chanted a roll call: "Comrade Neruda. Present! Now and forever!" The foreign press was out in force so Pinochet was helpless to stop the brave procession. Eventually Pinochet was prosecuted for war crimes.

The stream has not been restored but the house has and even the mural across the road is back.

I took a bus from Santiago to Valparaiso. I expected to have to deal with my luggage and find a taxi, but a handsome, smiling blond man greeted me as I stepped off the bus. Michael the German Pirate drove me to my Bed and Breakfast which it turned out was owned by his best friend, an Australian who had married a Chilean woman, as had Michael.

I was overwhelmed by Valparaiso. While Santiago was a pretty city, it looked like many other cities. NOTHING else looks anything like Valparaiso or as the locals dub it, Valpo. The city cascades down forty-two steep hills to the sea. The hills are so high that funiculars have to get people up and down them and are part of the public transit system. In fact, they are the only public transit beyond some daredevil taxis who can't get to much of the city. The architecture is primarily wood covered with corrugated metal painted bright colors giving it the nickname "the corduroy city". The port dominates the coastline, so great stacks of shipping  containers line the waterfront. The entire waterfront is owned by an international company and only 300 yards of it are open to the public – a remnant of the Pinochet government and a fact that angered Michael (and me) who felt the sea should be open to the public.

My B&B hosts poured some wine for us all and Michael and his buddy joked about loving South America, even its dangers.

"When I first landed here, I was met by a mate who warned me 'Beware of Peruvian drinks, Argentine police and Chilean women'," he said, and his wife swatted the back of his head.

Isla Negra

In the morning Michael and I set out to see Neruda's favorite home, Isla Negra. I did not have reservations but the minute Michael and I walked in, the receptionist at the entrance smiled radiantly.

"Michael, how nice to see you again," and she asked about his wife and children who were vacationing with her relatives. I was to learn quickly that EVERONE near Valpo knew Michael. Some just called him "Pirate." He turned out to be my key to the city.

Neruda was raised in the forests of Chile's southern wilderness where his father worked for a railroad. He was old enough that when he first saw the sea, he remembered it vividly and it invaded all his poetry. All his life Neruda loved the sea but suffered horribly from seasickness. At Isla Negra he satisfied his nautical passion without risking his digestive system.

About sixty miles south of Valparaiso, his house sits on a stunning cove above brilliant blue waters, a white sand beach, and jagged black rocks. Gardens spill down the hillside to the beach and the home, Isla Negra, sprawls among the rocks. Isla Negra, the area, was and still is a quiet artists' colony. Neruda just became the most famous of them to settle there. There's a small stone tower that defines the house, but Neruda kept adding to its structure to house his ever-growing collections of ships items, pottery, shells, books, statuary – you name it.

He began working on the house with his second wife Delia del Carril. He had begun an affair with her while still married to his first wife, a Dutch woman, Maria Hagenaar, from Indonesia.

Delia, a gifted artist, his best editor and critic, and an ardent political colleague, was also from a privileged Argentine family with many servants. As such, she never learned such basic domestic skills as cooking, cleaning and entertaining. Neruda, a thorough Latin male, was no help, and was always adding messes to the construction-zone they lived in, so the early years of Isla Negra tended to be messy and chaotic, but fun.

Delia and Neruda were married eighteen years before he divorced her to marry Mathilde. Despite being twenty years older than him, Delia got a form of vengeance by living to be one hundred and outliving both Neruda and Mathilde.

At Isla Negra Neruda built a bar that only he was permitted to tend since he loved dispensing drinks to his friends. He also beached a boat for cocktail parties saying "one does not need to go to sea in a boat to feel unsteady if one brought a drink". He installed a great ship's bell he would ring to let his neighbors know he was home and the party was about to begin.

In his living room he installed most of a collection of ships' mastheads, reserving a couple nudes to surprise guests in other parts of the house such as a bathroom. Artist friends contributed various works to Isla Negra as well as his other houses. A stone mason had given him a magnificent fireplace. Michael and I roamed his dining room where large windows looked out over the sea and on the opposite side, over the garden. We noticed he had placed his collection of blue and green vinters' jugs on the sea side, the earth-toned ones on the garden side.

A long hallway revealed Indonesian carvings and a collection of masks. I remembered Neruda as a young man had been Chile's ambassador to Indonesia and had a passionate affair with a wild and violent native woman. Rooms revealed collections of seashells, fabrics – you name it.

I pointed out a plaque to Michael. It had been donated after his death to Isla Negra by the descendants of the Winnepeg. That was a

Canadian fishing ship he managed to commandeer in France when he was an ambassador there, that he used to rescue 2000 refugees from Spain's Civil War who were dying in concentration camps. They escaped to Argentina then Chile on the Winnepeg.

His writing studio in a separate building below his beached boat, featured a desk made of a hatch cover. He saw it bobbing in the waves and told his third wife, Mathilde, "I see my desk coming." He waited on the beach all day until the sea delivered it.

His bed upstairs in the main house, was set at an angle so he could see the sea from all directions. He had furniture built to maintain the angle after the housekeeper insisted on moving it to sweep.

Towards the end, he lay ill and dying on the bed looking at his beloved sea. Pinochet, ordered his soldiers to invade and trash the house of the communist poet. But when the young officer burst into the room, Neruda said, "Look around - there's just one thing of danger for you here - poetry." The soldier was overwhelmed at actually seeing the revered man. He apologized, ordered his men out and left Neruda and Isla Negra in peace.

Michael and I shared a lunch at a small café at Isla Negra and marveled at Neruda's life. He got a text from the B&B that my friends had arrived. We left, stopping at an elegant winery where I bought a bottle of champagne for the occasion. I learned the winery was at the same latitude as Sonoma and Napa Counties, just on the reverse side of the Equator, so wineries on either side of the Equator exchanged help during each other's harvest time.

My friends Nancy and Roger were as enchanted as I was with Valpo. The following day Michael was to lead us and a few others on a tour of the city and then take me to La Sebastiana – Neruda's Valpo home.

Michael's tour of Valpo was one only he could conduct. When I travel on my own dime I am a very frugal traveler, but his fee was so low and the value so high I made up my mind to tip him lavishly when my friends and I finally departed Valpo to go around the Horn on our cruise.

We went into the home of a magician who performed tricks for us, we were smuggled into a lavish mansion of a corrupt Chilean politician who used the residence to store loot he had garnered. I wondered if some of it belonged to Neruda. On the tangled, hilly streets of Valpo we came across marvelously artistic graffiti that often included portraits of the beloved Neruda. Massive retaining walls preventing whole blocks of residences from tumbling down Valpo's hills were graced with his portrait and lines of his poetry. At the top of a funicular a street violinist embraced Michael and in his joy at seeing his friend gave us an impromptu concert.

After the wildly odd tour, we ended up at a lovely rooftop restaurant for lunch where all the other tourists went their own way. My friends, Michael and I left and headed for the new destination.

That evening we all gathered at a tango club near the waterfront that had a colorful history and celebrated glorious Valpo.

La Sebastiana

Valparaiso is a gritty port town, sometimes dangerous, but Neruda loved it. Once, hiding from the government that had declared him a dangerous rebel, the port workers of Valpo had safely hidden him there for six months until he could be smuggled out on horseback (his first ever equine experience) across the dangerous Andes to Argentina. In that six months he fell in love with Valpo as so many of us do.

Years later, his status restored, no longer a political fugitive, he came back to build a new home at the very peak of a high hill. In Valpo the higher you get, the poorer the neighborhoods so it was in keeping with his love of the working people that he chose a peak, not a shoreside location for his home.

Smaller than the other homes, the ship-like feeling still permeates this house. A porthole replaces a window, blue and green tiles in a bath suddenly take you underwater. The bedroom at the top of the house seems to hover over the seaport below like a crow's nest. Mathilde's dressing robes still hang in the closet.

This house, too, was demolished by Pinochet's soldiers after his death. Mathilde got a frantic call from neighbors to come to Valpo and see if she could somehow seal the house. Even the front door was gone. Shortly afterwards a friend of Neruda's was in Valparaiso when he saw a huge crowd gathered around the house in an uproar. It turned out an angry eagle had flown into the rooms at the top through the broken windows, frightening everyone and it wouldn't leave. This struck all who knew the poet because Neruda had always said if there was such a thing as reincarnation he would come back as an eagle.

La Sebastiana is not only the smallest, but seems in some ways, the most personal and private of Neruda's homes. Despite his love of entertaining and the ever-present bar for him to tend, this home feels as though two people shared many close times here.

Neruda wrote a poem about watching La Sebastiana growing organically like a flowering bush, and it is still on his desk written in green ink as he wrote all his work – saying it was the color of hope.

It took ousting Pinochet and prosecuting him for his crimes, before the Chilean people could demand that La Chascona in Santiago be restored, and that all of Neruda's homes be opened to the public as he had wanted. Isla Negra had to be sealed for years to legally protect it from being seized and destroyed by Pinochet, so it was the only one to survive intact. Mathilde was active in making it all happen. She wanted a foundation in his honor established, but while she put all the pieces in place, the foundation couldn't actually operate until after her death when Pinochet was finally gone, charged with crimes against humanity.

Neruda would get a chuckle out of the prosperity of the once poor neighborhoods in Santiago and Valpo whose inhabitants capitalize on visitors' interest in his homes today. Souvenir stalls abound;

handicrafts as well as refreshments are hawked outside La Chascona and La Sebastiana.

His and Mathilde's bodies were eventually moved to Isla Negra where he wanted to be buried and they lie beneath the slope. It is the most peaceful of the three homes he built, and even free of the souvenir stalls.

The houses are the fruit of a life lived fully, richly, generously, without restraint. The collections are not merely acquisitions, but were obviously loved and honored. Like his work they excite, depress or anger you, but they always enrich you.

Thank you, Michael the German Pirate for giving me the key to Neruda's homes. Pablo Neruda, I think I begin to know you now. I think I can begin to understand your beloved Chile.

Me and Julio

Michael the German Pirate and I were driving north to Valparaiso from Isla Negra when he said, "I have a friend in the next town, Quintay, that you should meet."

We stopped in the village of Quintay to admire it. It was a pretty little fishing village on a peaceful cove full of families enjoying the beach and boats. Michael's friend lived a little way north of the cove. I realized that Quintay had probably been an indigenous Mapuche village at one time. Most names with a Q in them were of Mapuche origin.

"I don't take many people to visit him, but I know he will like you. His name is Julio. He's an extraordinary man and he will remind you of Neruda, but please don't mention Neruda's name to him. He hates Neruda because he was a communist," Michael warned.

Julio's house was made of stone – rounded stones set carefully in mortar. "He built this house himself by hand," Michael told me as he rang the doorbell.

Julio did remind me of what I had seen of Neruda in films.

"Michael," he greeted us with a big smile. "Who is this that you have brought to me?"

He spoke perfect English and began flirting with me instantly. We walked into his living room that had a huge picture window framing the sea and a garden gone riot with flowers. A life-sized replica of Venus de Milo was next to his fireplace.

"Let me introduce you to my wife," he joked and bowed formally to the statue.

"I think I met her before, in Paris," I quipped to his delight.

"Andrea has told me she likes tall ships and I think she'd like to see yours," Michael told Julio who beamed (and) me then led us downstairs to a large studio. I stopped in amazement. Michael had said something about model boats, but I expected some like people put in bottles or on their mantles. Julio's models were about six feet long. He had undertaken to reproduce every boat in the Chilean Navy at the time it had a war with the Peruvian Navy in 1879. The Chileans won in 1884.

Each model had everything replicated from casks of wine and cheeses hanging in galleys to what was in the holds. He had done meticulous research and the models were cleverly designed so you could lift off a section to look inside and then replace it. I was spellbound. I've always had a soft spot for tall ships. I have read all twenty-one books of Patrick O'Brian's *Master and Commander* series, not just once but five times. My daughter, when she saw me reading one, would announce "Mom's been press-ganged by the British Navy again."

After exploring the wonderful ships Julio said, "Let me show you my museum."

"You are the director of a museum?" I asked.

"No, the owner. I built it."

Michael was grinning so I knew I was in for an unusual treat. He led us through the back of his property to a concrete block building, drowning in flowers and vines. He unlocked strong double doors made of steel. It was all one large room with some work benches at one end. The first thing that stopped me was a creature that looked like a pterodactyl.

"I studied skeletons of prehistoric animals. I recreated this using some fossils and the skeleton of a condor," he explained. He had made all sorts of creatures mixing pre-historic and current bones. Then I saw a Spanish Conquistador's armor. Michael donned a helmet.

"I used to manage a mine in the Atacama Desert. Whenever I could I went exploring. Most people hide from the desert. I embraced it. I found the casualties from a battle," Julio explained.

Like Neruda, there was nothing he wouldn't collect. Unlike Neruda he also made things. He had a collection of sculptures he had made.

My afternoon with Julio sped by. Finally, Michael said we had to go if I were to meet my friends arriving from California. Julio tried to persuade me to stay with him and move in. He was in his eighties but had so much energy and excitement about life he seemed much younger.

"You are too young for me," I told him and made him laugh.

"That's what all my ex-wives said," Julio shook his head ruefully.

Domesticating the Demon - Rounding the Horn

Just the name used to strike dread into sailors' hearts – Cape Horn. It has taken untold lives and terrorized those that made it around the infamous passage. The Horn is home to the roughest waters on the planet.

On our ship it was just beginning to get light. Stewards appeared on the eleventh story deck with its wrap-around views, wheeling in carts with coffee urns which they set up with trays of pastries for us early risers. Some of us had binoculars, and we sat in the padded chairs we had set our alarms before dawn to claim, staring ahead through the mist.

Suddenly we saw it: that great peak, shaped, oddly enough, like Diamond Head on Oahu Island. But this monster did not preside over placid tropical waters. This was the dreaded Cape Horn that looms large in sea shanties and sailors' lore. It is the end of all habitable land at that end of our planet, where the Andes plunge into the sea, and where two mighty oceans come together in a titan's clash.

Some sailors fell victim to the Williwaws, the wind phenomenon peculiar to those latitudes. Cold air builds up behind steep slopes then suddenly spills over the top of a mountain and falls into the sea at hurricane speeds, like an invisible iceberg, making a temporary dent in the water and a great splash. Woe to any boat that is not securely tied up at both ends below a Williwaw. Of course, now, the Panama Canal provides safer, even pedestrian, passage. I kept my eyes peeled, but never saw a Williwaw in action.

Sir Frances Drake claimed to have reached the end of land and seen open ocean – the historical jury is still out on it. The story is that the dapper, red-bearded privateer climbed up the banks and crawled his way through the gales to reach the end for bragging rights, as he came back and told his men, "I have been the farthest south of any man yet known." Historians all have to agree he did make it around South America and enter the Pacific where he ravaged the Spanish towns and treasure ships. The sea passage south of the Horn is still called Drake's Pass.

But it took the Dutch to really use it for trade purposes and name it. During California's Gold Rush, the Horn saw a lot of traffic. Later, around the turn of the 20th century, large steel, square rigged sailing ships were specially constructed for heavy hauling around the Horn. Coal and nitrate were the usual freights. The last tallship to make the passage was the *Pamir* in 1949.

In the terrible winter of 1905 of the 200 or so ships to leave for the Horn, 55 went missing.

"We are exceedingly fortunate," a ship's officer told us over the loudspeaker from the bridge. "We are seeing the smiling face of the Horn today."

While the skies were gray and winds fierce, the seas were relatively smooth, just long slow swells. There were white caps but no mighty waves. I was still glad we were not on a sailing ship. I felt secure on our great, motor driven ship.

"In the next few moments the bow will be in one ocean, the Atlantic, and the stern will be in another, the Pacific," said the officer. "However, fortunately we are still joined," he added chuckling.

There were no trees, but lots of moss and grass covered the promontory. Then came the announcement that because the weather was cooperative, the captain of our ship planned to circumnavigate the Horn island so we would see it from all sides before we headed off into the Atlantic.

As we came into the lee side we poured on deck to take photos and gawk at the island. A ferocious wind was still blowing. Soon we could see the residence of the Chilean naval officer and his family in the loneliest place on earth.

Seven meters high, the metal diamond shape features a cutout albatross – the traditional spiritual guardian of the souls of sailors drowned at sea. The layered metal reflecting the sky and the scudding clouds makes it appear the albatross is flying. The Chilean poet Sara Vial from the port of Valparaiso wrote a poem that is carved there. The officer read it to us.

I, the albatross that awaits at the end of the world...
I am the forgotten soul of the sailors lost,
rounding Cape Horn from all the seas of the world.
But die they did not in the fierce waves,
for today towards eternity, in my wings they soar,
in the last crevice of the Antarctic winds.

Everyone grew very quiet as we passed the memorial, our thoughts reaching into the terrible past of the Horn.

These days there is little traffic around the Horn. The occasional cruise ship, such as ours, sometimes Antarctic cruises and expeditions pass, or even stop. Yachts sometimes try it, don't always make it. There are some insane yacht races to circumnavigate the globe every few years that include rounding the Horn. The albatross cares for the spirits of some of those blue water sailors. Local fishermen are too smart to chance its unpredictable ways.

In the 1980s Argentina's military government, looking for some conquest to distract their unhappy citizens from the "Dirty War" they were waging against their political opponents, made threatening noises about taking over the Horn. The Chileans responded by sending their navy and land mining it. So, the Argentine dictators turned to the Falklands instead with disastrous results for the country. .

In tallship days when sailors rounded the Horn they were entitled to put a small golden ring in their left ears and could put both feet on the mess table as well as sport a tallship tattoo. My ears were pierced already and I had no interest in tattoos. Still I felt strange – as if a part of me had indeed been marked – maybe my heart?

At last we were past the Horn and we could see that wave-torn, wind-scarred, brave marker of the seas fade into the mist behind us. We still had almost six degrees of latitude to pass before we reached 50 degrees and had officially rounded the Horn, but as I saw that wild outpost of land vanish in the distance I felt very privileged, like a great milestone had been crossed, and also, I felt as if a part of me had been left behind with the sailors' albatross – yes, it had to be a piece of my heart.

The End of the World– Tierra del Fuego

After rounding the Horn, our ship entered Argentine waters and took us to Ushuaia, the most southern city on the planet. It is in Tierra del Fuego. Just the name that means land of fire sent chills up my spine. There on the docks was the town motto. It read "The End of World, The Beginning of Everything." It all depends on which direction you are heading.

This busy little port is where most Antarctic expeditions and cruises set out. The buildings all have metal roofs and they are painted bright colors, making it picturesque against the snowclad mountains. The Beagle Channel is there. A small cruise ship had just rescued a shipload of passengers from an Antarctic cruise that had foundered.

I opted to go on a small boat to explore the channel. It was rich with wildlife. An ice floe covered with seals offered a sad sight. One of seals was doomed to die as it had a plastic six-pack ring around its neck stretched but still cutting into the animal's flesh. My boat mates were a collection of jolly Brazilians. I have yet to meet a Brazilian traveler who isn't jolly.

There were four cruise ships docked in Ushuaia tripling its normal population so there was no chance of getting a driver to take me to the mountains as I planned, so I just explored the town.

In a bookshop I saw a volume I had read before the trip to prepare myself for Tierra del Fuego. It was *The Uttermost Earth* by Lucas Bridges. He was a son of the first successful missionary to settle there. The preceding ones had starved to death or been killed by the locals.

Lucas' father established an estancia and provided for what natives there were left. They needed help. Argentine ships came by, sailing ships stopped to get water and each time they brought some disease like measles that proved deadly to the natives.

I ran into Nancy and Roger and we had lunch together in a small café. I saw an old woman in one port at a park and a sign on her table of baskets said she was the last Yaghan – one of the Tierra del Fuego tribes. I thought it was just hype and when I later saw a flyer about a documentary about the last Yaghan in Buenos Aires, I saw her picture and realized I lost an opportunity to buy a genuine Yaghan piece of work.

Despite colorful Ushuaia, it seemed to me life at the high latitudes seemed dismal. Natives dying, missionaries starving, people freezing. I saw the brave sign as we sailed from the port once more and looked forward to fewer degrees of latitude.

Outlaw Saints and Penguins

South America held many surprises for me. I expected penguins, but not so many of them as I discovered in Argentina. Nor did I expect a Welsh town in Argentina.

My ship had put in at Punta Madryn, a port in the Patagonian Desert. The ship would wait for its own overpriced tours if they were late but not for any private tours. I definitely wanted to see penguins but didn't want to be marooned by unreliable local tours. I decided to book through the ship. The van looked professional as did the young woman and man taking us to Punta Tombo Natural Reserve where Jackass Penguins liked to nest.

I learned that in the 1800s a ship called the Mimosa had brought a load of Welsh people who had been promised rich farmland. Instead they landed in Argentina's desert country – greedy scammers are always at work preying on the hopeful. The Welsh would not have survived without the help of the local tribe of indigenous South Americans much like the early Pilgrims in North America were saved by Squanto and his folks.

Our guides stopped at a roadside stand to leave an offering of a piece of red cloth to Gauchito Gil. A little farther down the road they left a bottle of water at another shrine, this one to La Difunta Correa. These are both outlaw saints not recognized by the church, but adored by the people.

Gauchito Gil was in love with a girl out of his league and was driven away by her family out into the desert. There he became a Robin Hood type outlaw. The people loved him and he was said to have healing powers. He was captured by the army. As they were preparing to hang him, he told an army sergeant that his son in a far-away city was very ill, but if the sergeant would ask him to pray for the boy before he was hanged the lad would live. The army fellow laughed then casually slit Gauchito Gil's throat. Reportedly, the sergeant's boy died. Before venturing out of town into the desert people leave red cloth at his shrines to ask his blessing.

La Difunta Correa was a young woman who learned that her soldier husband the mid 1800s had been wounded. She set off with her baby to see her husband. Out in the desert she died of thirst, but her body miraculously kept giving milk to her baby. When her body was found the baby was still alive. So before going into the desert you have to leave water for her, so she will protect you.

The Punta Madryn millennials who were our drivers, seemed sophisticated, but there was no way they were going to take their chances in the desert without supernatural assistance. It was a three hour hot drive. At the reserve there were boardwalks to keep the public off the nesting grounds of the penguins. The penguins were everywhere. I was told currently there were 250,000 birds at the reserve.

It was very hot. The railing of the boardwalk cast a strip of shade. Penguins chicks, fatter than their parents as they still had their baby feathers, lined up in single file in that strip of shade for the half mile walk to the beach. They complained loudly that they were hungry and wanted their parents to bring them some fish. At the beach the sea was full of adults fetching fish for their young.

With the water teeming with thousands of penguins no one was tempted to go swim with them. The grounds of the reserve were full of holes that were the penguin nesting burrows. Birds went in and out of them All the penguins were noisy. The smell was overwhelming in the heat. The penguins were very friendly. One came out of burrow and waddled in my direction braying.

I brayed back. It stopped, looked at me silent, then brayed to me and waited for me to bray back. I did, and we carried on an avian conversation for a few minutes. Some children nearby decided to start their own conversations. Their parents recorded the moment. The penguins went on to the beach and we all smiled at each other.

When I went back to the van to get my boxed lunch I ran into our guides.

"I can't get over the number of penguins. Are there really 250,000 of them?"

The guides laughed at me. "The nesting season is almost over. About six weeks ago we had two and half million penguins."

We drove back to the ship, stopping at two shrines again to honor the gaucho and dead mother. The box lunch had been in the overheated rear of the van away from the air conditioning. I didn't eat all of it, but had enough to give me food poisoning by nightfall. I muttered to the outlaw saints that they had failed to protect me. I wondered if my guides had suffered the same fate. I hoped so since they had been the ones to store the boxes.

Despite that, I felt satisfied by Punto Tombo. I had seen enough penguins to last the rest of my life.

Uruguay, Argentina and the Mighty Rio de la Plata

El Rio de la Plata, River of Silver, or as the Brits used to call it River Plate, boasts the widest mouth of any river in the world.

I found that out on our ship when we turned west and were told we were on the river. All I could see were some buoys in the distance. It looked like we were still at sea, but apparently the water was fresh, not salt. The mouth is 220 kilometers wide. Two mighty rivers join to form La Plata: the Uruguay and the Paranha. You could not see either bank of Rio de Plata. One side was Uruguay and the other was Argentina.

The first day we eventually landed at Punta del Este in Uruguay. I missed that port because, sick with food poisoning from a lunch I had shared amidst penguins, I was confined to my cabin. But my travel mates, Roger and Nancy, assured me it was much like any sea resort I had ever been to, so I hadn't missed much. The next day when docked at Montevideo, the capital of Uruguay it was very different.

I hired Juan, a genial taxi driver, to take me on a tour of the city. It was impressive. People say Buenos Aires is the Paris of South America, but Montevideo looks much more Parisian because of its very similar architecture, including many mansard roofs. It enjoyed a wide stretch of sand beach that looked like it was an ocean fronted city. The beach was on the fresh water of the river, which was still so wide we couldn't see Argentina.

Juan stopped once to refresh his mate gourd. In both Uruguay and Argentina people like a steady flow of caffeine. Instead of Starbucks, they have the gourd gals. Young women, some teens, fill a large backpack thermos with hot water. People fill their gourds with the mate mixture they like best in the morning, and all day pay the girls to refill them with hot water, sipping the hot brew through silver straws.

It took another day upriver to reach Buenos Aires. You couldn't see Uruguay from the banks of the river in Buenos Aires. Buenos Aires is an exciting, electric city. Just think Tango, and you have got it. This is where the wild, sexy dance originated.

Nancy, Roger and I left our cruise ship, taking note as we went through Immigration then Customs, of the couples we had seen who turned around and went right back through Customs then Irrigation and were greeted by their same cabin attendants they had just left.

We had discovered several California couples on board, laid off work during the Great Recession, had rented out their Silicon Valley homes and while cruise lines were offering excursions for $50 a day had decided to live on board until the economy got better. It was a clever idea. For less money than the rent they collected, they had board, lodging, entertainment and housekeeping services. Some people retire on cruise ships and are well known and pampered by the crews as they move from ship to ship.

We took a taxi and moved into a small apartment we had rented online and set out to explore this glamourous place. We took off for San Telmo, a neighborhood where we had learned there was an outdoor market and people tangoed in the street.

As we walked into the plaza a whole bunch of drummers came in and began playing a very African beat. Unfortunately, a thunderstorm also moved in on the plaza and drummers had to take shelter to keep their instruments dry. We darted into a café, starved. We ate slowly, we lazed, ordered drinks, hoping to outwait the rain, but it never let up. We tried calling a cab. I think cabbies don't like to drive in the rain. Finally, we saw a stray cab across the plaza, and made a run for it. When we were dropped off the driver was put out because we had drenched his cab with our soaking clothes, so we tipped him extra. When we had left we saw the drummers in doorways and under awnings trying to keep dry also trying to outwait the rain. The rain stopped in the morning.

Our apartment was in a great location. The transportation center was less than two blocks away so we could travel wherever we wanted, and we were a short walk from Florida Street, a pedestrian city center where everything happens.

It was Sunday and a lot of things were closed. I had read that El Tigre was a popular weekend getaway for the Porteños, as Buenos Aires residents call themselves. We hopped a train and a little over an hour later we arrived the delta of the Paranha River. It was green and tropical. From the small town at the station, to see El Tigre properly, we had to take a ferry.

The settlement at El Tigre, outside the small town by the depot has no roads, only canals and waterways. There was just one walking path that linked two small ferry docks. It was a stunning place. Sometimes there were grand houses with their own docks and large boats, sometimes small huts with rowboats. The waterways laced through them. There were frequent boats traveling the waterways. Some were locals going somewhere, others were delivery boats.

At last we hopped off at a wood dock while other passengers leaped down into the boat. We saw the path. As we strolled everything was in bloom. The smell of flowers and fresh flowing water made breathing a delight. We all breathed deeply. Along the way a beer delivery boat passed us and went around a curve. The smell of flowers and jungle was suddenly permeated by another delightful odor. Someone was barbecuing. We rounded the bend and the beer was being delivered to small outdoor restaurant. The afternoon had worn on and we were ready for a late lunch.

Ducks, egrets, and other birds busily worked the waters, other birds sang in the trees. The weather was warm, we were in dappled shade, the food was simple and tasty, the beer was cold. Life in El Tigre could be very fine we all decided.

Eventually we resumed our walk and found ourselves at a shaded dock where we waited for a ferry back to the train station. The pleasures are simple in El Tigre. Without a boat there was nothing much else to do. A young woman who lived there was on her way to a night job in Buenos Aires. We chatted and learned she was contented with her schedule. While we spoke, an unusually large boat for the waterways came by. It slowed hopefully at the dock. It was a floating store that held groceries, dry goods, and some hardware.

"Walmart of the river," joked the woman and we all laughed.

El Tigre was a lovely way to try to become a Porteño.

A few days later when Roger and Nancy said they planned to shop, I decided to go on my own to Uruguay and explore Colonia, another Porteño getaway, a Portuguese one. I bought tickets for a high speed hydrofoil ferry. It would take us over two hours to cross El Rio de la Plata. It was drizzly and a little foggy when I boarded early in the morning. I could see nothing ahead but what looked like open sea. Buoys marked a passage and I saw ships sail by. When I looked back I could not see the Argentine shore.

I have been on some mighty rivers. I have been on the Mississippi, I have been on the Nile where what's on the shores is singularly impressive. But never has river itself impressed me as much as the Rio de la Plata for its sheer width and amount of water it provides.

By the time we docked the mist had lifted and Colonia was in full sunshine. There I discovered two dear friends, fellow travel writers, from California. They had been on a different cruise line than mine but had followed our ship into every port along the way around South America and the Horn. We had compared notes, but off the Argentine coast they had gone to the Farallones, and I had gone to penguins. Now we were reunited in a gorgeous town.

I had been in countries where the Portuguese had settled – most notably Mozambique in Africa and seen ruins of the architecture. Here I saw it intact and realized how I preferred it over the Spanish architecture which dominates so much of South and Central America. Instead of walls hiding gardens, the Portuguese share their flowers. They spill out everywhere. Homes seem to reach for you in welcome instead of hide behind high blank walls.

I wandered thoroughly enjoying myself when I noticed a bank. It was built like a fortress. Once again, I had run into the contrast of the architecture of intimidation and the architecture of welcome. Banks like the former.

I met my friends for lunch and realized the Argentines were not flocking as much to Colonia as they were wont to do because prices in Uruguay were higher and the Recession was hitting everyone.

I crossed that mighty river again back to Buenos Aires where Roger and Nancy told me we had a superb steak restaurant just down the block. After I left they would spend another week in Buenos Aires. I advised them not to miss Colonia.

Dog Walkers and Crazy Graves

Buenos Aires had a lot of interesting sights. The first time I encountered its professional dog walkers I was gobsmacked.

I have seen dog walkers in the States, but Buenos Aires takes it to a new level. The first one I ran into was walking twenty dogs. Yep, twenty. The dogs all seemed to get along and behaved well, but everyone else on the sidewalk had to give them a wide berth so as not to get tangled in their leashes. A while later I saw another walker tie his ten dogs to a handy tree outside a café while he bought himself a coffee.

The dog walkers provide all sorts of services for the dogs: keep their nails trimmed, coats brushed, look after their teeth, tend to their general health. If a dog needs medical care they alert the owners. And of course, they keep them exercised.

Buenos Aires is full of lovely tree-lined boulevards and parks so there are lots of places for the dogs to explore. The walkers must do a conscientious job of cleaning up after their clients because I never ran into anything unpleasant to my relief.

Another bizarre sight was the Recoleta Graveyard. Only if you were very rich and connected to important families could you get buried there. Evita is interred there because she came from a connected family. Her husband is not.

The graveyard is enormous. You have to buy a map to not get lost. It's a city of graves. The graves themselves are over the top.

Many are actually rooms with locked glass doors. I saw stairs leading underground to where the beloved were stored. Others sport wild sculpture. There are many life-sized or larger angels, portraits and such, but some were surprising. A carving of a great tallship topped a high column over a sea captain's grave. It seemed through the generations people tried to outspend their neighbors as they mourned their loved ones.

I took my map and set off to find Evita's grave. It was very unassuming in that ostentatious cemetery. It was just one name on a wall that listed all the dead in her family. It was the only grave I saw with fresh flowers. A feral cat lives nearby, and dishes of catfood and fresh water were laid out in front of her grave, so she always has a mourner even if it is feline. It took a while to get her buried. Her husband while he was head of the government carried her embalmed body with him on state trips, insisting maids dress her body in glamourous clothes for each occasion and dress her hair. But finally he died and she got her spot in Recoletta.

Another interesting sight was a bookstore. It was big two-story bookstore and almost all the books were on psychology. Fiction, history, and other topics all had small shelves in out of the way corners. Every facet of psychology covered the tables and filled most shelves. I learned that Argentines are so into analysis they even have an on-call psychologist at the airport to help people who have a fear of flying. The Chileans, a mountain range away next door make fun of the Argentines about it. They have a more caustic and cynical view of life and think the Argentines constantly trying improve themselves are hilarious.

Gauchos

San Antonio de Areco was a bus ride away from Buenos Aires. It is the historical gaucho town.

I didn't know exactly what to expect; a dusty run-down cowboy town or some phony tourist attraction. I was pleasantly surprised to discover a charming real town. Many of its buildings were white-washed adobe, some of its sidewalks were wooden boardwalks. It was no Disneyland.

I was supposed to go out of town to an *estancia* (ranch) barbecue, but fell under the spell of San Antonio de Areco itself. There was a gaucho museum at one end of town and I walked in that direction. Horses were tied up or loose and grazing on the green grassy fields. A dust covered man rode in and took his horse to a stream so it could drink. As he dismounted he took off his red beret then knelt to wet his neckerchief and wrap it around his neck again.

A real gaucho. They still exist as much as cowboys do in the States.

The museum was set up like the home of a rancher. I watched as horses continued to graze. A couple of men on horseback came from different directions on the gravel road leading out of town and greeted one another as they passed. One went into his home after he turned his horse loose to graze. It was much smaller and definitely humbler than the museum estancia home.

I slowly strolled through town. I stopped to buy a mate gourd nicely decorated in silver. I stopped at a shop to pick up some mate.

I stopped to eat a light lunch and took the bus back to Buenos Aires. It was a nice, gentle, satisfying day. And I saw real gauchos!

Tango

There are lots of expensive, flashy tango shows for tourists in Buenos Aires. I was hoping for something more authentic. I was in luck.

Buenos Aires has a number of cultural centers. These are neighborhood gathering places where art shows, films, and performances are offered by locals for locals at very affordable prices. Our apartment was near the Borges Centro de Cultura. We had already enjoyed art receptions there, and I saw a tango performance advertised.

Roger, Nancy and I bought our tickets and found ourselves in a small, intimate theater. The show opened with a fog machine creating the smoky atmosphere of a dive bar. The show depicted the history of the dance. The energy was electric. The dancers incredibly skilled.

One woman wore stilettos so sharp looking, and her foot work was so intricate, close and fast, I feared she might accidently emasculate her partner. The show was breathtaking. As we were leaving some of the dancers, including the lady with the dangerous shoes suddenly tore past us and hailed a taxi.

A young stage hand told us, "They are going to perform a tourist show now, but they did this for the neighborhood first."

We also heard the La Boca had great tango dancers so we headed off for the notorious waterfront neighborhood. It wasn't easy. I had read it was best to get a taxi instead of a bus there as it can be a rough part of the city. So we hailed a taxi, told him La Boca, and he dropped us off. After we paid him he took off fast and we realized he had not taken us to La Boca, just to a bus stop. The chicken didn't want to risk his taxi there. So, we caught a bus after all.

The part of La Boca where the dancing happens is very colorful. The tale is everyone painted their homes which were metal clad with the paint ships left behind, so every part of a house can be a different bright color. It makes La Boca very interesting.

There was not just tango happening but group traditional dancing, and some were dancing with bolos, whipping them around and somehow avoiding hurting themselves or other dancers. They were all dancing for tips. Passing a hat after each dance. They were worthy of good tips.

Tango is more than a dance in Buenos Aires, it is a passion. Entire clothing stores are devoted to tango clothes: slitted skirts, murderous tango heels, kitten heels for little girls to learn how to tango. There are private tango clubs for afficianados. There for up to fourteen minutes at a time a couple can be tango-intimate and when the music ends, go home to wife or husband and resume normal life. It beats adultery.

We returned to San Telmo when the weekly flea market happened and where we had been rained out our first night in the city. The flea market was in full swing when someone brought out a wooden pallet about ten feet square. As soon as it was laid on the cobblestones of the plaza people began dancing the tango. A couple would take over, dancing to recorded music at first, and later to musicians who showed up. People took turns. It wasn't a performance for tips; it was just people having fun. Once an elderly woman hopped on the pallet and a young man took on the challenge. She was a superb dancer and the crowd applauded her as the young man bowed to honor her.

I had learned from the informative performance we had seen at our cultural center that the Tango came from the waterfront slums and then was adopted by the upper classes, and from there spread around the world to the most unlikely place for dance that had African beginnings to end up – Finland. The Finns get through their unending dismal winters in Tango parlors, doing that hot, sexy dance through their long, dark nights.

Belize and the Lucky Mugging

I went to Belize to get my teeth fixed. The same dental work in the USA would have cost $5000, but in Belize it was just $900. I chose Belize because English is the official language, unlike the rest of Latin America. I wanted my dentist to understand me.

I sent my x-rays, set up an appointment and called the tourism board to get some information on what to see in Belize. As a travel writer, I wanted to make it a business trip as well as a medical tourism trip. I also read about a nice little B&B in a guidebook, that was conveniently located in downtown Belize City. That was mistake one.

Never go to Belize City. It was so utilized by drug cartels as a transfer point that even the government of Belize has abandoned the city that used to be its capital. They claimed it was floods, but everyone in Belize City knows better. Almost everyone on the streets is drugged out. I think of the city as an ugly boil on the face of a beautiful woman because the rest of Belize is lovely.

I checked into my room and asked the innkeeper where I could get lunch. He waxed enthusiastic like he worked for the Chamber of Commerce if Belize City ever had one.

It was Sunday, a sleepy day in the tropics. I finally found a restaurant near a major intersection that was open and had a simple lunch. I had a guidebook I had borrowed from the library before I left home and read it as I ate. I almost walked out without it, but the waitress stopped me. So, I was carrying it as I left. I had not yet switched my passport and such back to my money belt and had it and my camera in my shoulder bag.

The streets were deserted. Everyone was having a nice little siesta and I decided to do the same as soon as I had a shower back at the inn. At the intersection of a major avenue a young man on a bicycle came pedaling up to me.

"Gimme dat!" he yelled as he ran me down.

I jumped back and as I did my shoulder bag swung around to my back just as the man jumped on me knocking me down in the street flat on my back.

He kept saying "Gimme dat!" as he struggled to get at my bag. He was sitting straddling me so his weight and mine kept the bag firmly behind my back. He grabbed my head and banged it on the pavement. I tried to yell and suddenly realized I was still gripping my travel guide.

The edges and corners of the well-built book served me as a weapon. I hit him repeatedly in the face and neck using the corner of the spine like an axe. He was startled. I kept yelling and apparently woke someone up because as suddenly as he had jumped me, he jumped up, hopped on his bike and took off full speed. The whole incident must have lasted thirty seconds. Some other men were coming out of their homes. I was afraid of being attacked again.

I began running back to the inn which was just a couple blocks away. I did not realize that the mugger had ripped open my blouse and scratched my face and neck so my chest and face were bloody. I was just terrified he would come back.

A kind man watering his garden saw me and called out, "Are you all right?"

"No, I was just attacked."

He took out his cell phone. "I am calling the police. Where are you going?"

"To my hotel. It's just there," I replied. I was wary. I didn't want any stranger near me after that frightening attack.

"I am going to walk with you to keep you safe as I call the police," he explained and keeping a distance of several feet, as he sensed my fear, he walked with me until I was safely inside the gates of the inn.

A group of young tourists had arrived and rushed to help me. I wasn't in the inn more than five minutes before police with automatic weapons showed up. I hastily changed my blouse as they insisted I come to the station. I was startled to see a whole truck full of armed police outside.

They drove downtown to a simple looking storefront that served as the entrance to the headquarters. Then they took me upstairs. I thought I had landed in a Graham Greene novel. I have never seen a police station so scary as that one. The walls and floors were raw concrete. Chunks of the wall were missing and floor was covered by ugly stains. I couldn't wait to get out of there, especially when I realized in the scuffle with the mugger I had wet myself and hadn't had time to change my black skirt. The police station was as traumatizing as the mugging.

The officer that questioned me asked if I thought I could identify the man. I didn't want to spend hours looking through mug books so I told him no, but I let him know that the man had been riding a new red bicycle that he had probably stolen. Two officers looked at each other nodding knowingly. Belize City has a small population (about 17,000) so they probably could locate him soon enough. I told them he had got nothing of mine and that he was covered with bookmarks. I held up the guidebook. The man looked at me, an older American woman, just 5'3". "You must be a strong woman," he told me.

"It's a strong book," I replied as I wondered how many other people had borrowed that book from the library and beaten muggers with it. I hoped there was no blood on it. I had really chopped at the mugger with it. At last the police took me back to the inn. On the way I saw that the truck full of cops with automatic weapons had been deployed at every corner of the avenue where I had been mugged.

At the inn I discovered the hot water heater was not working so there went the dreams of a hot shower. I overheard the innkeeper and his wife arguing. "You sent her out there on her own? You know how dangerous it is on Sundays, you idiot!"

The couple were about to break up. The woman came to my room to apologize. I told her I wanted a refund. The man invited me into the kitchen where he poured me a glass of rum and began complaining about his marriage. I couldn't imagine a worse innkeeper. Only cold showers, and the couple's arguments kept me up later that night.

I took a cab to an internet café and emailed home. I called the tourism bureau to let them know I was leaving the city early and couldn't keep my appointment as I had been attacked less than two hours after my plane touched down. The woman at the bureau begged me to come immediately in a cab. I walked in and I saw her gasp. The scratches on my neck and face revealed I had clearly been in a battle.

The bureau, terrified of what I might write, then told me I was their guest for the rest of my stay. She made arrangements for me to have a private driver and I would be staying in five-star hotels. They also arranged a stay at a jungle lodge, an archaeologist as a guide to Mayan ruins, and a cave tubing expedition. I was overwhelmed. I had been planning on doing all those things, and had been warned by other travel writers that the Belizan Tourism Board were not especially generous to them. My original plans had definitely been budget level, not red carpet luxury.

I thought maybe I should thank my mugger – a few cuts and bruises weren't much of a price to pay for the hospitality the Belize Tourism Bureau provided for the rest of my trip.

Where Pirates Ruled

I lay in my hammock enjoying the balmy breeze off the Caribbean, listening to the gentle lapping of the sea on the shores of Caye Caulker. I read a book and dozed in turns. In the distance someone was playing Bob Marley music. I was on the Caribbean Sea side of Belize as opposed to the jungle side in the west.

I had spent some time in the jungle exploring the many Mayan ruins and had crossed into Guatemala to visit Tikal, now it was time to chill out.

Belize is home to the planet's second largest barrier reef, pirates were the first Europeans to discover Belize or, as they called it, The Mosquito Coast. They had a few secret ways to get through the reef the English and American navies did not know about. Caye Caulker is where they patched their ships.

When the pirates came they found an empty countryside because the Mayans centuries before had fled a thirty year drought and moved north. The pirates became privateers – pirates with government permission and settled in to cut down the mahogany forests and claim the place for England. Since tree cutting was hard work they got slaves to do it for them.

In 1981 the Brits gave independence to Belize. Since, Belize has been run by corrupt locals instead.

The country has always attracted immigrants including a sizable settlement of Mennonites. I had been startled to see horse buggies on the roads with bearded white men driving the horses. They settled in Belize because they didn't want to pay US income taxes.

Caye Caulker was less than five miles long and less than a mile wide. Cars were not allowed, just golf carts and bicycles, and delivery trucks came via ferry only one early morning a week. It was lively place despite its small size.

Before sunset I left my hammock and went to the restaurant down the block. On the beach out back the tables had swings hanging from a palapa instead of chairs. I wanted to watch the show that entertained the locals every sunset. As the fishing boats came in with their catch of the day pelicans, frigate birds and gulls gathered screeching, hoping to get some fish guts.

The birds in turn excited the island dogs who came madly running out on the pier to chase them. The dogs jumped off the pier into the sea in their pursuit of the birds, who simply flew off when a dog came too close. The dogs were not discouraged. They swam back to the shore and ran madly down the pier again. The game went on for at least a half hour until all the fish were cleaned.

I ordered whatever fish had just been delivered for dinner and ate it with one of dozens of varieties of Marie Sharp's hot sauce they had that night. Marie Sharp must be the biggest employer in all of Belize. They sold her sauces everywhere. I wish they exported them; I have missed them ever since I left Belize.

One night I left my hammock to find Willy's – a part time restaurant. A couple nights a week Willy hauled lawn furniture out to a vacant lot to set up a restaurant with the cook turning out fresh fried fish dishes from a tool shed using a kerosene stove. It was terrific food.

I had journeyed out to the reef to play with rays but I did not dive and did not visit the Great Blue Hole in the ocean divers love. The hammock, the sea, the nightly dog and bird show, and the Panty Rippers, the national drink, were enough excitement for me for the five days I stayed on Caye Caulker.

Teeth fixed, library book in hand, not overdue and hopefully the tiny blood stain wouldn't matter, I prepared to leave the Caribbean and head home.

Prologue
Home Sweet Home

The best day of any journey is the first full day back at home. Long flights are hard. With plane changes and layovers any international travel seems to take at least twenty-four hours.

Once, returning from Italy, my son left my car at a hotel that was also a stop for the airport shuttle. After a startlingly intense security procedure at Fiumicino Airport in Rome, the nightmare of Heathrow awaited me. It featured pushy guards and bossy security and never having a chance to sit as we waited in hours long lines, as did one more US airport with a long layover before I landed at SFO in the wee hours. I caught the last airport shuttle to the hotel where I was to get my car and drive home.

I couldn't find it. I searched and searched. I finally went to the desk in tears of exhaustion and begged to use the phone to call my son. I got his answer machine, left a pitiful message, and in disgust went outside where I promptly found the car. He got my teary message and called the desk asking them to look for me. It was too late.

I drove home and as I pulled up in great relief I saw my two cats frantically throwing themselves against my French door entry. I tried to open the doors. I had asked my house/cat sitter to leave the door unlocked. I had no key. It was locked. I screamed in frustration, then noticed a ladder. Using my headlights, I propped it against my laundry room window hoping the sitter hadn't noticed it was unlocked. She hadn't.

I crawled in on top of my dryer as my joyous cats were all over me. After that trip, I arranged for my son to pick me up at the airport when I returned from an exhausting journey. Once, a travel companion found herself locked out when we returned after midnight.

My son won her undying gratitude by finding a way to break in and open her door for her. House breaking must run in the family.

After the first good sleep, then it's time to enjoy the true contentment of a traveler home from a journey.

Home is the sailor, home from the sea

Home is the hunter, home from the hills.

The old nursery rhyme is important to me. It helps that I return to a beautiful place after my travels. I live near the coast in a redwood forest next to a sheep ranch. It is quiet and peaceful country.

Once awake and full of coffee, I unpack any gifts I have brought back for my family and gloat over them, and as each telephones me, we arrange to gather. I go into my flower garden to see what changes have come about. My cats won't let me out of their sight when I first return, so we spend a lot of time purring together.

When the family gathers after initial hugs, we get caught up in all the news each of us brings. Like I said, the first full day home is the best day of a journey.

Now, thanks to the pandemic, I have spent over a year rejoicing in my home. I am ready to travel again once I figure out where I can go that is safe. I am not as interested as I used to be in going new places as I am in going places I know I love and getting to know them better.

I lost my daughter to cancer and that has since altered some of my outlook on travel. She was the one I emailed every chance I had, and she spurred me on to new discoveries with her enthusiastic replies. My sons are loving but would just as soon keep Mom at home or have her travel in protective groups, not my favorite way to see the world. I have decisions to make and places to see.

CPSIA information can be obtained
at www.ICGtesting.com
Printed in the USA
FSHW022336241021
85708FS

9 781647 197919